Rural Britain
A Social Geography

Rural Britain
A Social Geography

DAVID PHILLIPS
ALLAN WILLIAMS

Basil Blackwell

First published 1984
Basil Blackwell Publisher Limited
108 Cowley Road, Oxford OX4 1JF, England

British Library Cataloguing in Publication Data
Phillips, David
   Rural Britain.
   1. Country life—Great Britain
   I. Title   II. Williams, Allan
   941'.009'734 S522.G7

   ISBN 0–631–13238–4
   ISBN 0–631–13237–6 Pbk

Typesetting by Oxford Publishing Services

Printed in Great Britain by T. J. Press Ltd, Padstow.

Contents

To Frances and Linda

Preface

This book is intended as an introduction to rural social geography, a subject that until recently has received relatively little attention. Although the book was written mainly with students of geography in mind, we hope that it will be of interest to a wider readership. Rural social geography is a young and growing sub-discipline, and many of the suggestions we make in the book may well require modification as our collective understanding of the field develops. It will be some time before we can hope to achieve the levels of specialization achieved by urban social geographers; nevertheless, we feel that this book shows something of what has been achieved so far as well as indicating avenues for future work.

We believe that an analysis of political and economic changes should provide the starting point for interpreting changes in the countryside. Chapter 1 therefore seeks to place this approach in the context of methodological changes in rural studies, while subsequent chapters examine some specific implications that follow from changes in the political economy of Britain – for example in deprivation, transport, leisure and services. Within this framework, the emphasis is placed on the changing roles of areas and social groups in the larger social formation, as well as on the implications for such areas and groups of macroeconomic and political developments. So we have concentrated on neither the analysis of political economy itself nor the mechanisms of change, but rather on their implications for areas and groups. This does not permit any simple generalizations for rural research but reminds us, above all, of the variations that exist within areas and between social groups.

There are however substantial constraints on any attempt to write such a broad synthesizing review, not least of which is the availability of appropriate case studies pertaining to all types of groups and areas. Inevitably, the supply of material is very uneven, and some regions of Britain and some social groups have received greater academic attention than others. Some themes and some areas will therefore figure more in this review than might be ideal; and is important to avoid generalization from case studies that may be rooted in specific local circumstances. Nevertheless, we hope that we have been able to outline some of the main features of life in rural Britain, and to illuminate these from the perspective of social geography.

If we have been successful in fulfilling any of these aspirations, we owe this in no small part to a number of other people. At the University of Exeter, our colleagues Mark Blacksell, Mark Cleary and Mike Winter have all given valuable comments on specific chapters. Andrew Gilg has been a constant source of encouragement, advice and information, and has been most thoughtful and generous with both his time and his personal library. The Department of Geography provided a most congenial working atmosphere; more specifically, the drawing office staff have given practical assistance. Rodney Fry and Gary Moss drew draft versions of most of the diagrams in the book, while Andrew Teed provided photographic help.

Access to currently unpublished material was given by Sally Dench who provided data for a figure in chapter 3 and by Simon Nicol of the Building Research Station, Garston, who provided data for a table in chapter 5. Other individuals and publishers have given permission to reproduce copyright material and the sources of these are given at appropriate points in the text.

We owe a particular debt of thanks to Mrs Jane Hayman who, on this occasion as on many others, has helped to turn what we thought was English into a genuinely acceptable style. She has most generously read and commented on the manuscript at a number of stages. To her and to all the other people named above, we owe a huge debt of gratitude; but, as ever, we must admit that the fault for any errors that may have crept into the text lies with ourselves alone.

David Phillips
Allan Williams
Exeter

1 Rural Social Geography

The argument over the scope and definition of social geography has been long and wide-ranging (Watson 1957; Houston 1963; Pahl 1965a; But-timer 1968; Eyles 1974; E. Jones 1975; Jones and Eyles 1977). However, the debate concerning the scope for distinctive urban and rural social geographies is even more complex. Herbert (1972), for example, saw urban social geography as a broadly based discipline and concentrated on the study of social mosaics and activities in the city. More recently, in his *Urban Social Geography* (1982), Knox's view of the subject is largely coloured by the approach suggested by Jones and Eyles, although he does consider that urban social geography comprises an ill-defined, eclectic mixture of ideas. Neither Herbert nor Knox seems to feel it necessary to establish a case for a separate urban social geography, perhaps because they regard advanced capitalist society as being predominantly urban. This view is shared by Jones and Eyles in their *Introduction to Social Geography*. They felt constrained, mainly for pragmatic reasons, to write that 'this book is largely about urban society . . . reflecting the weight and distribution of studies in social geography. This does not unduly distort the real situation because we live in a predominantly urban society, and most of our problems lie in the city' (Jones and Eyles 1977, p. 2).

Social geography is therefore seen by some as being synonymous with urban social geography, and a number of arguments support this view. For example, Wirth's (1938) view of 'urbanism as a way of life' has been used to argue that a country such as Britain is completely urbanized in cultural terms even if not in physical terms. This argument suggests that, although all people do not necessarily live in an urban built environment, all are subject to the same cultural influences, irrespective of whether or not they live in 'rural' or 'urban' areas. Dunleavy (1982) argues that, in postwar Britain, both economic activities and socio-cultural life are orga-nized on the same basis in both city and countryside. There is no urban–rural dichotomy in advanced industrial society, and therefore there is no scope for an urban–rural dichotomy in contemporary social science. In sociology, many commentators have argued that a separate urban sociology is not really viable. A specifically urban sociology is seen as largely fruitless (Pahl 1970), as trivial (Glass 1962), or as an irrelevant pursuit (Mellor 1977). By the same token, a specifically rural sociology would also seem to stand condemned and hence, presumably, would rural social geography as well.

Despite these arguments, a case can be made for the study of rural social geography. At the simplest, if not very compelling, level, it is possible to suggest the need for rural studies to counterbalance the predominance of urban socio-geographical studies. This has been argued by Moseley (1980c), who considered that rural geography lags behind urban geography in its methodology, and by Cloke (1980c), who complained of the 'conceptual famine' of rural geography. Furthermore, if rural areas are viewed as the non-metropolitan built areas, then the scope of this book will encompass most of the land area and a not inconsiderable proportion of the population of Britain.

In the same practical vein, a case can be made for the study of rural social geography on pragmatic grounds. Herbert (1972) has written of the city as being 'a unit of convenience' for analysis, and Duncan (1976, p. 13) also saw 'urban' as being 'a convenience for dealing with some aspects of conflict, appraisal and access within a social and spatial structure. . . .' The same argument can be extended to rural studies, so that 'rural' is also a label of analytical convenience. A similar logic is evident in the following recent definition of urban geography as the study of 'the patterns and processes which occur among and within urban places; the objective form which these take, the subjective manner in which they are interpreted, and their mode of origin at both local and societal scales' (Herbert and Thomas 1982, p. 4). A corresponding logic can be used to justify rural geography and, perhaps, rural social geography.

The arguments for a rural social geography, however, go beyond the level of practicality and convenience. A more positive view is that it is important to develop this branch of study, partly to help counterbalance some of the romantic rural myths that have been fostered by an evident anti-urban bias of much British social science. There are also particular features in rural areas that give a distinctive character to their social geography.

The subjective feeling that urban life is somehow bad or unpleasant has contributed to a stereotype image of the countryside, summarized by Palmer *et al.* (1977 p. 739) as 'a place to preserve rather than a place to change, a place to visit rather than a place to live, a place of sentiment rather than a place of work'. Glass (1955) traces the anti-urban bias to its Victorian roots, when towns were viewed as being unhealthy and the sources of social discontent and political disorder, while the countryside was idealized as the repository of traditional values and the 'country seat' was the ultimate symbol of social status. This ideology has been a potent force in the development of British planning (Mellor 1977), and Geddes (1915), one of the 'founding fathers' of modern planning, saw cities as 'expanding ink-stains and grease spots' and the countryside as demanding protection. This anti-urban bias coloured attitudes to rural areas to such an extent that many of the features of poverty and deprivation and the lack of access to resources in the countryside were recognized only belatedly. The development of rural social geography has a role to play in identifying and publicizing the nature, extent and causes of these features of rural life.

The second argument in support of a distinctive rural social geography is that rural areas have particular features that distinguish them from urban areas. This is not to say that the underlying processes shaping socio-spatial patterns in rural areas are different from those in urban areas. On the contrary, the economic, political and social context provided by the development of capitalism is the framework for the study of both kinds of area. For example, changes in the distribution of income, or in the tax relief accorded to mortgage payments, or in the relative subsidies provided for public and private transport, will affect all individuals, wherever they live. However, the precise ways in which such macroeconomic and political changes affect individuals, or local social groups, depend on a number of local features. It is a basic tenet of this book that these vary between rural and urban areas consistently enough to allow generalization.

This is clearly illustrated by the current debate over deprivation, which only recently seems to have been identified as a problem in rural areas (Walker 1978a; Shaw 1979a). That there are similarities in the characteristics of deprivation in the two types of area is not surprising, for, as Knox and Cottam (1981a, 1981b) have argued, both urban and rural deprivation can be viewed as outcomes of the same underlying process, the development of late industrial capitalism. However, rural deprivation is distinctive because the 'rural environment' is itself distinctive, particularly in terms of inaccessibility and isolation. This point is further illustrated by Moseley (1980b), who suggests that, while urban and rural areas share a set of common economic, social and demographic problems (table 1.1), there are problems specific to urban and to rural areas that stem from their 'local' and place-specific features. In rural locations these are essentially problems of access, demographic imbalance and infrastructural costs, while in the urban areas the specific problems tend to be the quality of the physical environment, over-crowding and perhaps racial tension.

If we accept that particular local features distinguish rural and urban areas, then these require identification. Two features, in particular, seem important: distance–accessibility, and the rural political framework. The

Table 1.1   Urban and rural 'problems'

Inner urban	Urban and rural features	Outer rural
Quality of physical environment	Economic stagnation	Inaccessibility
		High per capita costs of infrastructure
	Population decline	
Racial tension and social pathology	Services decline	High percentage of elderly people
	Lack of new investment	
Overcrowding and high density		
	Gentrification	
	Housing 'traps' Low 'morale'	

Source: after Moseley (1980b)

former has already been referred to. As Dicken and Lloyd (1981) have emphasized, people derive most of their needs and wants from their local environments. The range of retailing, employment and service opportunities within rural areas is usually far more restricted than in urban areas, and access to jobs or shops in adjacent centres will also be more difficult. In the age of private motor transport, those without their own vehicles are deprived wherever they live; however, the options available either by public transport or by walking are far more severely restricted in rural areas. Location does affect life-chances, and the potential for associated deprivation is greater and more distinctive in rural areas. This point will be elaborated in subsequent chapters.

The local political framework is discussed in greater detail later in this chapter. An element in this is the nature of rural land use, for although urban life-styles may have permeated rural areas, land use in rural areas is both extensive and distinctive. It is the subject of competing, often conflicting, but not necessarily contradictory, multiple uses (Blacksell and Gilg 1981). The countryside is at the same time a workplace, a locus of social relationships, a place of recreation and a repository of inherited value-laden environmental beauty. As a result of the 'anti-urban' ideology in Britain, policy-makers have tended to emphasize the last-named function, even though this may inhibit economic and social opportunities for the local rural populace. This is the backcloth for many issues in rural politics, and furthermore, it is not only the *issues* that are distinctive, because the composition of rural councils is often markedly conservative. Working-class interests are far less likely to be represented directly on rural councils than they are in urban areas. There is therefore an inbuilt middle-class and usually 'conservative' bias in rural political structures.

In summary, the case can be made for presenting a distinctive rural social geography. It is partly to counteract the dominance of urban-based studies and to add to the growing literature that seeks to demystify the countryside. Inequalities, deprivation and unemployment exist among the green fields and picturesque villages of rural areas as well as in the dull and dismal back streets of urban areas. Many of the concepts and methods adopted by urban studies, such as territorial justice or housing classes, can be applied equally well, and with illuminating effect, to rural studies. At the same time, these applications have to be sensitive to the subtleties of social and political structures and to the constraints and problems imposed by distance and accessibility within rural areas. Studies of rural geography can be illuminated by bringing them within the orbit of developments in social geography, but at the same time a distinctive rural social geography, if one not independent of underlying societal forces, may be proposed.

The restriction of this study to a single country is considered to be important in a text where a new synthesis is being outlined. For example, access to medical services is dependent on the distribution of income levels, on the nature of transport provision and on health service policies. All these features vary from country to country, so care must be taken to avoid over-generalization in trans-national comparisons.

Although the details of rural social geography presented here are limited to one country, the basic approach outlined may be useful in examining the rural social geographies of other nations. Even with this areal restriction, it must be acknowledged that this book cannot survey all of the elements of the rural social geography of Britain. A 'complete' rural social geography is probably an impossible objective, and this book seeks instead to outline what are considered the salient features of this field of interest. The remainder of this chapter considers some of the approaches to rural studies which are important in rural social geography and suggests that a proper understanding of the rural scene demands some analysis from a political economy perspective.

DEFINING THE RURAL ENVIRONMENT

Most people are aware that rural areas are basically different from urban areas, and that there are internal differences within rural areas themselves (see Cloke 1979). Indeed, many know that something like four-fifths of the land area of Britain is rural by use or in appearance and that one-quarter or one-fifth of the British population live in such areas (Woodruffe 1976). If called upon to specify the exact factors that characterize an area as 'rural', the majority of people could define the gross features or extreme locations fairly easily, but would have greater difficulty in distinguishing the intermediate localities.

The problem of defining rurality, especially when the life-styles, spatial behaviour and aspirations of residents are taken into account, is recognized or commented on by virtually all authors in this sphere of research (Ashton and Long 1972; Jones 1973; Moseley 1979a). The task of translating the 'perceived differences' between urban and rural areas into spatial distributions for practical purposes is very difficult, but it is particularly important for geographers who do not wish to apply aspatial definitions based solely on sociological factors (Cloke 1979). Official designations are generally of little help in this today. The system of local government in Britain, institutionalized from the late nineteenth century until 1974, included many authorities nominally designated 'rural' and 'urban', but this often bore little resemblance to their current built form or the behaviour of their inhabitants. The 1974 reorganization of local government deliberately constituted authorities in many cases to combine towns with rural hinterlands, so that the new district councils cannot easily be defined as urban or rural.

There have, however, been a number of attempts to define the rural areas of Britain on other than administrative criteria. Shaw (1979a, 1979b) brings together four of these, ranging from largely intuitive definitions of rural areas by Green (1971) to more formal statistical definitions based on the multivariate analysis of various indices deemed to indicate rurality (figure 1.1). However, as Shaw (1979b) points out, few of the statistically derived classifications of Britain provide the basis for a definition of the rural areas that reflects their distinctive characteristics. Perhaps the most statistically sophisticated is by Cloke (1977a, 1979), building on work by the Department of the Environment. His 16 variables indicative of rurality (table 1.2) include measures of distance from urban centres of 50,000, 100,000 and 200,000 persons, giving some quantification of remoteness (however approximate), which were included in a principal components analysis to indicate links with other variables. Two 'degrees' of rurality–'extreme rural' and 'intermediate rural'–were designated in England and Wales, and these occur mainly in four major areas of 'rurality': the South West, Wales, eastern England and a discontinuous Pennine belt. However, it must be remembered that any index must be subject to sympathetic interpretation in the light of local knowledge and understanding of the statistical techniques employed.

In general terms, however, the rural areas indicated in figure 1.1 do suggest that rurality has strong links with remoteness and peripheral locations (in England and Wales at any rate; Scotland has been less well catered for in research to date). This is, of course, rather an oversimplifi-

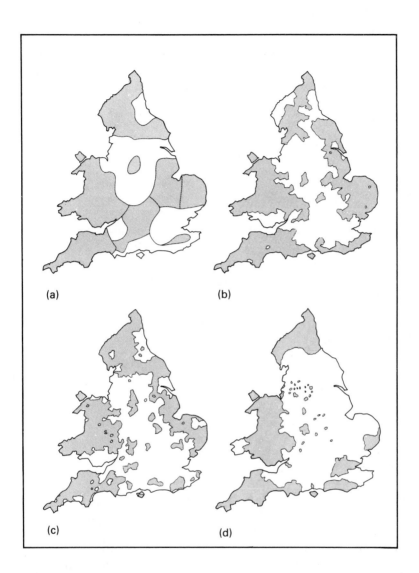

FIGURE 1.1 Rural areas of England and Wales. (a) Five intuitively defined rural regions (Green 1971). (b) Rural clusters – based on a multivariate analysis of 40 1971 census variables for new local authority areas (Webber and Craig 1976, 1978). (c) Extreme and intermediate rural areas – classified on the basis of a principal components analysis using 16 'rurality' variables for old local authority areas (Cloke 1977a, 1979). (d) Areas with low levels-of-living values for old local authority areas (Coates, Johnston and Knox 1977).
Source: after Shaw (1979b)

Table 1.2   Variables used in Cloke's 'index of rurality'

Variable name	Census data
1 Population density	Population per acre
2 Population change	% change 1951–61, 1961–71
3 Population over age 65	% total population
4 Population men age 15–45	% total population
5 Population women age 15–45	% total population
6 Occupancy rate	% population at 1½ per room
7 Occupancy rate	Household per dwelling
8 Household amenities	% Households with exclusive use of: (a) hot water; (b) fixed bath; (c) inside WC (1971)
9 Occupational structure	% in socio-economic groups: (13) farmers – employers and managers; (14) farmers – own account; (15) agricultural workers
10 Commuting-out pattern	% residents in employment working outside the rural district
11 In-migration	% population resident for less than 5 years
12 Out-migration	% population moved out in last year
13 In/out migration balance	% in/out migrants
14 Distance from nearest urban centre of 50,000 population	—
15 Distance from nearest urban centre of 100,000 population	—
16 Distance from nearest urban centre of 200,000 population	—

Source: Cloke (1979)

cation, as we shall point out. Although some places may be disadvantaged in terms of location and lack of centrality, not all people in them will be equally disadvantaged. In addition, problems related to access to services and to opportunities can be as great for some persons in relatively accessible country locations, which do not emerge as particularly rural on the indices.

COMMUNITY STUDIES AND THE RURAL-URBAN CONTINUUM

Defining the rural environment is one matter but understanding its social and economic functioning requires a different approach. Community studies, developed mainly by sociologists, provide one useful methodology although there cannot be said to be a single type of community study. Methodologically, they are based on a mixture of observer–participant and questionnaire data. Community studies share a common objective of taking a 'rounded' view of the community, attempting to study the inter-relation of institutions in any given locality. However, sociologists them-selves have been critical of this approach, and Stacey (1974) lists a number of arguments that have been directed against community studies. They are 'mere descriptions', non-replicable works of art, committed to a holistic approach; and they abstract from empirical social reality at a point where such abstraction is neither feasible nor useful. Needless to say, advocates of the community study approach, such as Stacey herself, have counter-arguments to these criticisms, the most important of which is probably that 'social relations must be seen not only in combination with each other but in the two dimensions of time and space' (Stacey 1974, p. 18). Community studies establish the social milieux in a particular time and place within which individual institutions or the relations between institu-tions can be analysed. This seems to be of considerable value to a study of social geography, and the fact that so many of these studies have been undertaken in rural communities makes them of particular value to rural social geographers. There is no doubt that studies such a those of Rees (1950), Williams (1956) and Littlejohn (1964) can provide rich material for colouring our view of socio-spatial features in particular types of com-munities at particular times.

Although of great value to those interested in rural social patterns, it should be said that the geographical element in these studies is fairly dormant. The definition of 'community' is usually geographical; however, there is generally little concern for geographical features, such as the spatial organization of the communities, beyond the definitional stage. In the seminal work among British studies, Stacey (1974) abstracted 31 tentative propositions about communities, but only two of these were explicitly concerned with spatial features within the communities, and these dealt with the effect of physical proximity on social relations.

A few studies have paid more than passing attention to the explicitly spatial features of social activities within rural communities. Pahl's (1965b) analysis of two commuter villages in Hertfordshire showed that there were important differences in life-style between newcomers and the traditional social groups. These differences, and also social class divisions, were deepened by the spatial segregation of social groups within the villages. Ambrose (1974) produced a study of a very different nature, an account of social change in the Sussex village of Ringmer. Using a variety of primary and secondary data sources, he described the main features of village life at three points in time; 1871, 1925–35 and 1971. As in Pahl's research, a recurrent theme was the relationship between newcomers and the traditional village residents. He analysed social networks and their relationship to settlement form and was able to show that both residential layout and distance from the village centre affected the integration of newcomers into the community.

On their own, community studies provide a valuable backcloth for any attempt to portray a rural social geography. There is much implicit detail on the socio-spatial features of village life, as well as on the organizations, institutions and values that condition the way in which social groups view and use space. For the geographer, however, the greatest value of community studies probably lies in their contribution to the debate about urban–rural contrasts in ways of life.

An important question has been whether particular types of social relationships or institutions are affected so greatly by the size of social groups or the nature of the environment in a locality that distinctive ways of life can be associated with rural as opposed to urban areas. There are three major viewpoints about this. First, there is the traditional view that there is a rural-urban dichotomy; second, there is a modified view which states that, although there are rural–urban differences, these are arranged along a continuum; finally, there is a critical view that it is over simplistic to try and associate particular social patterns with particular types of settlement.

A number of theories have dealt with rural–urban contrasts, often at a societal level, comparing more and less economically advanced societies. Reissman (1964) has provided a useful summary of these 'theories of contrast' which is shown in table 1.3.

There is no need to detail all of these theories here, but one in particular merits closer attention. This is the work of Tönnies (1963), who contrasted *Gemeinschaft* and *Gesellschaft*, concepts that really referred to the

Table 1.3   Theories of contrast

Author	Urban category	Non-urban category
Becker	Secular	Sacred
Durkheim	Organic solidarity	Mechanical solidarity
Maine	Contract	Status
Redfield	Urban	Folk
Spencer	Industrial	Military
Tönnies	*Gesellschaft*	*Gemeinschaft*
Weber	Rational	Traditional

Source: Reissman (1964)

differences between community and association but, partly through misconception, later became grounded in particular geographical locales, and were crystallized as belonging to the village and town as opposed to the city. *Gemeinschaft* was the 'community', which was characterized by intimate relationships, and a prescribed status, and where the population was physically and socially immobile, with a homogeneous culture and enduring loyalties to both the place and the people of the community. By contrast, *Gesellschaft*, or 'association', was characterized by large-scale impersonal and contractual ties based on market and legal relationships, high social and spatial mobility and relationships chosen for their efficiency in achieving specific ends (Bell and Newby 1971). The difference is between the community found in the town or village, with limited mobility and close, intimate relationships, and the association found in the city, where relationships are more impersonal and where a higher mobility ensures stronger links with society beyond the immediate locale. The dichotomy originally had been concerned with the differences in the forms of association but, unfortunately, 'from being a typology of social relationships, Tönnies' concepts became a taxonomy of settlement patterns' (Newby 1977, p. 95). As such it has obtained a central and enduring place in the literature of rural sociology and geography.

As an alternative to the theories of contrast, some sociologists have proposed a rural–urban continuum, along which communities can be arranged. The most notable British proponent of this idea has been Frankenberg (1966), who reassessed the findings of a number of community studies, and arranged these along a typological continuum (table 1.4). The choice of studies on which the continuum was based was necessarily restricted; nevertheless, the communities ranged from those of 400 people earning their livings mostly from agriculture in relatively isolated areas to large housing estates located in and around the major cities. Frankenberg suggested that there was a continuum of types of social relationships in these communities, based essentially on organization and levels of technology. He elaborated 25 themes that summarized the nature of this continuum, covering such matters as simple-versus-diverse economy; multiple-versus-overlapping role relationships; the division of labour; status-versus-contract; closely knit-versus-loosely knit networks; and segregation. Frankenberg denied that there was a dichotomy between rural and urban communities in terms of these themes. Instead, any community would contain some social groups that could be considered 'more urban' or 'more rural 'in terms of certain characteristics. Therefore the 'truly rural' communities would have largely rural characteristics, but some groups would be 'more urban' in terms of certain aspects. The inverse of this pattern was that a community such as Bethnal Green would be largely 'urban' but that some social relationships, for example the pattern of support within the extended family, would be more akin to those found in rural areas, as Young and Willmott (1957) had observed.

Table 1.4   The community studies in Frankenberg's rural–urban continuum

Author	Date of study	Community	Environment
Arensberg and Kimball	1940	Lough and Rynamona	Truly rural
Rees	1950	Llanfihangel	Truly rural
Williams	1956	Gosforth	Truly rural
Frankenberg	1957	Glynceiriog	Village in the country
Dennis, Henriques and Slaughter	1956	Ashton	Town that is a village
Birch	1959	Glossop	Small town
Stacey	1960	Banbury	Small town
Young and Willmott	1957	Bethnal Green (London)	Community in a conurbation
Lupton and Mitchell	1954	'Liverpool estate'	Urban housing estate
Hodges and Smith	1954	'Sheffield estate'	Urban housing estate
Mogey	1956	Barton (Oxford)	Urban housing estate
Young and Willmott	1957	'Greenleigh' (outer metropolitan London)	Urban housing estate
Durant	1959	Watling (London)	Urban housing estate

Source: after Frankenberg (1966)

The thesis proposed by Frankenberg satisfied some of the critics of the rural–urban dichotomy theory. Others remained unconvinced, and Pahl launched a blistering attack on the concepts of both dichotomy and continuum. He considered that 'in a sociological context the terms rural and urban are more remarkable for their ability to confuse than for their power to illuminate' (Pahl 1968, p. 263). Several arguments are advanced in support of his ideas. First, face-to-face contacts were not destroyed by urbanism, for they remained important in offices and factories; therefore there was no simple process in which social relationships became anonymous in urban areas. Second, Pahl considered that all of Britain is now culturally urbanized. Whether an individual lives in a city, a town or an isolated cottage, he or she has broadly the same range of consumer goods to choose from, is subject to the same television and newspaper coverage of events, and is inevitably drawn into 'urban society'. Third, there is no simple link between place and occupation, for this has been modified by transport changes which allow commuting to 'urban' workplaces from 'rural' residences. The result has been the growth of urban villages that, in terms of physical characteristics, are identical to the traditional rural villages, but are economically dependent on metropolitan areas. Finally, the development of communication and information systems, especially the telephone, has transformed the effects of distance so that physical isolation need no longer imply the existence of social isolation.

Pahl argues against the view of life-style as being dictated by a particular urban or rural location. For him, life-style is dependent more on class and stage in family life-cycle, and to a lesser extent on whether a social group has a 'local' or 'national' orientation. Therefore some of the important differences in life-style are between the locally orientated middle class, the nationally orientated groups of middle-class spiralists, and the working-class families who work in the towns but are forced by the housing market to live in rural areas. Pahl's position is best summarized by his own much-quoted phrase, that 'any attempt to tie particular patterns of social relationships to specific geographical milieux is a singularly fruitless exercise' (Pahl, 1968, p. 302). In terms of social patterns, some people are of the city but are not in it, whereas others are in the city but are not of it. The particular value of Pahl's work is that it prevents any oversimplified association of social and spatial milieux, and should alert researchers to a more sensitive analysis of social relationships.

One reservation should be placed against Pahl's thesis; in criticizing the oversimplification of the rural–urban dichotomy and continuum theories, he has perhaps overstated his own case (Newby 1977). In some circumstances, the geographical milieux may define some patterns of social relationships as a result of the constraints that are applied to the local social structure. For example, improvements in communications may have reduced the social isolation of those in small, physically isolated communities, but distance still imposes a constraint on the choice of jobs or the number and type of face-to-face contacts that are possible. Pahl himself recognized this, and he considered that there were five important differences between rural and urban societies: availability of facilities, density of role relationships, degree of occupational choice, problems created by the commuting rural population, and the strong ideological bias in the attitudes to urban and rural societies (Pahl 1970). Therefore, as argued earlier, it seems that there are important differences between rural and urban areas, even if these do not amount to distinctive ways of life.

SOCIAL PATTERNS AND ACCESSIBILITY IN RURAL AREAS

One of the underlying themes in the literature on community studies and the rural-urban continuum concerns the nature of social change in the countryside. Broad national-scale developments such as the de-skilling of work (Wood 1982) or the growth of white-collar jobs affect both rural and urban areas, to some degree. Also important are specific migrations which bring new groups into rural areas either to work or to live. Those who take up residence in the countryside may be retirement migrants, commuters, workers in local industries, 'drop-outs' from conventional society, or other social groups. The particular composition of this influx will differ within rural areas; as an obvious example, commuters will be more numerous in the more accessible districts. Partly because of the complexity of these changes, there has been no common agreement on the definition of rural social groups; Stamp (1949), Pahl (1966), Thorns (1968) and Ambrose (1974), among others, all agree that there have been and remain substantial social changes in rural areas – but they have all produced quite different typologies of rural social structure (see chapter 4).

Nevertheless, there have been some dominant themes in these social definitions, particularly with respect to the continuing importance of the agricultural community, the division between 'newcomers' and 'locals' and the significance of social class. These themes are all developed more fully later. In reality, the social divides and the definitions of social groups may involve all three of these major components of rural social structure. Nevertheless, although complex, this involves more than an exercise in social theory, because the differences between social groups are the key to interpreting the experiences of those living in rural areas. Nowhere is this more evident than with respect to accessibility.

In fact, accessibility has both a social and a spatial dimension. The main social constraints are the availability of income to purchase transport and services and the acquisition of education which improves job opportunities. The spatial constraint is the limitation imposed by distance on access to jobs and services. The two sets of constraints are of course linked, because those with higher incomes are more likely to own private means of transport which will reduce their problems of spatial access. Therefore, the problems of spatial accessibility are usually greatest for those with least social accessibility. This is a theme that will be developed below, especially in chapters 6, 8 and 10. Details of these variations in accessibility and of the policies that have aimed to improve (mainly) spatial access are not important at this stage. However, it is important to note that, since the fading of the debate on rural and urban differences, there has been a substantial growth in the literature concerning rural accessibility and the related problems of deprivation in rural areas. This has stemmed mainly from the work of sociologists, geographers and planners.

The growth of such studies has been relatively recent, for even as late as 1978 Walker (1978a) edited a book on rural poverty for which he claimed that the main aim was to counter the overwhelmingly urban image of poverty and deprivation. Collections such as those edited by Moseley (1978, 1982), Walker (1978a) and Shaw (1979a) have helped to dispel some of the myths that surround rural areas, and there is now a growing corpus of such research. However, many of these studies appear to abide with the spirit of Pahl's dictum that it is fruitless to attempt directly to relate social and geographical milieux. Rather than argue that there are distinctive problems of service or employment provision related to some distinctive rural way of life, they emphasize that there is a variety of social groups in a variety of rural environments with differential levels of accessibility. Accessibility can be seen to vary both between remote and developed rural areas and between higher and lower income groups. At the same time, the abilities of social groups to circumvent these problems are very different; the more wealthy may more easily move house to achieve greater accessibility, or run two or more cars. This emphasis on the variety of social groups and rural environments is important, because it should help to prevent over-generalization of problems and solutions. However, it still leaves unresolved the question of how differential accessibility is to be analysed and explained.

MANAGERIALISM AND RURAL MANAGERS

Rural geography has tended to lag behind some of the other branches of geography with respect to explaining the production of needs and resources (Harvey 1973). For this reason Moseley (1980a) considers a comparison of rural and urban studies instructive. In the 1970s studies of urban geography passed through four overlapping phases: quantitative model-building, behaviouralism, managerialism, and political economy (Robson 1979). By contrast, Moseley sees rural geography as still being firmly ensconced in the first two of these phases, which imposes limitations on the capacity for explanation. This can be illustrated by the example of housing. A quantitative model-building approach would aim to provide a sophisticated description of the distribution of needs and resources in housing and, through statistical analysis of aggregate data, would suggest some of the variables, such as income levels or demand, associated with this distribution. Behaviouralism, on the other hand, would direct attention away from the aggregate level to the individual householder or aspirant, and would examine such features as housing search processes, residential mobility and changing needs. It would reveal how individuals react to constraints in the housing market. By contrast, managerialist and political economy perspectives highlight, respectively, the operation and production of such constraints. The remainder of this chapter will outline the elements of such approaches and will attempt to assess their value for rural social geography.

Pahl (1970) is usually recognized as the formative influence in the development of the managerialist approach. He argues that there exist spatial and social constraints on the access to scarce urban resources and facilities. The emphasis is on constraints rather than choices, with the constraints reflecting the distribution of power in society. Control over the distribution of scarce resources is in the hands of 'gatekeepers' such as building society and bank managers and local authority planners, who operate according to bureaucratic rules and procedures. These rules are not value-free, and tend to favour some social groups over others. According to this view, social groups are the dependent variables while the 'gatekeepers' or managers are the independent variables in the allocation process.

The basic approach outlined by Pahl inspired a number of studies of the activities of 'gatekeepers'. These have been mainly urban-based and have been concerned predominantly with access to housing; for examples, see Boddy (1976), Gray (1976a) and P. R. Williams (1976). Although the thesis of managerialism has been developed mainly in urban studies, it could nevertheless be applied in rural areas. Pahl (1970, p. 203) himself emphasized this, writing that 'education, jobs and housing as scarce resources are all potential sources of conflict: access to such resources is systematically structured in a local context. Such contexts may be physically 'urban', 'rural', or a mixture of the two.' As the emphasis is on the actions of the managers, managerialist analysis can be as valid in a rural setting as in an urban one.

Moseley (1980a) considered that the most prominent challenge for rural research was to investigate the managerialist thesis in order to lay bare the realities of decision-making. This challenge has been taken up in recent years, and the major advances, as in urban studies, have been in the housing field (Niner 1975; Shucksmith 1981; Phillips and Williams 1982a). However, research has not been totally restricted to housing and Heller (1978, 1979), for example, has examined some of the managerialist features of the provision and planning of health services. Local authority planners have also come under scrutiny – Harrison (1972) has discussed the attitudes of local planners to what constitutes 'acceptable' development, and how their views are influenced by central government decrees.

It is clear that the managerialist perspective has considerable potential for drawing attention to differences in decision-making at a local level. Although the decision-making process itself may be similar in urban and rural areas, the implications may differ; for example, a decision to concentrate educational provision in a few, large-scale units would have widely differing implications for remote mid-Wales and suburban London. Above all, the value of this approach is that it 'provides a useful way of penetrating the complex relationships that structure . . . areas at the points of contact between consumers and allocators of scarce resources; it may help both to expose the allocation processes and the rationalities on which they are based' (Herbert and Thomas 1982, p. 48).

Nevertheless, one reservation must be made. Up to this point, the bureaucratic decision-makers within rural areas have been treated as the 'real' local decision-makers. This view takes no account of the power of elected representatives, and to some extent bureaucratic decisions are constrained by, or possibly reinforced by, councillors. As there are notable differences in politics in urban and rural areas, this feature requires further consideration, although it is important to note that central government has reduced the autonomy of local authorities in recent years.

THE LOCAL POLITICAL CONTEXT IN RURAL AREAS

The relationship between councillors and their professional officers has been a matter of great debate. In theory, the professionals or bureaucrats merely advise the councillors and execute their decisions, but this model division of responsibilities rarely occurs (Gyford 1976). There are many, such as Dennis (1972) and Goodman (1972), who believe that, in the face of the rising complexity of local government, it is the professionals who have the upper hand. Knox (1982) has summarized the techniques by which bureaucrats maintain control over decision-making: these include overloading and stifling councillors with long and very technical reports, withholding information, and slanting its presentation. Most councillors therefore have to rely heavily on the advice given by their officers. Against this, it has been argued that councillors do have a decisive influence because they fix the total budget for the local authority (Rich 1979) and thereby the total amount of scarce resources to be distributed. The prolonged struggle over the annual budget of the politically 'hung' Berkshire County Council during 1982 illustrates the importance of this argument.

Of course, power need not lie exclusively with either the elected members or the bureaucrats. Buchanan (1982, p. 5), in a study of structure plan preparation by Suffolk County Council (SCC), found 'the existence of a small core in SCC which directed the procedures of plan preparation. That core comprised the two chairmen of the planning committees and three senior officers in the county planning department.' This elite 'exercised considerable influence over the content of the plan, its preparation, discussion and final form'. They gave the plan a distinctive 'conservationist ethos' at an early stage, and this conditioned all later discussions. At the stage of public participation they favoured information dispersal techniques, such as public meetings and exhibitions, rather than more widespread household survey methods. They also seemed to consult disproportionately more amenity groups than economic and community interest groups, so that the whole process of plan formulation could perhaps be viewed as a cynical exercise in manipulation by a small elite group.

Pahl, who did so much to foster the managerialist thesis, has recently suggested that more attention should be paid to the local political context in which decisions are made (Pahl 1979). In addition to socio-economic factors he considers that there are important local political determinants of variations in life-chances in Britain:

1 the political history of an area;
2 the organization and social affiliations of local political parties;
3 the organization of professional officers;
4 the degree of overlap between economic and party political interests;
5 the existence of alternative public or private power bases and interest groups in the local area;
6 the pattern of relationships with central government.

This provides a framework that allows some of the key elements in the rural political context to be identified. With regard to the first point, the Labour Party historically has had little grass-roots support in many rural areas and, hence, relatively little political power. A review of local government election results indicates consistent dominance by the Conservative Party (or by the Liberal Party in a few areas such as mid-Wales or Cornwall), by Independents or by Ratepayers' Associations representatives (Butler and Stokes 1971). These tend to be conservative in outlook if not of the Conservative Party. The extent of this political control is indicated in figure 1.2, which shows the almost total lack of Labour Party majorities in 'rural' areas.

The second point on Pahl's list – the organization of local political parties – can also be a distinctive element in rural areas depending on the balance between newcomers and traditional groups. Newcomers are often urban commuters or those who have retired from jobs in the town to live in the countryside. Although there can be a conflict of interest between newcomers and traditional groups, this does not always arise. For example, newcomers who have retired to an area because it is environmentally attractive are often the most belligerent and articulate in seeking to protect the rural landscape. This may involve excluding industry, which is seen as an ugly intrusion into the countryside. In this respect Newby *et al.* (1978) have shown that the farmers may sometimes be the allies of the newcomers, because they may wish to exclude alternative industrial employment in order to protect their own supply of farm labour.

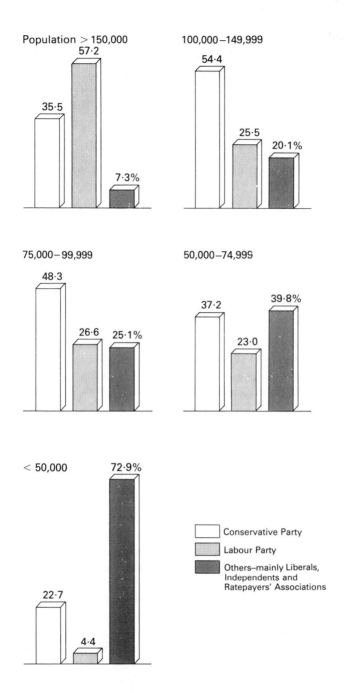

FIGURE 1.2   Political representation on district councils in England and
Wales, classified according to population size
Source: based on information from *The Municipal Year Book and Public Services
Directory 1982* (London: Municipal Publications Ltd)

The thesis proposed by Newby *et al.* has been challenged by some commentators. Buller and Lowe (1982), for example, argue that, although the interests of farmers and middle-class preservationists coincide on many issues, particularly in a generally restrictive attitude to urban and industrial development, there are important differences between them.

> Though for both groups property may be a means of accumulating wealth as well as a place of residence, for the farmer land is also a factor of production. To the middle class resident, in contrast, the surrounding countryside is an amenity – i.e. an extension of his interest in his home as a pleasant residential and recreational environment. . . . [Buller and Lowe 1982, p. 34]

The main conflicts between the groups are therefore often over the use of agricultural land. Farmers may want to intensify agriculture while middle-class newcomers may oppose this on amenity grounds.

The organization of the professional officers in rural authorities is a third factor determining variations in life-chances. Prior to the 1974 local government reform, most of the old rural district authorities tended to be relatively small and to have weak local rateable bases, partly because of the lack of highly rated premises. In consequence, many rural local authorities had relatively weakly organized administrations, often employing only one or two officials. This was certainly the case in housing, where in some localities, with relatively small stocks of council houses, the whole business of allocations and lettings could be in the hands of a single councillor (Larkin 1979). In such authorities the power of the civil servants was weakened by their small number and by the apparently straightforward nature of the administration. Such arrangements are less likely to occur since the reorganization of local government, which tended to increase the size of local authorities.

The degree of overlap between economic interests and party membership is another source of distinctive features in rural areas. Bracey (1959) has shown how, at least before 1974, the Conservative/Independent political groups were dominated by different economic interests at each tier of local government. The county level was dominated by the gentry, the professionals and the owners of larger farms; the district level was dominated by the 'lesser' gentry and the 'lesser' professionals; while the parish level was dominated more by working farmers, tradesmen and clerical workers. More recently, Buller and Lowe (1982) have indicated that one in six of the members of Suffolk County Council are farmers or landowners, and that this group often holds key positions on committees. Newby *et al.* (1978) have shown that this overlap of interests can have important implications; for example, farmers may oppose the building of council houses with the apparent aim of keeping down the rates, but also to reinforce their control over workers who live in tied cottages.

Where there are a number of alternative power bases in rural areas (e.g. farmers and various rural protection bodies), the conflicts between them, which are often centred on their attempts to influence physical planning decisions, can have a decisive effect on the social composition of rural areas. Working-class groups, by contrast, are relatively poorly organized in rural areas, particularly because the trade unions are so weakly represented, although this may change with the amalgamation in the early 1980s of the National Farm Workers' Union with the much larger Transport and General Workers' Union.

Finally, although the rural political scene is arguably distinctive, it is important to view it in the context of the changing relationships between central and local government. The 1950s and 1960s were a period of rapid expansion of local government activities, when local government expenditure grew at a faster rate than total public expenditure. However, local government expenditure has subsequently fallen, from a peak in 1973–74, when it accounted for 31 per cent of all public expenditure, to only 26 per cent by the late 1970s (Conference of Socialist Economists 1979). This reflects a strengthening of central government control over local authorities, which has been achieved in four ways. First, local authorities wishing to raise commercial loans currently have to obtain central government sanctions for these. Second, since 1967 the Rate Support Grant (a transfer from central to local government) has been paid as a 'block' grant rather than as a series of grants to particular departments within local authorities. This in itself allows tighter control over expenditure; in addition, since 1975 mid-year supplements to local authority budgets have no longer been made. Third, since 1974 control of many functions, including water, sewerage, public transport and some health services, has been transferred from local government to other statutory public bodies. Finally, in the 1980s central government has imposed very strict borrowing and spending limits on local government, backed up by severe financial penalties for overspending. All these measures have severely eroded the autonomy of local government, and make a general political economy perspective even more valid and necessary.

RURAL POLITICAL ECONOMY

So far, we have examined the relative importance of the bureaucracy and the local political structure in influencing the distribution of scarce resources. However, some argue that this exaggerates the importance of local decision-makers (Norman 1975; Duncan 1977; Harloe 1977). They stress that the managers operate within wider economic and social constraints than suggested by the managerialist thesis, and that to emphasize their independent role exaggerates their importance. Furthermore, the managers are only the distributors of resources, and managerialism does not allow for the analysis of the production of such scarcities. Pahl (1975, 1977) came to accept these criticisms, and in later works sought to reinterpret the role of the managers, linking managerialist theory to a corporate view of the State, in which managers may be viewed as mediating between the State and the private sector. Not all critics accept this reformulation (for example, Mellor 1977; Bassett and Short 1980), but the move towards an appreciation of the wider societal context was generally welcomed. Pahl, in effect, was shifting towards a political economy perspective on the allocation of scarce resources in urban areas.

The political economy approach analyses the interrelated set of social, economic and political features of a society in conjunction with each other, rather than as separate social phenomena (Shaw 1972). Most recent developments in political economy have been Marxist-inspired, although there are considerable differences between the orthodox and the neo-Marxist approaches (see Desai 1974 and Evans 1975). However, one point that Marx barely touched upon, but which has been of great importance in recent attempts to develop political economy perspectives, is the role of the State in capitalist society (Colletti 1975). Pahl's initial view of managerialism envisaged managers as the servants of a neutral state which served the community as a whole. This is rejected in political economy approaches, which see the State as being either instrumentalist or semi-autonomous within the structural constraints of the capitalist mode of production. The first conceptualization, which sees the State as the instrument of class domination, is usually considered too simplistic, and will not be developed further here. The structuralist view is more subtle and regards the State as the arena where different classes compete for political power. However, whichever class has control, the power of the State is seen to be limited by the structure of capitalism, and basically supports the interests of the dominant class.

Gough (1979) advances three arguments to support the structuralist view. First, most of the key posts in the 'commanding heights' of the State are occupied by members of the dominant class, who share certain common ideological and political positions which condition their actions (Miliband 1969). Second, through its ownership of economic resources, the dominant class has greater power than the other classes and is therefore able to exert greater influence on the State. Third, the capitalist economy has its own rationality to which the State must sooner or later submit; for example, if the State threatens the interests of capital this might lead to future investment being diverted abroad.

It has been argued that the State has two basic and often contradictory functions (O'Connor 1973). The first is to support the process of capital accumulation: through social investment (for example, in infrastructure or in subsidies to industry), in order to increase the productivity of labour, and through social consumption (for example, housing and health services), in order to lower the reproductive costs of labour. The other function is legitimization, which involves social expenditure such as income subsidies in order to maintain social harmony. The total amount of expenditure by the state in Britain in fulfilling these and other functions has risen enormously in the twentieth century, from 29.4 per cent of GNP in 1921 to 57.9 per cent in 1975. The reasons for this are that, 'as accumulation proceeds and the laws of motion of capitalist development unfold, increased State intervention and activity is required in order to overcome the barriers to profitable accumulation that arise' (Campbell 1981, p. 174). The role of the State is therefore an important area for research, as is also the related discussion about the role of the 'local state'.

One view of the 'local state' stresses that it is part of the State but that, as it is relatively autonomous, there is scope for variation in local policies. According to Saunders (1979), following closely O'Connor, the main functions of the 'local state' under capitalism are threefold: first, social investment, which includes expenditure on infrastructure and education, and aiding the reorganization of production through the planning process; second, social consumption, which includes the provision of low-cost housing and cultural facilities; third, social expenditure on the police and social services. In fulfilment of these functions, local government expenditure has increased markedly; in the early 1970s it amounted to almost one-third of public expenditure in Britain. However, the 1970s and early 1980s also saw a reduction in the power and autonomy of the 'local state', as noted in the previous section. And within local government, the introduction of corporate management techniques has centralized power within the bureaucracy.

The outline provided so far of the political economy perspective and of the functions of the national and 'local' states provides some useful concepts to relate to social geography. In particular, the nature and location of expenditure on services and resource provision can be reinterpreted in terms of the state's continuing need for legitimization and support of the process of capital accumulation. However, although the stress on the 'local state' provides an insight into the variations between local authorities, there is nothing so far in it that would allow for the development of either a specifically urban political economy or a rural political economy.

Castells (1976, 1977a, 1977b) sought a suitable definition of the term 'urban'. He rejected definitions based on production (for which he considered that the regional level was significant), institutions (as there is little congruence between 'real' urban areas and administrative urban areas), or ideology (there being no distinctive cultural formations at the urban level). Instead, he sought a definition of urban areas in terms of *collective consumption*. This is consumption organized by the State, including housing, education and health services, in order to ensure the reproduction of labour power. In short, urban areas in capitalism are the loci of state actions to guarantee adequate supplies of suitably housed and educated segments of the labour force. Harvey's view of urban studies is not entirely different; he emphasizes consumption processes but also considers that investment in the built environment is an important and distinctive urban element of the capitalist system. 'Whatever else it may entail, the urban process implies the creation of a material infrastructure for production, circulation, exchange and consumption' (Harvey, 1978a, p. 101). Therefore it is essential to analyse the vast flows of capital into the built environment.

This view has been refined to emphasize that the mobility of capital and labour is a necessary condition for the accumulation of capital in the advanced capitalist system (Harvey 1982). Also, the reproduction of the labour force entails some geographical specialization, which is supported by investment in social infrastructure. Crises occur at the local level because of the increasingly rapid and erratic movement of capital, in an extreme form termed 'hypermobility' (Damette 1980), which can 'abandon' labour, plant and social infrastructure in particular areas. This theoretical view is underlined by the empirical work of the Community Development Project (1977), which has noted the decline of some inner-city areas as they have become redundant in the national economy. This approach can help to explain growth and decline in specific localities by reference to their position in the national and international political economy.

Where does this leave rural political economy? In the absence of any separate, substantive attempt to develop a rural political economy perspective, the foregoing discussion is valuable, for it does provide some guidance. First, rural areas are the loci of distinctive forms of production, namely agriculture and forestry. However, with the decline of subsistence farming in Britain, agriculture does not lie outside the production process of capitalism but, rather, becomes a distinctive part of this process. It could be argued that the growth of highly intensive factory farming may lessen this distinctiveness somewhat, but agriculture and forestry still remain land-intensive activities closely influenced by the limitations of the natural environment.

Second, although Dunleavy (1982) argues that the number of workers employed in agriculture is so small that in most areas it is unable to support a distinctive socio-cultural system, Castell's notions concerning collective consumption can probably be applied to rural areas. Agriculture poses its own problems for the reproduction of labour power, both in remoter areas experiencing substantial population losses and in urban-dominated rural labour markets where there is alternative employment. The continued use of tied cottages is one of the farmers' responses to this potential crisis, but special problems are also raised for the local state in the provision of public housing in rural areas (see chapter 5). Beyond agriculture, the well documented counter-urbanization trend (Spence *et al.* 1982) also poses problems for the reproduction of social relations and of non-agricultural labour power outside the immediate metropolitan areas. This can be reinterpreted as the creation of a new division of labour involving core–periphery (Massey 1979, Lipietz 1980) and urban–rural production shifts. The establishment of industry and office employment in the smaller towns in turn creates the need for State intervention to increase and ensure collective consumption in these areas. This may involve investment in, for example, infrastructure or training in new commercial or industrial skills, as well as the provision of housing, education and health services.

Furthermore, contradictions may arise in an acute form in rural areas between collective and individual consumption. Collective consumption needs may require the construction of new housing estates, roads or factories, but individual consumption needs may require that rural areas be preserved for landscape value or recreation. This may give rise to conflict between social groups divided by class but also according to whether they are rural or urban residents, and whether they are newcomers or long-term residents of the countryside. In Britain many of these conflicts are acted out on the public stage provided by planning inquiries, and the outcome of such conflicts clearly influences the nature of life-chances in the rural areas.

Finally, Anderson's (1976) work on the meaning of 'urban' can be used to advantage in rural studies. He argued that 'urban' signified a particular interaction of social processes with spatial structures, with the spatial structure being produced by the processes of production, of class relations, and of the State within a particular social formation. Boddy (1976) takes up this theme and considers whether 'urban' is therefore more than just a 'convenient' description based in empiricism. He decides that it is, because these larger social processes do occur in a real, spatial setting which actually affects their operation. Furthermore, Boddy argues that the effects of spatial structure are strongest in urban areas, which brings out more clearly the contradictions in production and intensifies problems of labour reproduction. However, this is debatable, and depends on the definition of the term 'spatial structure'. Here, it is sufficient to turn the argument slightly and to state instead that some of the spatial effects in rural areas are different from those in urban areas, depending as they do on, for example, social and spatial constraints on accessibility. This implies that there is a worthwhile, even if not a theoretically distinctive, rural political economy perspective.

The arguments presented in this section are inevitably rather complex and, in view of the infant status of the study of rural political economy, are mostly indeterminate. No simple conclusions can therefore be formulated, not least because rural political economy currently lacks a coherent framework. However, this review of the theoretical literature does provide a general perspective.

Rural areas do not exist in isolation, for they are part of larger national and international structures. Neither do they possess fixed characteristics, because the roles ascribed to them change as part of the process of capitalist development. The more accessible rural areas are in many ways indistinguishable from urban areas, not simply because of similarities in built form or in levels of non-agricultural employment, but because they are the loci for the collective reproduction of segments of the labour force. However, rural areas may also be distinctive, especially in terms of the nature of agriculture and forestry as forms of land-intensive production. Moreover, the requirements of such production may conflict with individual consumption requirements for a locale for relaxation and leisure. In addition, particular features of spatial structure in rural areas – such as the distribution of settlements and economic and social functions – affect the process of capital accumulation; and the nature of these distributions and associated levels of accessibility poses particular problems for both individual consumption (for example, access to shops) and collective consumption (for example, the centralization of services) in rural areas. Therefore policies adopted by the State in pursuit of its social investment and legitimization functions, whether in transport, housing or education, may well have very different implications for rural areas than for urban areas. Furthermore, the particular nature of the local State in rural areas may add to the distinctiveness of the policies adopted by some local government agencies. It is this broad perspective that will underlie, usually implicitly, the remainder of this book.

2 The Rural Economy I: Living Off the Land

THE ECONOMY OF RURAL AREAS

Labour markets, along with housing markets, fundamentally shape the nature of life in rural areas. Most of the themes and problems dealt with in later chapters, such as deprivation and accessibility, can be clearly appreciated only if the basis of the rural economy is understood. As a first step, we need to dispel some of the myths that surround the rural economy, and the most important of these is the belief that it is an agricultural economy.

In terms of land use, agriculture and forestry certainly dominate the countryside, although some industrial and mining activities may be visually impressive in particular locations. However, agriculture and forestry are extensive forms of land use, and most people living in rural areas do not make a living directly from the land. Agriculture in Britain now employs just over 2 per cent of the economically active population, and accounts for only a small proportion of employment even in the most rural areas. Gilg (1976), in a survey of some of the more rural areas of England and Wales in 1971, found that less than 20 per cent of employment was in the primary sector even in counties such as Devon, Kent, Norfolk and Westmorland. Therefore, more than four-fifths of employment will be in the secondary and tertiary sectors, with the service sector usually accounting for more than half of total employment. Where tourism is particularly important, as in parts of the national parks or in some coastal areas, the significance of the service sector may be even greater. Manufacturing employment may also be important, especially in the more accessible countryside, and can include both rurally based activities (such as food processing or the manufacture of fertilizers) and firms that have no direct links with the local primary sector (such as electrical engineering).

Another myth to be dispelled is that of uniformity: the assertion that labour markets are similar in all rural areas. This is not true; and a spatial division of labour (see Lipietz 1980) within rural areas has at least two distinctive geographical elements, the regional and the local. The regional element is based on the fact that there are faster rates of employment growth and fewer agricultural jobs in the more accessible rural areas, as in the South East, the West Midlands and south-east Lancashire. By contrast, the economies of more remote and upland areas are more likely to be stagnant and to have larger proportions employed in agriculture (Countryside Review Committee 1977a).

At the local scale, the density of agricultural employment varies according to the fertility of the land and the organization of farming but it does provide a relatively even spread of jobs throughout rural areas, whereas factories and service centres provide concentrations of employment. Therefore, given the growth of manufacturing and services in the rural economy, there has also been a spatial redistribution of jobs, which have tended to become increasingly concentrated in the larger settlements. Access to jobs can therefore vary markedly over relatively short distances. Those living in or near the larger settlements or towns have better access to a wider range of jobs; there will be opportunities to commute to nearby towns, and there will also be greater opportunities for part-time and hobby farming. As a result, labour markets are being transformed and extended so that they cut across the traditional rural – urban divide. This is a change that is being reinforced by the out-migration from towns of workers who may subsequently commute back to urban jobs. One of the critical divisions in the rural economy, therefore, is between those places and groups of people that have access to urban labour markets and those that do not. It is possible to envisage a typology of areas within the British space economy (table 2.1). Employment opportunities and diversity are greatest in the metropolitan regions and in the more urban localities, and fewest in the remoter rural localities. Commuting levels are rather more complex and are highest in localities adjacent to, and within commuting distance of, towns. They are lowest in the least urban localities beyond commuting range, and also within the towns themselves (Spence *et al.* 1982).

This simple classification of economic areas gives an insight into some of the problems of rural areas, especially with respect to maintaining viable communities. The Countryside Review Committee (1977a, p.6) recognized the crucial role of the local economy, since 'without opportunities for employment, there can be no community.' Hodge and Whitby (1981, p.3) also stressed that 'economic viability will usually be a necessary, but not a sufficient, condition for social survival.' The problems of some rural communities, such as out-migration or the persistence of low incomes, stem from the character of the rural economy. The nature of these

Table 2.1 Some employment characteristics of the space economy

Characteristics of employment	Type of area		
	Metropolitan areas	Accessible rural areas	Remoter rural areas
Agricultural employment	Low	Intermediate	High
Employment diversity	High	Intermediate	Low
Importance of commuting	Low	High	Low

problems will vary according to whether the community is in a metropolitan region or a more remote and inaccessible area.

In order to understand how the rural economy has changed in recent years, we have to consider the national and even international framework. For example, British agriculture was fundamentally affected by the rapid growth of international trade in foodstuffs in the late nineteenth century (Perry 1973). In the postwar period, agriculture has been subject more than almost any other industry to price controls and guarantees, first by the British government and latterly by the EEC. The growth of manufacturing can be understood in terms of the changing requirements of production, especially industry's needs for cheap, non-unionized, unskilled labour in the face of the 'deskilling' of work caused by technological change (Massey 1979; Wood 1982). This has made non-metropolitan areas more attractive locations than previously for many manufacturing firms. Changes in service employment have also resulted from fundamental alterations in economy and society such as the expansion of state activities, and the growth of recreation and tourism.

We need therefore to move away from the traditional view that there is a distinctive rural economy based on extensive and almost exclusive land use by agriculture and forestry, because this is not really true except for a few locations in some remoter regions. Instead, we must recognize the roles of manufacturing and service employment, especially with regard to the increasingly complex interlinking of places within spatially expanding labour markets.

THE STRUCTURE OF BRITISH AGRICULTURE

The current agricultural returns for Britain show that about half the surface area of the country is under crops or grass, and that about one-third is under rough grazing. Therefore, more than three-quarters of the country is used for some form of farming activity, and the predominant source of farming income, according to the *Annual Review of Agriculture*, is livestock and livestock products (Ministry of Agriculture 1982). Livestock, especially cattle and pigs, account for 36 per cent of receipts; and livestock products, especially milk and eggs, account for a further 27 per cent. By contrast, arable crops account for only 25 per cent of income, which partly explains the high level of food imports, particularly cereals, to the UK. The relative composition of farm income has remained remarkably stable since at least the 1930s, disturbed only by enormous arable conversions during the Second World War (Britton 1974), although more recently the contribution of crops has been on the increase. The underlying organization of farming, however, has changed considerably over the twentieth century, especially in terms of levels of specialization, farm sizes and ownership of farm land.

The organization of farming

Since the 1930s, agriculture has increasingly been organized in more specialized units. Only 40 years ago, it could be said that most farms were mixed and would have perhaps six or even twelve different products. This was a strategy that offered some protection against climatic risks, spread work more evenly throughout the year, and helped to preserve soil fertility. However, improved methods have reduced risks and mechanization has relieved some of the demands of labour at peak periods (Britton 1974). Therefore farming units have become increasingly specialized; in the most extreme form, this has led to factory farming of single products. The capital-intensive battery chicken production unit employing a dozen or so unskilled workers in routine chores of feeding, killing, cleaning and packaging is one result of this process, and the work practices and skills involved are clearly very different from those required of the farmer and his few employees on the more traditional, mixed farm. It has been estimated that, by the early 1970s, about 90 per cent of full-time holdings were specialized, and that only 10 per cent could be classified as mixed farms (Britton 1974), although this is based on a very broad definition of specialization which includes both single-product farms and those with two or three products. In the analysis, part-time units, including many smallholdings, were more likely to be mixed.

Specialization has also been accompanied by an increase in the scale of farming units, which has been most marked since 1945. Earlier forms of mechanization, such as the substitution of tractors for horsepower, could usually be accommodated in the existing pattern of farms. However, with the marked increase in the capital-intensive nature of farming in the postwar period, involving for example larger and more expensive machinery, there have been important economies of scale, necessitating an increase in the size of farms. In practice, there are considerable difficulties in measuring farm size, especially with regard to the minimum size of units to be included. Britton (1974) has estimated that the average size of agricultural holdings of larger than 1 ha increased from 51 to 62 ha between 1964 and 1972. Other data show that, between 1976 and 1981, the average size of full-time holdings (those requiring at least 250 standard man-days per year) increased from 112 ha to 119 ha, indicating that the trend of concentration is still continuing. As a result, the number of farms declined by about 2 per cent per year during the 1960s and 1970s. Although the rate of decline has now slowed, there was still a 5 per cent decrease in the number of holdings between 1976 and 1981. An associated change has been the reorganization of farms during the same period, especially with the enlargement of fields and the removal of hedgerows (Countryside Commission 1974). This has profoundly transformed the landscape, especially in eastern England.

Although there has been concentration of farm units, this does not necessarily mean that agriculture is dominated by enormous farms. In 1981, most farms in the UK were relatively small; and 96,000 of the 235,000 units were smaller than 20 ha, compared with only about 30,000 units of over 100 ha (figure 2.1). However, the latter group account for about 50 per cent of cropland and grassland, compared with only 7 per cent for the former. These figures are a little misleading, however, because they include 'all farms', not only 'full-time' units. In 1981 it was estimated that the average size of holding required to occupy fully one person for a year was over 20 ha, and just over half of the farms were therefore economically capable of being full-time units. The precise nature of these smaller farms is, however, very varied; some are genuinely part-time, while others are viewed by their owners as providing full-time work. The important point is that the nature of the work, the form of organization and the level of capitalization will all vary according to the size of the farm. Farming may involve combining similar inputs to produce identical products irrespective of farm size, but the skills required and the work patterns involved in managing a very large farm are obviously very

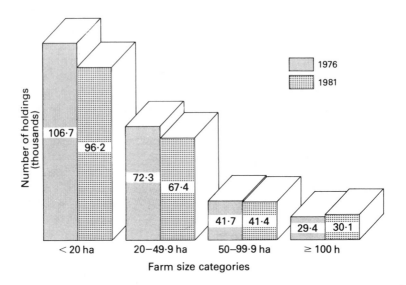

FIGURE 2.1   Number of farm holdings in England and Wales, 1976 and 1981
Source: data from the Ministry of Agriculture (1982)

different from those required of the farmer who runs his enterprise without any paid assistance.

The third major change in the organization of farming has been in the ownership and tenure of farms. Before the First World War most farmers in England were tenants and only about 10 per cent were owner-occupiers. In the interwar years there were fears of legislation being passed restricting landlords, and many owners sold to their tenants, and by 1981 the level of owner-occupancy had reached 66 per cent (Ministry of Agriculture 1982). The relative merits of the two systems are much discussed, and it has been argued that, while the owner-occupier has far greater scope for innovation, he is also more likely to be saddled with large debts from having borrowed money to buy his farm. Therefore, the owner-occupier is more likely than the tenant to have a smaller farm and to be under-capitalized even though he has greater freedom of action (Edwards 1974). However, such a view is an oversimplification. Many tenants also own land; furthermore most have quite good security of tenure and can be as heavily in debt as many owner-occupiers. At the same time, owner-occupiers may have paid off their loans and can have considerable freedom of action with their current investments. It is therefore difficult to attribute any pattern of farm investment simply to tenure. Nevertheless, there has been a shift from renting to owner-occupancy, and one factor underlying this has been the relatively low level of rents: they have consistently lagged behind the value of land, which has encouraged many landlords to sell their farms.

There have also been changes in forestry in the UK. After decades, if not centuries, of decline in the size of forest area, this trend has been reversed or at least halted since the mid-twentieth century. The major responsibility for this lies with the Forestry Commission, established in 1919 with the dual roles of planting new forests and encouraging private forestry (Gilg 1978). The Commission planted 149,000 ha of trees during the interwar period, and in 1943 set itself the target of planting a further 2 million ha by the end of the century. Although substantial planting has been achieved, the anticipated target is unlikely to be met, mainly because the Commission has experienced difficulty in obtaining large tracts for afforestation. Ultimately, the reason for this is the preference given by the state to agriculture than to forestry (Matthews *et al.* 1972).

THE POLITICAL AND ECONOMIC CONTEXT OF FARMING

The economic context for understanding the changing structure of agriculture in Britain is provided by the levels of farm costs and receipts. The latter have been influenced greatly by state intervention, while costs have been affected particularly by increases in the price of land and by the changing ratio of capital to labour. These are not the only considerations that have influenced the shape of agriculture, but they have probably been the most significant. (The relationships between government and agriculture are fully discussed by Bowler 1979.)

The price of farm products

State intervention in agriculture began during the First World War, but it was only with the Agriculture Act 1947 that there was a concerted move to guarantee prices (Tracy 1976). This Act aimed to promote 'stability and efficiency' in the industry, through a system of guaranteed prices which were negotiated in an annual price review. In the immediate postwar years the emphasis was placed on expanding production, but this was modified in the mid-1950s as world commodity prices started to fall and the cost of supporting prices in the UK increased.

This approach to intervention was fundamentally altered by Britain's entry into the EEC in 1973 and the adoption, soon afterwards, of the Common Agricultural Policy (CAP). CAP protects farmers, since imports to the EEC are taxed to increase their prices to agreed internal levels. This is quite different from the previous British system, in which prices were set at world levels and farmers were paid the difference between these and a set of guaranteed prices. As EEC prices were at first considerably higher than world prices, this proved to be a costly policy for both government and consumers in the UK; more recently, the gap has narrowed.

Farmers generally welcomed the system of intervention in agriculture, even though this sometimes seemed to conflict with their own attitudes towards the role of the state. Bell and Newby (1974a, p. 87) succinctly state that 'one of the most striking paradoxes of the farmer's market situation is that a group that so vehemently and continually espouses the values of independence and free enterprise has long been in the vanguard of state interference in, and control of, the free market.' In economic terms there is, of course, no contradiction. Farmers stood to benefit substantially from price agreements, which offered them some protection against fluctuations in prices and the low income elasticity of demand for food, especially for non-livestock products (Metcalf 1969). Moreover it is widely considered that farmers have managed to negotiate advantageous terms in the price reviews, although there have been variations among products.

The means by which farmers have been able to achieve supposedly favourable terms provide an insight into the nature of agricultural organization. Farmers, through the National Farmers' Union (NFU) and to a lesser extent, the Country Landowners' Association, have been exceptionally well organized in defence of their own interests (Wilson 1977; Newby 1979). They have considerable solidarity as a group in spite of their wide geographical distribution, and have always shown formidable expertise in publicizing their case. The NFU has argued that higher prices will guarantee food supplies and reduce imports, as well as assuring reasonable incomes for their members. However, the strength of the farmers' lobby goes beyond this, and it has been argued that, although farmers and their families are numerically a small group, electorally they form significant minorities in a number of constituencies (Self and Storing 1962). The real political influence of the farming group probably lies in their traditional links with the Conservative Party, which still has a number of important landowning members (Howarth 1969; Roth 1973), as well as in the ability of the NFU to represent its members' interests.

The cost of farm production

The cost of labour is relatively low, both because of the use of 'unpaid' family labour and because of the level of agricultural wages (the average weekly wage for 45.7 hours work was £86 in 1980). Indeed, agricultural wages have, if anything, fallen further behind general wage levels in the postwar period – from 73 per cent of the wages of those employed in manufacturing in 1950 to less than 70 per cent in 1970 (Gasson 1974*a*). Labour costs, therefore, have probably not been paramount in shaping agriculture, and generally there has been a surplus of labour available, except in areas most accessible to urban employment. More important have been technological developments, which have required an increase in the capital–labour ratio in agriculture. Larger and more expensive machinery, requiring greater minimum usage for efficient running, has led to an increase in average farm size as well as to greater specialization. For example, economic use of a combine harvester may require a larger area of cereal land than that currently cultivated by a farmer; two possible reactions to this are the conversion of grassland to cereals (increasing specialization), or the purchase of additional land. Both of these trends are visible, although their influence has been modified by the greater use of hired equipment.

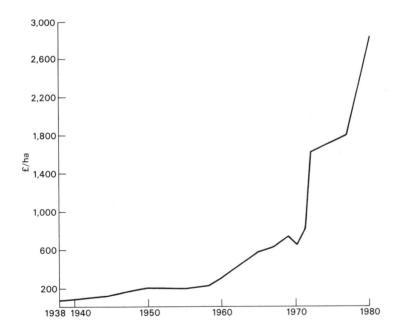

FIGURE 2.2   Sale price of agricultural land, 1938–80
Source: data from Edwards (1974) and Ministry of Agriculture (1982)

The other important element of costs is the price of land, which has risen substantially in the postwar period, especially in the late 1950s and the 1970s (figure 2.2). An apparently surprising feature has been the way in which the price of land has outstripped the returns from land. Several reasons have been suggested to explain this apparent economic paradox, including the willingness of farmers to pay higher prices in order to purchase land adjacent to existing farms so as to achieve economies of scale, the desire to obtain the amenity value of land, and a general awareness of the scarcity of land (for all purposes) in the United Kingdom (Edwards 1974). Land also has the appeal of retaining its value quite well during periods of inflation. An additional, although usually overrated, factor has been the increasing intervention of City institutions in the agricultural land market; Munton (1976, 1977) estimated that by the mid-1970s, in spite of considerable land-buying, institutions held less than 1 per cent of all agricultural land in Britain. However, institutions have tended to purchase better quality land and this has been regionally concentrated, mainly in eastern England (figure 2.3).

The implications of the general rise in price levels are important, even though no more than about 2 per cent of agricultural land comes on to the market each year. Higher land costs would increase the mortgage loads of entrants into farming and this, combined with high interest rates in the 1970s in particular, leads to pressure to use the land to its maximum capacity, usually implying greater specialization. Higher land prices also induce some small farmers to sell in order to capitalize their assets, especially if they lack the resources to farm efficiently (Brett 1972). Institutions, however, usually lease their land, often to the previous owner, as they prefer to purchase tenanted land which is generally cheaper. Institutions also expect high returns on investments, and this also increases the pressure to specialize. Furthermore, larger units minimize managerial costs, which has added to the tendency for concentration (Edwards 1974).

EMPLOYMENT IN AGRICULTURE

Direct employment in agriculture in the UK now amounts to little more than 2 per cent of paid employment. However, a more realistic idea of the importance of agriculture is given by the estimate that indirect employment, the processing of farm inputs and outputs, amounts to about 10 per cent of total employment (Gilg 1976). Nevertheless, Britain has one of the lowest rates of direct employment in agriculture in the world, comparing with 5 or 6 per cent in countries such as Sweden and the Netherlands and 9 per cent in France (Hodge and Whitby 1981). This relatively low level of

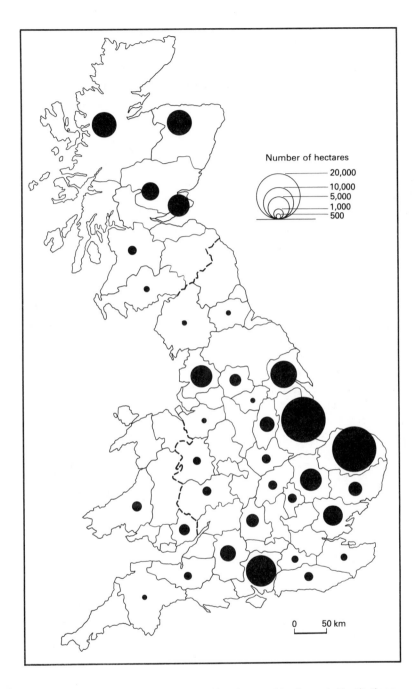

FIGURE 2.3   Distribution of agricultural land owned by financial institutions, 1975
Source: Munton (1977)

agricultural employment is the outcome of a steady 'drift from the land' that has occurred since the late nineteenth century.

The sharp decrease in the proportion employed in agriculture began in the first quarter of the nineteenth century. By 1891 only 10 per cent of employment was in farming; since then there has been a slower decline to the present low level (figure 2.4). As mentioned earlier, however, these figures are somewhat misleading because there is considerable indirect employment in agriculture, the relative importance of which seems to have been increasing. Many jobs previously undertaken on the farm are now carried out elsewhere. For example, chemical fertilizers are made in factories instead of manure being processed on the farm; feedstuffs are bought in instead of being locally produced; and more of the final processing of crops is likely to occur in factories.

Recent Trends

During the 1970s, the number engaged in agriculture fell from 716,000 to 639,000 and within this total the number of employees fell from 418,000 to 344,000 (table 2.2). The change seems to have occurred a little less painfully than in some other industries, for there have been relatively few redundancies. About 10 per cent of the workforce has left the industry each year to be replaced by an intake of only about 5 per cent (Wagstaff 1971). This relatively gentle turnover of labour was important in maintain-

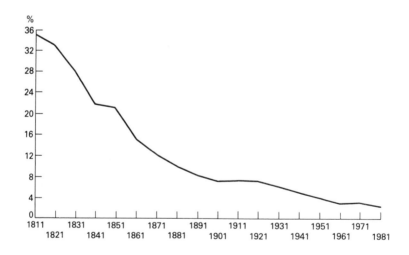

FIGURE 2.4   Percentage of the labour force employed in agriculture, 1811–1981
Source: after Gasson (1974a) and Ministry of Agriculture (1982)

Table 2.2   Employment in agriculture (thousands)

	1970–72 average	1981
Full-time, regular		
Hired male	177	129
Hired female	15	12
Family male	55	30
Family female	15	5
Part-time, regular		
Hired male	25	19
Hired female	26	24
Family male	16	12
Family female	16	7
Seasonal		
Male	38	58
Female	36	41
Salaried managers	–	8
Total employed	418	344
Farmers, partners, directors		
Full-time	224	205
Part-time	69	90
Total farmers, etc.	293	295
Total	716	639

Source: Ministry of Agriculture (1982)

ing the paternalistic nature of employer–employee relationships on non-family farms (Newby 1977).

The reduction in the labour force has not affected all groups equally. The drift from the land has been strongest for hired workers; there were 1,472,000 regular employees in agriculture in 1851, but only 238,000 in 1981. In terms of hired labour, the largest decrease was in the number of full-time males, which during the 1970s fell from 177,000 to 129,000; but the substitution of capital for labour has usually involved the substitution of machinery for both male and female employees, especially on the larger farms. The importance of relatives in farm employment has also declined, and the children of farmers are increasingly less likely to work on the family farm, both because of the attraction of alternative employment elsewhere and also because the demand for labour may have fallen (Nalson 1968). The number of full-time regular family employees has fallen by half during the 1970s, and the number of part-time family workers has fallen almost as quickly. The trend may have been reduced in recent years because in a period of recession there are fewer job alternatives off the farm. It also seems that during the 1960s the rate of reduction in the number of males employed was greater than in the number of females, but that during the 1970s this trend levelled off. One group that has not declined, however, is seasonal workers. It is true that the 'migrant armies' of hop pickers and harvest labourers, well documented by social historians (Samuel 1975), are now a feature of the past – they have largely been replaced by harvesting machinery or, increasingly, by the subcontracting of some parts of farm work to specialist firms. However, mechanization has meant that farmers can now dispense with the services of some full-time or part-time workers for most of the year, replacing them with temporary labour at times of particular intensity in the work of the farm, which has contributed to a modest increase in the number of seasonal workers in the 1970s (table 2.2).

The overall picture is therefore one of decline in the number of almost all occupational groups engaged in agriculture, but especially of employees. One of the few sub-groups that has shown an increase in numbers is the specialists, especially on stock farms, mirroring the increasing specialization of agriculture as a whole (Gasson 1974a). One other major group has not been mentioned so far – the farmers themselves, whose number remained remarkably stable between 1851 and 1961. Only subsequently, with the increase in scale of farming units, has this declined. During the 1970s, however, their number actually increased slightly, owing to a growth of part-time farming. The number of full-time farmers fell by 8 per cent over the decade.

Farms are frequently transferred from one generation to another. Nalson, in his study of the mobility of farm families in an upland area in north-west England, found that 'all but one of the single farmers, 81 per cent of the married farmers and 69 per cent of their wives have fathers who are or were farmers' (Nalson 1968, p. 81), and most of these had worked the same farm land. However, this tradition was weakening, and fewer of the children of the then current generation of farmers were in farm work. Among the sons, for example, 5 per cent were in quarry work, 6 per cent in factory work, 5 per cent in transport, 8 per cent in building and 5 per cent in engineering. However, in general terms farmers have resisted the drift from the land more successfully than their employees. This is not really surprising, as becomes clear when we consider why farm workers leave agriculture.

Reasons for leaving agriculture

Two reasons are usually given to explain the drift of farm workers from the land. First, there is a definite 'push' provided by the substitution of capital for labour, a trend marked both by the increased concentration of farms and by specialization. An example of this is provided by milking; modern machinery operated by one person can milk as many cows as it previously took ten persons to milk (Hodge and Whitby 1981). However, most commentators stress a second reason – the 'pull' factor – and Tyler (1974) emphasizes that about two-thirds of farm workers who leave the land do so of their own accord. It is important not to exaggerate the degree of choice here; farm workers are really responding to a limited set of opportunities within a set of close constraints (such as the access to alternative work). Nevertheless, it is useful to emphasize the features of alternative work, especially higher wages and easier jobs, which have made leaving farming an attractive option.

Wages in non-farming jobs certainly tend to be higher; it is estimated that agricultural wages often have been only about 70 per cent of average wage levels. During the 1970s this gap closed a little but the differential remains important (Hodge and Whitby 1981). The gap is substantial even after account is taken of the provision of tied cottages (a questionable privilege, discussed in chapter 5) and fringe benefits such as free milk and vegetables. Farm workers also suffer from the lack of a career structure in their industry because, as most farms employ only one or two workers, there are few opportunities for advancement to higher-status jobs or to higher wages. The only exceptions to this would seem to be in the larger 'agribusiness' farms, although these are still relatively few. Even in these cases, managers usually have far better formal qualifications than the average farm worker is likely to possess (Gasson 1974a). This lack of opportunities is further compounded by the soaring price of agricultural land, which has made entry into farm-tenancy or owner-occupancy very difficult. It is significant that, in Nalson's 1968 study, very few farmers had been the sons of farm employees. This lack of opportunity for advancement partly explains the predominance of young men among those leaving agriculture. The consequence is an ageing labour force; in 1970, 20 per cent of farm employees were aged 16–20, 52 per cent were over 35 and only 28 per cent were aged 21–34 (Gasson 1974a).

The nature of agricultural work has also contributed to the drift from the land, as it can involve long, erratic hours and is frequently arduous and boring. Furthermore, many farm workers dislike the relatively solitary nature of the work and some also resent the paternalistic nature of their relationships with their employers. Finally, many farm workers leave the industry for social reasons, for example in order to improve their access to schools, shops and services (Bracey 1970).

The position of farmers is quite different. Many prefer to remain in agriculture because, as owner-occupiers, they have an employment status that they are unlikely to be able to achieve in any other sector. Many farmers also lack the formal qualifications and training that would enable them to obtain managerial posts outside farming. A study in the Fens and Hertfordshire found that many farmers had started their careers during the Depression years when there was little alternative to staying on the family farm; furthermore, three-quarters had left school before the age of 15. Many were also rather elderly – nearly half of the farmers studied being over 50, and few employers would wish to train someone of that age (Gasson 1969). Therefore most farmers would have to give up their independence and the status of being self-employed or employers in return for uncertain prospects in other industries. On the more positive side, it can be noted that many farmers would be loath to give up what they see as the attractive features of their jobs, including work in the open air and a variety of tasks. In Gasson's study it was the younger farmers and those who had better access to alternative employment who tended to stress the positive features of farming, and she concluded that,

> contrary to expectations, farmers with a higher opportunity cost, through location, age and experience, showed stronger attachment to their present job. Since those who could change their occupation will not and those who would change cannot, there seems little prospect of encouraging small farmers to leave farming before they reach retiring age. [Gasson 1969, p. 279]

Although a decline in the number of farmers has begun, therefore, it is likely to be a slow process and one that will have distinctive geographical features according to the types and locations of farms, and the opportunities available locally and regionally.

AGRICULTURE: A SOCIAL PATCHWORK

The agricultural industry is one of the most complex and varied forms of economic activity. Considerable variations have already been identified in the sizes of farm units, in the crops that they produce and in the social characteristics associated with these. A more systematic classification of farms, according to socio-economic organization, is provided by Bell and Newby (1974a), who concentrate on the manual-versus-administrative roles of the farmer and on the market orientation of the farm. Whether a farmer is directly involved in manual labour or acts in a purely administrative role depends partly on the size of the enterprise. They suggest that 'a certain size of enterprise will necessitate a division of labour that constrains the farmers to a purely administrative role, with only the occasional symbolic tramp across a field or poke of a pig to reinforce his self-definition. . . .' (Bell and Newby 1974a, p. 95). At the extremes the relationship is very simple, for a one-man farm must involve the farmer in manual labour, while very large farms are so complex as to have administrative structures that are little different from those found in factories. In the intermediate range of farm sizes, however, the degree of bureaucratization is often a matter of choice for the farmer.

The second element of the classification is the degree of market orientation of the farm, for, 'whilst all farmers produce for the market, by no means all farmers behave in a market-orientated manner in the work situation. For many farmers, farming is much more an expressive and affective form of behaviour than an instrumental one' (Bell and Newby 1974a, p. 96). Again there is some correlation between this and the size of the enterprise. Taking the two dimensions together, Bell and Newby propose a simple four-fold classification of farm type (figure 2.5) which identifies family farms, hobby farms, 'agribusiness I' (high administration content) and 'agribusiness II' (high manual labour content).

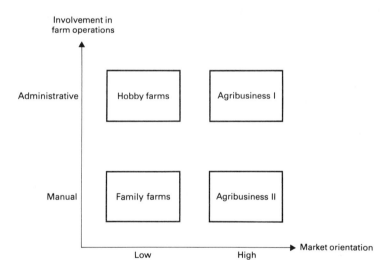

FIGURE 2.5   Socio-economic classification of farms
Source: after Bell and Newby (1974a)

Hobby farmers

Hobby farmers are one group whose orientation to the market is minimal and who do little direct manual work. The pioneering research on hobby farming was undertaken by Gasson (1966) in a study of Kent and Sussex. She found that, between 1941 and 1964, the proportion of farmers with a substantial source of non-farm income had increased from 30 to 50 per cent. Three-quarters of this group of part-time farmers had other non-manual jobs, mainly professional and administrative, while only 8 per cent had another job in agriculture. Therefore she concluded that part-time farming in this region was becoming more of a hobby than a means of boosting agricultural income. Part-time farmers were more likely to see 'improving the general appearance of the farm' as the main criterion of their work, rather than 'increasing farm incomes' or 'economic efficiency'. In the extreme cases, the farm had become no more than a place of recreation, with farming activities being phased out and only a few horses being kept.

Family farms

In the second type of farming enterprise, the farmer is considerably involved in manual work but is not particularly market-orientated. Instead of income maximization, the main aim may be to pass on the farm intact to succeeding generations. These farms are usually 'family farms', defined as 'a holding of land, together with a farmhouse and outbuilding, which is occupied by a farmer and his family and which is maintained as an economic unit without the use of hired labour' (W. M. Williams 1973, p. 117). This is a rather rigid definition, however, and it is usually relaxed to allow for the use of hired workers during certain periods. Given this definition, family farms tend to be fairly small units, but their acreage will depend on their precise activity and location.

The retention of the farm within the family has been taken to be one of the main aims of this group, although their actual ability to keep the name 'on the land' is limited in reality. Nalson (1968) found that only 48 per cent of the farmers in his study occupied holdings that were previously owned or tenanted by their parents or other near relatives, and he estimated that fewer than half of this group had grandparents who had lived on the same farm. W. M. Williams (1973), in a study of family farming in Ashworthy in Devon, found a similarly low level of continuity between generations. Only one of the 75 farms had been continuously occupied for more than a hundred years, and at the other extreme there was one family that had lived on eight different farms during the same period. Generally, there seems to have been a high rate of migration within the parish and continuous adjustments to existing farms, so that 'only a small proportion of the parish has been occupied and cultivated by the same families for more than one generation; there are hardly any farms which have the same layout today as they had at the beginning of the century and many have been changed several times' (W. M. Williams 1973, p. 125).

Many family farms are officially classified as part-time (Ashton and Cracknell 1961), and the majority of these farmers supplement their incomes from a second occupation, such as factory work or road transport (Kirk 1974). This group is differentiated from the hobby farmers in that they do regard farming as their main occupation. They are also more willing to devote their time to the enterprise and will therefore undertake labour-intensive activities such as dairying, which hobby farmers would normally ignore. The hobby farms are also more likely to be specialized while the family farm undertakes a greater variety of tasks, such as raising chickens and growing vegetables, to supplement the family budget. Since many members of the household will help in running various enterprises in the family farm, social and economic organization will tend to be very closely interwoven, especially in terms of the division of labour between home and work.

Agribusiness

These are farming organizations that seek to apply modern technology and management techniques to large areas of land, with the aim of maximizing income. Agribusiness I is very bureaucratic and, indeed, 'the farmers' expertise lies in administration and financial accounting rather than husbandry' (Bell and Newby 1974a, p. 97). However, there is another type of agribusiness, type II, in which the farmers take an active interest in husbandry, spending as much time on the land as in the office. Relatively little is known of this type but, of necessity, they are generally medium-sized farms. The typical agribusiness type I usually operates as a limited company in which ownership and control are divided, and the most publicized examples are owned by financial and commercial city institutions.

The managerial organization of such farms involves systematic cost accounting, devolution of responsibility for day-to-day decisions to the managers and foremen, and centralized control of buying and selling (Gavin 1967). Commentators have taken different views of these farms. It has been suggested that they may have a 'galvanizing effect . . . on the thinking and attitudes of many larger farmers' (Wallace 1981, p. 218), but it has also been suggested, perhaps a little unkindly, that 'large farms are less economic than small ones; the hidden factors of subsidies, grants, tax allowances, loans, guaranteed prices, etc., seldom appear in the calculations of profitability, and milking 100 taxpayers makes larger profits than milking 100 cows' (John 1981, pp. 256–7). Whichever of these views is more accurate, it is undeniable that agribusinesses undoubtedly transform the rural economy. They introduce a clearer career structure into farming; in the extreme case, factory farms have totally eradicated traditional styles and patterns of farm work. They can also modify the traditionally dominant roles of large-scale farmers in the rural community because many of the owners of agribusinesses either do not live in, or do not take any interest in, the affairs of the immediate community, and therefore do not participate in local politics.

In summary, it can be said that agriculture may no longer be the dominant rural industry but it is still important in particular areas, not the least for its effects on the landscape and sometimes for its role in employment. Even the negative feature of the decline of agricultural employment is important because of its link with the drift of population from some rural areas. Agriculture can still influence evolving social and political structures in rural areas, and therefore the agricultural mosaic should form at least the backcloth for any attempt to analyse rural social geography.

3 The Rural Economy II: Non-agricultural Employment in Rural Areas

The rural economy has never been completely agricultural, for most villages used to support a number of craftsmen serving local needs. Although industrialization has tended to eliminate traditional crafts, the non-agricultural element of the rural economy has increased in importance since at least the nineteenth century. Apart from agriculture, what are the other important elements in the rural economy? First, there is mining and quarrying, which in particular locations can be a major source of employment. Most commercially exploited minerals in Britain tend to be in the older geological strata located in the more remote western and upland regions, while sand and gravel occur in coastal or valley sites or in glacial deposits, particularly in the south and east of England. Of more widespread importance is manufacturing, especially in the smaller towns, and there is evidence of movement of manufacturing firms away from metropolitan regions into more peripheral regions of Britain including many rural areas. Of greatest importance, however, is the tertiary sector, as the majority of employment in most rural areas is in services and transport. The distribution of tertiary activity is uneven within rural areas, especially with the increasing centralization of public sector employment in recent years. Tourism is also of particular importance in some regions and may dominate the local economy.

An interesting feature of the rural economy is the way in which these sectoral employment changes are interlinked. As a result of the increased relative importance of part-time farming and farm work, many individuals seek a second job in manufacturing or services. In addition, many farmers, particularly on family farms, have sought to diversify their enterprises, for example by catering for tourists. This may involve using a field as a camping site, offering bed and breakfast or providing 'farm teas'. Other farmers have entered the retail trade, through 'pick-your-own' or 'farm shop' methods of selling produce.

Another feature of the rural economy is its relationship with urban labour markets. The extension of commuting hinterlands has increasingly brought rural areas within the daily journey-to-work range of nearby towns. The result has been a two-way movement. Some people have moved out of towns to live in the countryside, sometimes adopting a second part-time job in the rural area, while many inhabitants of rural areas have been able to obtain jobs in towns. Occasionally, as with the case of part-time farms or even some full-time farms, one or more family members may work in a factory or shop in the town in order to support the family farm. Therefore, the increased separation of home and workplace in the modern economy has acted to strengthen the interlinkages between the rural and urban segments of the economy.

Underlying these trends has been the increasing importance of the state in the management of the economy. In addition to the macroeconomic policies of the state such as levels of taxation or public expenditure, which affect rural residents as much as urban residents, there are two specific facets of government intervention in rural areas. The first involves the statutory local planning process; for the location of quarries, mines, factories or holiday complexes in rural areas has become a source of conflict among local social groups. While some have welcomed the jobs provided by these developments, others have opposed them in order to preserve existing landscapes or to further their own economic interests (Newby 1979). The means for the resolution of such conflicts is the statutory planning process. The other specific role of government in the rural economy has been the attempt to create jobs, mainly by fostering manufacturing. Some rural locations have been designated as 'assisted areas' which can benefit from regional policy, while special development boards have been established in some regions such as mid-Wales and the Highlands and Islands. Furthermore, the Council for Small Industries in Rural Areas (COSIRA) and the Small Industries Council for the Rural Areas of Scotland (SICRAS) have also promoted small firms in rural areas.

MANUFACTURING INDUSTRY IN THE COUNTRYSIDE

Manufacturing accounts for a relatively small proportion of employment in rural areas, and in the more remote regions it has been estimated that this can be as low as 10–20 per cent (Gilg 1976). Rural manufacturing tends to be polarized into two main types. One involves craftsmen, operating on a small scale, producing custom-made or individual products such as quality pottery or fine furniture. On a larger scale, this type of production can incorporate such enterprises as Ercol furniture or Dartington glass. The other group of industries involves the processing of raw materials. Some of these are footloose industries, such as the aluminium plants in Scotland utilizing cheap hydroelectric power, while others are based on the processing of agricultural products, including milk, meat and vegetables. In these cases the locational attraction of rural areas can be considerable, and one of the most remarkable locational shifts in manufacturing in recent years has been the closure of port-based, imported cane sugar processing plants in East London in favour of sugar beet processing factories in East Anglia (Community Development Project 1977). However, the establishment of processing plants in rural areas can have unexpected effects on agriculture. In the eastern Scottish borders, for example, the establishment of pea processing plants led to a switch from sugar beet and potato production to peas, which require less labour than the crops they replaced, and the result was a net decrease in agricultural employment (Hodge and Whitby 1979).

In recent years, however, there has been a reversal in the relative fortunes of rural and urban areas with respect to a broad range of manufacturing activities. Fothergill and Gudgin (1979), in a study of manu-

Large scale modern industry in a rural setting (source: authors and A. Teed)

facturing in the UK between 1959 and 1975, show that there has been rapid expansion in rural areas, while Spence *et al.* (1982) confirm that decentralization of employment was prevalent throughout the British urban system during the 1960s. Two processes contributed to this: the out-migration of firms from urban areas, and, more importantly, a growth in indigenous firms in rural areas. Firm mobility usually accounts for only a small proportion of employment growth in any area, with most coming from existing or new indigenous firms (Cross 1981; Watts 1981). However, there are some regional exceptions to this. For example, 80 per cent of employment growth in the small-firm sector in Cornwall in the 1960s and 1970s was accounted for by exogenous firms (Perry 1982).

This growth of manufacturing employment can be explained partly by the quality of rural environment and partly by the changing structure of manufacturing. One view is that rural manufacturing growth stems from the preferences of employers for rural environments. Oakenshott (1979) found a preference for small towns among employers because of their more pleasant physical environments and easier access to the countryside, compared with the larger cities, while Spooner (1972) found that the attractiveness of the area was the most important factor influencing firms moving into the South West. In Cornwall, which has a very attractive image, in-migration of firms seems to be in some cases linked with a form of semi-retirement by owners. One survey indicates that their average age was over 55; they had a strong leisure orientation, and had few plans to expand their businesses (Perry 1982). Many were also now operating smaller enterprises than before the move to Cornwall. This group, therefore, had chosen to run their businesses less intensively in order to enjoy the benefits of living in Cornwall, possibly to prepare for retirement.

The second explanation of the shift to rural areas focuses on the changes that have occurred in the production process. Technological change has led to a de-skilling of industrial work, so that a major requirement of many employers is now for cheap, non-unionized, semi-skilled labour (Massey 1979; Wood 1982). The increased scale of enterprises, combined with improvements in management methods and telecommunications, has also contributed to spatial separation of functions within the firm (Goddard 1975, 1978). Different functions require different conditions of production and therefore may have different locational requirements. The result is that many manufacturing firms have decided to locate their physical production processes outside the metropolitan regions. Many small towns in rural areas have been chosen as the sites of branch plants because they have ready supplies of labour which (drawing on low female activity rates) is flexible, is relatively cheap, and has little tradition of trade unionism. In addition, even medium-sized plants can dominate the labour markets of small towns (for example, in the cases of Westland at Yeovil and Clarks at Street), and this places them in a strong position in their dealings with the labour force (Lever 1978). The major drawback for all immigrant firms has been the difficulty in recruiting the few highly skilled key workers essential to production.

THE STATE AND RURAL MANUFACTURING INDUSTRY

Although the factors outlined above have probably been the most important considerations in the growth of rural manufacturing, an additional reason can be found in the role of the state. State intervention in rural manufacturing really dates only from the Second World War, after the report of the Scott Committee in 1942 assessed the advantages and disadvantages that would result from rural industrialization. It was recognized that the advantages were outweighed by disadvantages, including the loss of productive agricultural land, disruption of the labour supply for farming, despoliation of the landscape, and modification of traditional village life. Therefore the Scott Committee recommended that, within rural areas, factories should be sited on vacant land in small towns rather than in villages or the open countryside. This has been the predominant view in planning until the present (Blacksell and Gilg 1981). Nevertheless, in response to the persistent problems of unemployment in rural areas, the

From school to workshop: is this the appropriate scale for village manufacturing? (source: authors and A. Teed)

government has increasingly become involved in attempting to stimulate industry in these areas. Hodge and Whitby (1981) classify such state activities into three types: the improvement of locations as sites for industrial development; the reduction of relative costs, and the improvement of information flows.

Both direct and indirect methods have been used to improve rural locations as sites for manufacturing industry. Indirect methods include attempts to improve accessibility, technical education and training; direct methods include the provision of factories and industrial estates. Such direct measures were first undertaken in rural areas by the Development Commission, established in 1947. Until 1976 the Commission had responsibility for England, Wales and Scotland, but thereafter its role in the latter countries has been taken over by the Welsh and Scottish Development Agencies (Carney and Hudson 1978, 1979). The actual construction of factories has been delegated to two agencies: the Industrial Estates Corporation, responsible for rural areas that are also assisted areas in terms of regional policy (such as parts of Scotland, Wales, the North and the South West), and COSIRA, responsible for the remainder of the country. The most important feature of the programme of advance factory building is the emphasis on concentration, particularly since the mid-1960s when the policy of 'trigger areas' was adopted, involving in effect a strategy of growth centres within areas of serious population loss. Such a strategy recognizes both the negative attitudes of local planners to industrial development in the open countryside and also the advantages of concentrating investment in infrastructure in the few locations that have reasonably large labour markets.

The same strategy seems to have characterized the work of most development agencies in rural areas. For example, the Mid-Wales Industrial Development Association was established in 1957 by the five counties of mid-Wales in order to promote industrial development as a means of alleviating unemployment, low incomes and a prolonged population loss of 25 per cent between 1871 and 1971 (Howes and Law 1973). From the beginning, the Association limited its activities to the 21 small towns in the region and, effectively, to the main settlements within this group (Garbett-Edwards 1972). After the report on *Depopulation in mid-Wales* (Ministry of Housing and Local Government 1964) this approach was formally adopted, and future factory building was concentrated in Aberystwyth, Bala, Brecon, Llandrindod Wells, Newtown, Rhayader and Welshpool. The scheme has certainly helped to attract manufacturing firms, and it has been estimated that between 1957 and 1977 some 5,000 new jobs were created in 113 factories, many of which were engineering or clothing firms (Broady 1980).

The literature on factories in rural areas has tended to over-emphasize the role of the Development Commission, for there are a number of other agencies that provide industrial premises. In Cornwall, for example, Perry and Chalkley (1982) have shown that the Development Commission built only one-fifth of the small premises (less than 5,000 ft^2) provided between 1975 and 1981. Substantial proportions were provided by the local authorities and the Department of Industry, and the largest share of all, one-third, was accounted for by private developers (figure 3.1). The same variation characterizes the provision of industrial estates in Cornwall (figure 3.2). There is a dispersed distribution of industrial estates within the county (Shaw and Williams 1982b), which were developed and managed by a number of organizations including the Industrial Estates Corporation, the county and district councils and commercial establishments. The estates varied in size from a few units in piecemeal developments to 30 or 40 plots on well serviced, carefully planned schemes. Some have the full range of infrastructural provision enabling them to accommodate all but the heaviest industries, while others are capable of occupation only by light industry or warehouses. All industrial estates, however, have one common characteristic: they are all located in, or adjacent to, major

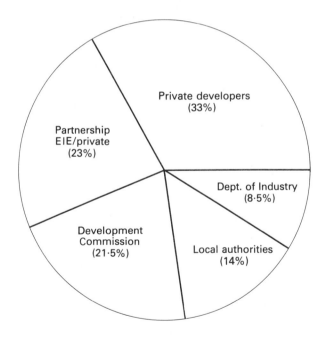

FIGURE 3.1   The developers of small industrial premises in Cornwall, 1975–81
Source: after Perry and Chalkley (1982)

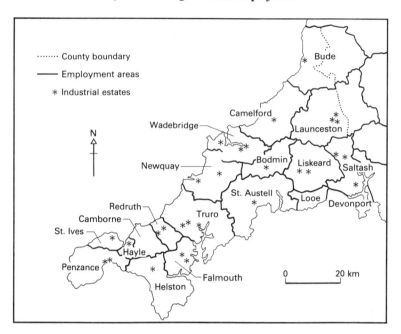

FIGURE 3.2   Industrial estates in Cornwall, 1981, by employment areas
Source: after Shaw and Williams (1982b)

settlements, and given their labour requirements perhaps this is inevitable. This reinforces the advantages of the more accessible rural areas.

A second form of state intervention to promote rural industrialization is the use of direct subsidies to change manufacturers' relative costs. These include grants for buildings and equipment, tax relief and rent-free factory lets. These incentives, together with controls on the location of industry, have formed the main body of regional policy measures developed to promote industrial growth in the assisted areas. The policies date from the Special Areas Act 1934 (McCrone 1976), but only in the early 1950s was the first rural region (North West Scotland) designated. Subsequently, most Scottish rural areas, mid- and North Wales, the Pennines and parts of Devon and Cornwall have at one time or another been designated as Assisted Areas (see figure 3.3a). The changes in definitions of Assisted Areas and in the financial assistance available to firms are too numerous to recount here, but useful summaries are available in a number of texts (Manners *et al.* 1972; Keeble 1976; McCrone 1976; Law 1980). As unemployment has increased and high rates have become more widespread geographically, so more rural zones (particularly upland areas) have benefited from regional policy measures.

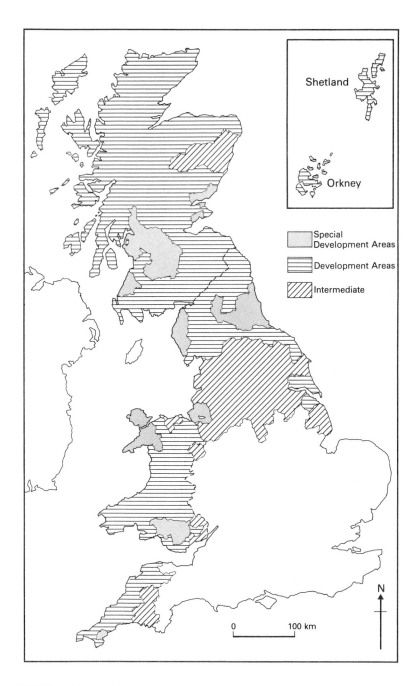

Shetland

Orkney

Special Development Areas

Development Areas

Intermediate

N

0   100 km

FIGURE 3.3(a)   Assisted areas, June 1979
Source: after Townsend (1980)

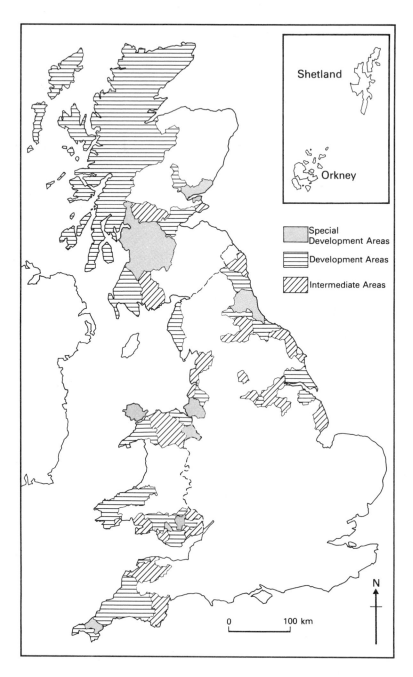

Shetland

Orkney

Special
Development Areas

Development Areas

Intermediate Areas

N

0   100 km

FIGURE Figure 3.3(b)   Revised assisted areas, August 1982
Source: after Townsend (1980)

Since 1979 there has been a reversal in regional policy. The newly elected Conservative government decided to reduce the extent of designated areas, through a programme of phased withdrawals, over the following three years (see Townsend 1980). Some of the most significant changes have affected rural areas, and Development Area or Intermediate Area status has been withdrawn from large parts of rural Wales, Scotland and northern England (figure 3.3b). As this has been combined with a general relaxation of Industrial Development Certificate controls on the location of industry and reduced real spending on regional policy, it is clear that resources are being redirected from rural areas. The corollary of this is the increasing emphasis that has been placed on urban policies, such as Inner-City Partnerships and Enterprise Zones. However, many specific rural employment policies survived the reductions in state expenditure in the early 1980s. The Development Board for Rural Wales and the Development Commission were little affected, and COSIRA, as a result of its commitment to small businesses, seems to have been favoured (Gilg 1980). Whether these agencies will be able to compensate in the mid-1980s for the loss of assisted area status is doubtful.

A third form of assistance to industry is the improvement of information. This can be either through the provision of market research data or through advice on accounting and management. An important role in providing such information is played by COSIRA and SICRAS and by the industrial development bureaus operated by many local authorities. Such bureaus may also adopt a promotional role, seeking to 'sell' the advantages of their areas to industrialists who are relocating their firms. The small North Wales town of Wrexham is one example of an authority that has taken a particularly active role in industrial promotion, and figure 3.4 shows one of their many eye-catching advertisements placed in the national press. Many, if not most, local authorities now have some form of industrial promotion campaign, and Burgess (1982) has shown that the more rural authorities are aware of the environmental attractions that they offer. For example, in promotional slogans Kings Lynn is 'a place to live, work and breathe'; the Isle of Wight is 'a unique living and working environment', and Shrewsbury is 'where town and country meet'. However, most of the campaigns are run by authorities in the more accessible countryside; there are few campaigns organized by those in the remoter or upland areas, either because they deem them undesirable or consider the likely returns insufficient.

The different approaches to industrial development have absorbed an enormous amount of resources and effort in the postwar period. Industrialization in rural areas has increased, and has been more rapid than in metropolitan areas. However, it is not clear whether this has been the result of state intervention or of changes in the structure of production.

GKN, Kelloggs, Metal Box Public Company Ltd., Continental Can, G-Plan, Fibreglass Ltd., Lego U.K. Ltd., Tetrapak (Rausing) Ltd. and Hoya Lens U.K. Ltd. are between them investing over £100,000,000 in industrial development in Wrexham.

In fact every month since 1974, a new project has commenced in the area.

Why?

Because the pioneering range of services and incentives offered by this progressive Borough Council are second to none.

Here are some of them:–

★ **An excellent Industrial Relations record.**
★ **Rent free periods in advance factories.**

★ **Easy access to major markets.**
★ **Special Development Area, British Steel Corporation and E.E.C. financial incentives.**
★ **Welsh Development Agency assistance.**

To beat the rush and stake your claim come along and talk to us at Wrexham.

The Chief Executive Officer,
The Guildhall, Wrexham LL11 1AY,
Clwyd, North Wales, U.K.
Telephone (0978) 364611

FIGURE 3.4   Industrial promotion by Wrexham Maelor Borough Council
Source: based on material supplied by Impact Information Ltd., Shrewsbury, with the permission of Wrexham Maelor Borough Council

Furthermore, industrialization has rarely been the panacea for rural development that had been hoped. A number of reservations have been expressed with regard to the employment created by rural manufacturing industry, concerning both type of jobs and type of firm.

The type of employment offered by manufacturing industry in rural areas has been questioned for a number of reasons. It has been argued that the jobs thereby created do not fit the aspirations of local residents and also perpetuate low incomes, since low wages may have been the initial attraction to employers. On the other hand, rural industrialization is considered essential to stem the outflow of population from rural areas (Saville 1957), although this depends on a matching-up of potential employees and potential jobs.

The type of manufacturing firm that is established is also important, with a fundamental distinction being made between indigenous and exogenous enterprises, and between parent companies and branch plants. Several useful reviews have examined this question, including Keeble (1976) and Watts (1981). In brief, the available evidence suggests that branch plants are likely to provide some unskilled but few managerial jobs, and are likely to be less stable employers, although the surviving firms may have greater growth potential than their indigenous counterparts. Perry (1982) has provided a useful detailed study of the employment characteristics of small manufacturing businesses in Cornwall, classified according to whether they are new starts or movers, and exogenous or indigenous firms. Figure 3.5 illustrates that new starts are less stable than established firms, and that exogenous firms are less likely than indigenous firms to create male and skilled employment.

Another important difference between exogenous and indigenous firms concerns their linkages with the local economy. The available evidence suggests that, in terms of both the purchase of services and material inputs, indigenous firms are likely to have the higher level of local linkages (Lever 1974; Marshall 1979; Watts 1981). This is supported by the few studies specifically of rural areas; Moseley and Townroe (1973) found that inmigrant firms in East Anglia retained most of their original linkages

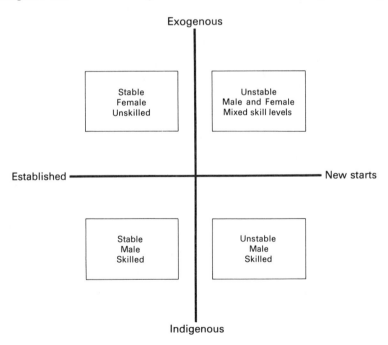

FIGURE 3.5 Employment characteristics of small manufacturing businesses in Cornwall
Source: based on Perry (1982)

outside the region, and Hodge and Whitby (1979), in a study of the eastern Scottish Borders, found that few in-migrant firms had important local linkages. Therefore, the impact of manufacturing employment in rural areas will depend on the precise nature of the firms that have been established.

SERVICES AND TOURISM

Services provide more than 60 per cent of employment in most rural areas, and are the mainstay of job opportunities and incomes in these localities. This is an economic sector that has a number of social features, usually with distinctive geographical dimensions. The ratio of service to manufacturing jobs in most rural areas is of the order of 2:1, but in the remoter rural areas this rises to 4:1 (Gilg 1976); service employment however also tends to include more part-time work and self-employed workers. For example, Marquand (1979) has shown that in 1976 23 per cent of female workers in manufacturing were employed part-time, compared with 51 per cent in the distributive trades, 57 per cent in miscellaneous services and 47 per cent in professional and scientific services. The self-employed form a larger proportion of the workforce in services (8.2 per cent in 1975) compared with manufacturing (1.6 per cent). Both these features of service employment have specific social implications; for example, part-time workers are often lower paid and need to work quite near home, while the self-employed usually must have their own transport and also have less security at times of sickness or slack employment.

There is a lack of readily usable statistics on service employment in rural areas, but some idea of its form and extent can be obtained from considering the national trends in service employment (table 3.1). The most rapid rates of growth have been in the professional and scientific services, in insurance and other financial services, in miscellaneous services and in public administration and defence, while employment in distribution and transport has stagnated or declined. Up to 1973 nearly all the fast growing services were of the type used by other industries. Employment in education and health, the two largest non-market publicly provided services, also increased. Consumer services, including most branches of retailing, did not expand, although this was accounted for by technological and organizational changes (for example, the growth of supermarkets) rather than by decline in demand. In very general terms, these developments represent a shift in employment from the more ubiquitous services to those that are footloose (Marquand 1979). In regional terms, there is evidence of a strong concentration of most footloose service industries in the South East, especially London. Furthermore, the avail-

Table 3.1   Growth in the UK service sector, 1960–77

	Employees	
	Number in 1960	Percentage change, 1960–77
Transport and communications	1,652,000	−11.8
Distributive trades	2,737,000	0
Insurance, banking, financial and business services	660,000	74.2
Professional and scientific services	2,040,000	76.9
Miscellaneous services	1,790,000	32.9
Public administration and defence	1,287,000	26.8
All industries and services	21,894,000	3.8

Source: after Marquand (1979)

able evidence suggests that the two strongest growth sectors – professional and scientific, and insurance and other financial services – have become more spatially concentrated during the postwar period (Daniels 1978). Only public administration and defence have become less concentrated, the result of growth in local authority functions and government policy to disperse the civil service. In order to understand how these trends have affected rural areas, it is necessary to consider separately the main types of service employment.

Office employment was one of the major growth sectors of the economy in the 1950s and 1960s, and by the early 1970s it was estimated that one-quarter of total employment was in offices (Goddard 1978). All forms of office employment reveal a marked concentration in the South East, which has nearly half of the total. However, there has been some decentralization of office employment since the mid-1960s, with a redistribution away from London to the outer-metropolitan areas. This change, and the more modest gains in the South West and East Anglia, has meant that many smaller towns have experienced increases in office employment (Marquand 1979). The reasons for this decentralization are lower rates and rents outside London, the desire for an attractive environment, and the availability of cheap female labour. Furthermore, many office jobs are routine clerical operations which could be located almost anywhere, while telecommunications are reducing the locational requirements of higher-order professional and managerial jobs (Goddard 1975). Regional policies have also sought to decentralize office jobs from London and the South East.

The dispersal of office activities may have resulted in an increase in employment in some of the smaller towns in more rural regions within the South of England. However, the bulk of tertiary employment in rural areas is in consumer services, both public and private, and in retailing. These activities are closely linked to the populations that they serve, and therefore there are only limited possibilities of interregional redistribution. However, changes have occurred at the local level, for there has been a strong centralization trend evident in both. Retailing, in particular, has been affected by economies of scale and by enhanced mobility offered by increased car ownership rates (for some social groups). As a result, village shops have tended to be replaced by supermarkets or shopping centres in nearby towns (Harman 1978). In some remoter villages mobile shops play an important role, but these rarely create jobs in these villages themselves.

There has also been centralization in the public services. This will be discussed more fully in chapter 8, but essentially, the reorganization of schools, health and social services has led to a closure of many local service outlets. This trend has been reinforced by reorganization of the public sector bodies such as the National Health Service, local government, gas, electricity and water authorities. Larger administrative units are usually associated with a greater concentration of service outlets. The selected settlement strategies proposed by local planners, discussed below in chapter 7, have also reinforced the concentration of resources and new development in a small number of key settlements. Therefore, although the service sector may be the mainstay of rural employment, it has a very uneven spatial distribution at the local level.

An uneven geographical distribution is also characteristic of tourism, one of the few industries that does tend to be found in the remoter rural areas (see chapter 9 below). The state has actively sought to develop tourism, both to attract foreign visitors and to act as a counter-magnet to holidays abroad for Britons. The most important policy instrument has been the Development of Tourism Act 1969, which allowed grants and loans to be made by the tourist boards for tourist projects in Development Areas. There was an upper limit of £50,000 on the amount of aid, and only about 500 projects were approved between 1971 and 1977 (Marquand 1979). In May 1977 the policy was amended, when it was decided to concentrate on a few tourist growth points in areas of rural depopulation where there was unrealized tourist potential. This led to a number of interrelated projects being financed in three limited areas; the High Pennines, the area around Scarborough, and between Bude and Wadebridge in the South West. In addition, COSIRA and the Countryside Commission can also help to finance some smaller tourist developments.

Tourism does bring economic benefits to rural areas, but it is usually considered to be a mixed blessing, even by those who depend on it for their living. The advantages are fairly clear and straightforward; both directly and indirectly, it brings about an increase in employment and incomes in rural areas. Income from tourism can account for a sizeable proportion of an area's total income; it has been estimated that, in Cornwall in the 1960s, this was equal to the income generated by manufacturing in the county (Cornwall County Council 1966). This can be particularly important to farmers, and Denman (1978) has shown that in Scotland approximately 6,100 private landholders, many of whom were smallholders or crofters, were involved in some form of tourist or recreational provision. Against this, a number of disadvantages have to be noted. Tourist receipts are volatile, for holidays are usually one of the first casualties of reduced family expenditure during a recession. Furthermore, tourism tends to provide unskilled and low paid jobs, which are highly seasonal, many lasting only three or four months during the summer. It can also contribute to congestion on the roads, various forms of pollution, and rising house prices if there is a demand for second or holiday homes. For all these reasons, it is probably not as beneficial or stabilizing to the local economy as an increase in other retailing or service jobs, or in office employment, would be.

RURAL DEVELOPMENT BOARDS

In addition to the economic policies already discussed, development boards have been established in some rural areas where particularly acute social and economic problems exist. To date, there have been three boards: the short-lived Northern Pennines Rural Development Board (1969–71), concerned mainly with agriculture; the more recent Development Board for Rural Wales, established in 1976; and the longer established Highlands and Islands Development Board, initiated in 1965. Discussion here will be limited to the last-named agency since it has had more extensive impact.

There are acute development problems in the Highlands and Islands, because of a sparse population living in dispersed settlements, and the relative isolation of the region. The economy has a weak base, and only 7 per cent of the land is cultivated, most being under rough grazing (Turnock 1974). Some 15,000 crofts, small family farm units that offer marginal incomes and mainly part-time employment, have survived. Incomes in the area have therefore been lower than in the UK as a whole, and out-migration has reduced the region's share of Scotland's total population from about 20 per cent in the mid-eighteenth century to about 5 per cent today.

There have been a number of attempts by central government to intervene in the region to stem the loss of population, dating from the 1886 Crofters Act (Turnock 1969). None was really successful, however, and as a policy departure the Highlands and Islands Development Board was established in 1965, covering some 3.6 million ha (one-sixth of Britain's area) with a population of only 340,000 (Grieve 1973). The aims of the Board have been to improve economic and social conditions as well as to increase the contribution of the region to the national economy. The Board prepares specific proposals for the region and submits these to the Secretary of State who, after consultation with the local authorities, has the power to approve them. Thereafter the Board has considerable means at its disposal to implement these schemes, and is empowered to acquire land and buildings to promote activities and enterprises (including the provision of grants and loans for these ventures) and to offer advice and training.

However, although its brief is exceedingly broad and its powers substantial, the activities of the Board have been fairly selective, both sectorally and spatially. In view of its relatively small budget and the size of the region, this is probably inevitable. The main sectors to be supported are tourism, fishing and manufacturing; between 1965 and 1974, each of these was allocated about £5–6 million, while by contrast, only about £2 million was spent on agricultural projects (Gilg 1976). This pattern has continued, with the three main activities absorbing 66 per cent of all loans and grants between 1971 and 1980 (Shucksmith and Lloyd 1982). A broad spectrum of projects has been supported, including repair yards for fishing boats, bulb growing, hotels, craft industries and an aluminium smelter.

The Board's activities have been concentrated into three growth areas – around Fort William, Inverness and Caithness, where almost one-half of the labour force of the region live – and the aim is to strengthen them further as both industrial and service centres. Plans include the provision of new housing, advance factories and industrial estates. This growth area strategy has been complemented by the designation of an additional 27 rural development points considered to be capable of further economic growth, whether in industry, as in Kirkwall, or services, as in east Sutherland. However, this leaves uncovered the larger part of the region in which 10 per cent of its population live.

The Board has achieved a measure of success although this has been boosted by the development of North Sea Oil. Population decline has been halted in many areas since the mid-1960s to its present level of 346,000, with employment in manufacturing trebling in this period and total employment growing by one-half (Shucksmith and Lloyd 1982). Incomes had also increased to 90 per cent of the national level by 1973 (compared with only 65 per cent in 1960). However, the Board has been criticized for over-concentration on economic development at the expense of social development (Carter 1974). The economic strategy has also been criticized for having placed too much emphasis on manufacturing, especially on large-scale, capital-intensive schemes such as the paper mill at Fort William. Instead, it can be argued that more attention should have been given to services and small-scale manufacturing. The recent closures of the paper mill and the aluminium smelter at Invergordon lend weight to this argument. However, there are no easy solutions to the problems of an area such as the Highlands within the constraints of the existing national economic structure, and there is no certainty that small-scale industries would have provided a better base for employment growth. Some of the features of deprivation that may be associated with life in such regions are discussed in chapter 10.

COMMUTING FOR WORK

The discussion so far has shown that the structural changes in the rural economy have had important spatial implication. Agriculture is an extensive activity with dispersed employment, but this sector has seen the largest decline. By contrast, in the growth sectors of manufacturing and services within the non-metropolitan regions there have been strong tendencies of concentration in the main settlements. This has led to an increasing separation of place of work and place of residence for many rural residents, a trend that has been reinforced by the decentralization of population from towns (chapter 4). As a result, an increasing proportion of the rural population no longer work in their home parish or village but instead commute for their living.

It is difficult to establish an accurate picture of commuting in rural areas, but some insight into its extent is provided by the work of Spence *et al.* (1982) on the urban system. This is a large-scale analysis which used local authority units in order to define metropolitan economic labour areas (MELAs), of which 126 were identified in Britain. Each MELA was divided into three zones – cores, with minimum employment sizes and densities; metropolitan rings, with 15 per cent or more of their labour force commuting to work in the cores; and outer rings, with up to 15 per cent of their economically active labour force employed in a core. The areas outside the MELAs were treated as 'unclassified' but, although there is only the crudest correspondence between these zones and the rural areas of Britain, the results of the analysis do give some indication of the extent of commuter hinterlands.

The MELAs clearly dominate the UK space economy. Even in 1951, less than 5 per cent of the population lived in unclassified areas (table 3.2). By 1971 there had been a further reduction in this proportion, so that only 4.3 per cent of the population lived beyond what may be considered practical limits for commuting to metropolitan labour market centres. There were also changes within the labour markets, with strong evidence of decentralization from the cores to the metropolitan rings and outer rings. At the same time, depending on personal mobility (chapter 6), more and more people have the possibility of commuting to major urban centres. The available evidence suggests that this has become less of a choice and more of a necessity for many people. Another feature of the MELAs is their geographical extent (figure 3.6); they cover almost all of England, particularly the South East, East Anglia, the Midlands, Lancashire and Yorkshire. The major regions excluded are those that may be identified as the more remote rural areas – the extreme South West, the Lake District, the northern Pennines, mid- and North Wales and Scotland. Even within these areas, there is smaller-scale, shorter-distance commuting for the few jobs in the larger villages and the smaller towns. Only the most remote of rural localities now lie beyond the influence of town-based labour markets.

Table 3.2   Distribution of 'urban' population in Britain, 1951 and 1971 (percentages)

	1951	*1971*
Cores	52.7	47.4
Metropolitan rings	26.4	32.2
Outer rings	16.0	16.4
Unclassified	4.8	4.3
Total	100.0	100.0

Source: after Department of the Environment (1976)

FIGURE 3.6 Metropolitan Economic Labour Areas and the 'unclassified' areas of the British space economy
Source: after Spence *et al.* (1982)

One major reservation must be added regarding commuting. Although we have emphasized the outer limits of commuting, this is realistic only where suitable public or private transport is available to link home and workplace. Given the decline of rural rail and bus routes (chapter 6), it is private transport that is most likely to be important, and access to cars and motorbikes is highly selective in terms of age, sex, income and social class.

INCOME, ASPIRATIONS – AND UNEMPLOYMENT

Income

The employment problems of the rural population concern not simply jobs, but also the rate of pay received. Thomas and Winyard (1979) have shown that, of the ten counties with the lowest average net incomes in the 1970s, seven were very rural: Gwynedd, Cornwall, Isle of Wight, Powys, Devon, Norfolk and Clwyd. Although these low average incomes may be affected by the large numbers of pensioners' households, there does seem to be a clear difference between urban and rural areas. Gwynedd is the county with the lowest average net income in England and Wales, and its position actually seems to have deteriorated in recent years. In the mid-1960s its average income was 90 to 94 per cent of the national average, but by the mid-1970s it had fallen to 85 per cent. Variations can also be expected to exist between the more and the less accessible rural areas, but few published data exist that allow this to be illustrated. A study of Cornwall in the early 1970s revealed that average earnings in the more rural employment office areas (in the west or the north-east of the county) were as much as 6 per cent below the county average, while earnings in the more urban areas (for example, near Plymouth or Camborne – Redruth) were 6 to 7 per cent above the county average (Cornwall County Council 1979).

The lower incomes may be due to the types of jobs available in country locations or to lower wages being paid in rural areas compared to urban areas for the same jobs. There seems to be evidence to support both of these arguments. Rural areas have relatively larger proportions employed in low-paying industries such as agriculture, distributive trades and tourism. However, lower wages are also paid in many other industries in rural areas; for example, in 16 of the 19 industries examined in the South West, earnings were as much as 13 per cent below national levels. These problems are further compounded by the extent of part-time and seasonal employment in rural areas (Thomas and Winyard 1979).

Two questions seem particularly relevant: why are agricultural earnings relatively low, and why are earnings less in rural areas than in urban areas for comparable work? There has been considerable research into the question of low pay in agriculture. The wages of farm workers are set by the Agricultural Wages Board (for England and Wales). The Board fixes minimum rates, although farmers and farm workers locally may agree higher rates and in practice this is fairly widespread – in 1976, 94 per cent of full-time male farm workers were paid more than the minimum. However, only 43 per cent were paid more than £5 per week above the minimum, and full-time male farm workers in 1977 still earned only 77 per cent of the average earnings of all male manual workers. The position of women is even worse: 8 per cent were paid below the legal minimum while over one-half were paid barely above it (Winyard 1978). It is true that there are some fringe benefits available to farm workers (as there are for many occupational groups), but their value amounted to only an estimated £1 per week for free food and a net £2 per week for low-rent tied cottages (Brown and Winyard 1975). Although only a small proportion receive free food, about half of all farm workers in Britain live in tied accommodation. However, the agricultural tied cottage is a doubtful privilege, because of its insecurity of tenure and the poor quality of accommodation (chapter 5). The result is that many farm workers are caught in the poverty trap between exemption from taxation and receipt of means-tested benefit (Winyard 1978).

The consistently low wages paid to farm workers have been explained by five main considerations. First, there does seem to be genuine preference by agricultural workers for the 'non-economic' conditions of their jobs compared with non-agricultural work. For example, Newby (1972a, p. 20) writes that, 'compared with most manual work in industry, agriculture offers greater non-economic rewards in terms of job interest, judgement, discretion, challenge, responsibility and control. On most farms the division of labour has not reached anything like the level of most factories and there is a wider variety of jobs to perform and more job rotation.' A second reason is that many smaller farms simply cannot afford to pay higher wages because of the low price elasticity for farm products (Bellerby 1956; Metcalf 1969). However, this does not generally apply to larger farms, and it is paradoxical that some of the lowest earnings are in East Anglia, where the largest and probably most profitable farms are located. More important may be the third reason – the poor trade union structure for agricultural workers. The geographical dispersion of agricultural work among predominantly small units makes it very difficult to organize union activities effectively (Newby 1972b). It is perhaps significant that the last strike organized by the National Union of Agricultural and Allied Workers was in 1923 and nearly bankrupted the Union; although, having amalgamated with the Transport and General Workers' Union in 1982, farm workers may now find themselves in a better bargaining position. The fourth consideration concerns the informal but patern-alistic social relations that exist between employer and employees on farms which make it difficult for farm workers even to consider industrial action. Finally, it may be argued that farm workers have to accept low wages because they are relatively immobile. A lack of capital, the tied cottage system, and the workers' age and lack of formal qualifications make it impossible for many to move to better jobs elsewhere (Newby 1972a).

As to the question of lower earnings paid in rural than in urban areas for the same industries, four reasons can be suggested for this, although there is some overlap with the earlier discussion of low agricultural wages. First, the types of manufacturing activities attracted to rural regions have included many enterprises that specialize in the routine semi-skilled and unskilled parts of production, often employing females. There is, there-fore, a preponderance of lower paid posts, and a lack of professional and managerial posts. Second, although many of the enterprises in rural areas are relatively small, some may dominate limited local labour markets (Lever 1978). As a result there may be lower rates of unionization, fewer strikes (Bean and Peel 1976) and more informal work relations resulting in lower wage rates. Third, all of these problems are compounded by the part-time and seasonal nature of much rural employment. Finally, the fundamental problem of a lack of suitable alternative jobs in rural areas, compounded by the effects of economic recession in the early 1980s, serve to keep local wages low.

Aspirations

Most of the recent research in this field has concentrated on school-leavers' job aspirations. Drudy and Drudy (1979), in a study of north Norfolk, found that 31 per cent of their survey group aspired to professional and intermediate non-manual jobs and that a further 31 per cent aspired to other non-manual jobs, so that little more than one-third aspired to manual work. Toyne (1977), in a study in Devon, found that only 16 per cent of school leavers' first-choice employment was manu-facturing, while 59 per cent preferred jobs in offices, retailing or the public sector. Manufacturing industry had a very unattractive image to school-leavers, especially because of the nature of the work, the working hours and the wages. The most detailed research, however, has been undertaken by S. Dench in mid-Devon. Again it has been shown that jobs in services, clerical work, agriculture and construction are attractive, but factory work is only the fifth choice, preferred by only 11 per cent (see figure 3.7). The most interesting feature of this study, however, is the way in which it compared the preferred jobs of school-leavers with those

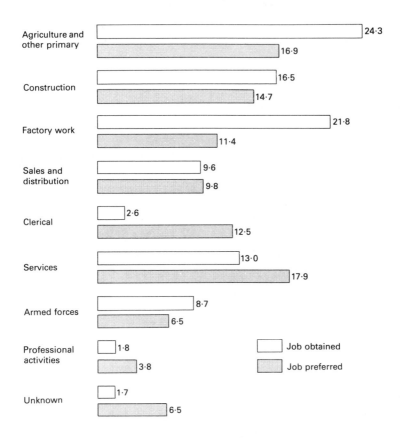

FIGURE 3.7 Jobs preferred and jobs obtained by school-leavers in mid-Devon (percentages)
Source: unpublished data provided by S. Dench

obtained, revealing the gap between aspirations and reality. The reality is a lack of suitable clerical and service jobs, leading many to take what are viewed as less satisfactory alternatives in agriculture or factories. Those living in rural areas are likely to meet barriers to the fulfilment of their aspirations. Faced with this fact, there are three possible options: accepting less desirable jobs, being unemployed, or migrating from the area. There is strong evidence that many will choose the last-named option. Toyne's study showed that one-third of his survey group expected to leave the region within the next 10 years, and the main motive for this was better career prospects. Drudy and Drudy also found that 22 per cent of

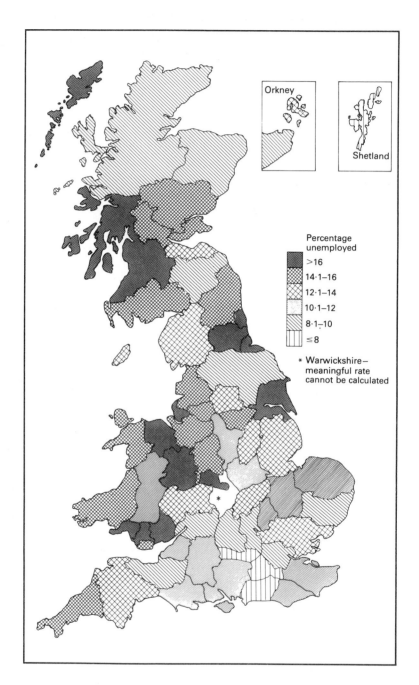

FIGURE 3.8 Unemployment rates in Britain, July 1982
Source: data from *Employment Gazette*

their survey group wished to leave the area, although they did not seek to establish the motives, while Dench found a willingness to leave mid-Devon if career prospects were frustrated.

Unemployment

Unemployment rates arguably provide the most sensitive indicators of local employment opportunities. Apart from the traditional urban-industrial Assisted Areas, the higher rates of unemployment may be seen in the South West, West and North Wales, Cumbria, and the Scottish Highlands and Islands (figure 3.8). The more accessible countryside throughout southern and eastern England and Scotland has relatively lower rates of unemployment. But there is a second, more local, level at which substantial differences exist in unemployment rates. This can be illustrated by an analysis of 1977 unemployment rates in Norfolk. The average male unemployment rate was 7.3 per cent in urban areas compared with 10.5. per cent in the rural areas. The two extremes were represented by 'urban' Thetford, with only a 5.4 per cent unemployment rate, compared with 14.6 per cent in rural Cromer (Packman 1979). These spatial variations, both at the regional and the local scale, are directly related to the structure of the rural economy.

Unemployment also affects social groups unevenly and four groups are especially susceptible: the young, the old, females and the unskilled (Packman 1979). Rising unemployment among school-leavers is sadly a national trend, and in particular there has been a lack of training opportunities and apprenticeships (see chapter 8). Females are more prominent among the unemployed for two main reasons: they are disproportionately employed in seasonal work and, as there are now more economically active women than ever before, they are as likely as men to lose their jobs because of recession. As a consequence, the proportion of women among the unemployed in Norfolk increased from 12 per cent in 1971 to 22 per cent in 1978 (Packman 1979).

The outcome of low incomes, frustrated job aspirations, restricted career structures and unemployment can be a poor quality of life. These conditions can also lead to selective out-migration, which has been an important feature shaping the social geography of certain rural areas. As this has been a recurring theme in the literature, it warrants further attention when the more general question of rural population change is discussed in the following chapter.

4 Population and Social Change

The British countryside has long been regarded as a source of out-migration and a pool of reserve labour for urban areas. Lawton (1973), in his analysis of Britain's nineteenth-century population, observed that between 1801 and 1911, while the total population increased four-fold, that of rural areas was stagnant, and in fact decreased after 1861 (figure 4.1). The rural population, as defined in the census, fell from a peak of 9.1 million in 1861 to a low of 7.3 million just before the Second World War. As a proportion of total population, this represents a decrease from 65.2 per cent in 1801 to just under one-half in 1851 and to 17.6 per cent in 1939. Britain had become the most urbanized nation in the world by the late nineteenth century, and has probably remained so ever since.

Lawton (1977) gives a most useful summary of the nature of those population changes and of the balance between natural change (the differ-

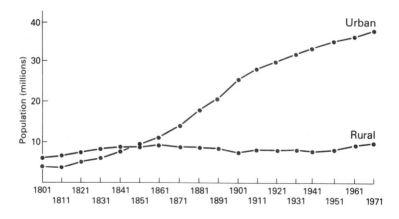

FIGURE 4.1   The urban and rural populations of Britain, 1801–1971
Source: after Lawton (1973)

ence between births and deaths) and migration. Between 1831 and 1861 the increase in the rural population was slackening as out-migration (especially to London) strengthened, although most moves were over short distances. After 1881 birth rates fell; this, combined with continuing out-migration, ensured the decline of rural population. Out-migration, however, had become more interregional, a trend that became even stronger during the interwar depression years. This period saw a levelling-out of both the absolute fall in rural population and the decline in the proportion of total population living in rural areas. By 1951 rural population was on the increase, a trend that has continued throughout the postwar period. Although a surge in the birth rate until the 1960s contributed to this, there is also evidence that the balance of net migration has turned in favour of rural areas.

This reversal provides the framework for an analysis of demographic change, but the trend has been uneven both spatially and socially. The spatial differences are mainly between the more remote areas and the accessible countryside; while some of the latter areas experienced population growth from the 1920s, many of the more remote rural areas experienced population losses of more than 15 per cent even between 1951 and 1971 (Countryside Review Committee 1977a).

The 1970s saw a further shift in population trends. The regions with the most rapid growth rates were two of the more rural, East Anglia and the South West. A county-level analysis also reveals that there are two different types of rural growth areas; those such as Shropshire or Sussex, which are accessible to the major conurbations, and those such as Cornwall or Powys, which are considered to be remote (Gilg 1983a). Therefore many traditional notions about rural decline have to be modified to take account of the remarkable turn-around in demographic trends. The precise reasons for these changes are hard to establish without further analysis of census material, but it should be noted that some of the population increases in rural areas (sometimes of more than 10 per cent) are from very low population bases and therefore are not great numerically.

The two-fold classification into more remote and accessible countryside areas is somewhat simplistic, but it does provide a useful guide to understanding spatial differences in rural population change. These changes have also been socially differentiated, because in-migrants and out-migrants have been selective in terms of age, sex and socio-economic characteristics. As a result, there has been a demographic and social differentiation of rural areas that reflects their economic and social functions. These spatial and social variations provide the framework for interpreting the themes of accessibility, service provision, recreation and deprivation that are examined later in this book.

Accessible, gentrified lowland England. The rural village of popular images
(source: authors)

THE DRIFT FROM THE LAND

The phrase 'the drift from the land' as a description of rural depopulation
is something of a misnomer, for both natural change and out–migration
contribute to this process. It is possible, for example, to distinguish
between two types of population decline in an area such as mid-Wales. In
the first there is natural decrease and out-migration:

these are the areas which are reaching the final stages of the demographic cycle in which, as a result of migration of the child-bearing age-groups, the residual population is unable to maintain, let alone increase, its own level by means of natural growth. There is no 'in-migration' of younger people, and the whole process becomes one, therefore, of cumulative decline. [In the second type there is] . . . a natural increase which is offset by outwards migration so that the overall result is one of population decline. . . . [Thomas 1972, p. 72].

Although it is important to note these differences, it is nevertheless possible to agree with Lowenthal and Comitas (1962) that out-migration is still the prime factor in rural depopulation.

Rural population changes can be observed at the regional level, where the pattern is one of population loss from the upland areas – the more remote and agriculturally poorer parts of the country. The main regions involved are mid-Wales, the Lake District and the remoter areas of the Pennines, the Scottish Highlands and some parts of the South West peninsula, although many lowland areas also lost population until comparatively recently. In the more remote regions population losses have been as high as 10 per cent in many of the intercensal periods during the twentieth century (Dunn 1976). Mid-Wales provides one example of a region where population has fallen during every decade, from 217,277 in 1901 to only 174, 604 in 1971 (Dunn *et al*. 1981).

These broad regional variations conceal substantial differences at the sub-regional level, although, again, these can be classified in terms of the more accessible and the less accessible areas. Jackson (1968), in a study of the north Cotswolds, observed that the main zone of depopulation was the area of hill farming, while the fringes of the Cotswolds, which are accessible to the West Midlands urban areas, had received large numbers of in-migrants. In Herefordshire, between 1951 and 1971 Hereford Rural District grew by 10 per cent as a result of expansion in the nearby city, and the remainder of the rural districts lost population at rates ranging between 3.8 and 20 per cent (Dunn 1976). This is not a very remote county, but some districts still lost up to one-fifth of their population in only 20 years, roughly equivalent to the 17.6 per cent decrease that occurred in the population of the Scottish Islands during the same period (Dunn *et al*. 1981).

Analysis at the local level provides a more detailed insight into the nature of population change. This is amply demonstrated by House's (1965) research on the rural areas of north-east England. In overall terms, there was a net gain of 9 per cent in the population of rural districts between 1951 and 1961, mainly owing to overspill from towns like Darlington and some growth in market towns such as Barnard Castle. But

Inaccessible and isolated Welsh farm (source: authors)

the remaining rural areas actually experienced a net loss of 2 per cent, while one rural district – Norham and Islandshires – had a 12.5 per cent loss. A more recent example of population loss is to be seen in the Wells area of north Norfolk (Drudy and Wallace 1971). Between 1951 and 1966, three parishes had population gains of between 5 and 22 per cent, but ten parishes had population losses, the largest of which (52 per cent) was in Warham. The importance of studying these demographic changes is underlined by Neate (1981, p. 9) who stressed that the depopulation of an area 'is the ultimate protest and arguably one of the most potent indicators of relative disadvantage or deprivation'.

Causes

In explaining rural out-migration, emphasis is usually given to economic factors, especially the problems of employment outlined in chapters 2 and 3, although factors such as planning policies, housing markets and the decline of services are also important. Nevertheless, it is the economic change in rural areas, and especially the decline in agricultural employment, that are often stressed as root causes of depopulation (Drudy and Wallace 1971). The decline in the agricultural labour force, continuous since the nineteenth century, can be observed in all regions, not only in the more remote ones. Drudy (1978) saw changes in agriculture as contributing significantly to population loss even in relatively prosperous rural areas such as north Norfolk. Furthermore, even if agricultural jobs are available, they may not be attractive to those who live locally; Cowie and Giles (1957) found that 40 per cent of a sample of out-migrants gave low pay and long hours of farm work as reasons for deciding to leave their home areas.

The lack of alternative employment is also a cause of rural out-migration. This was discussed in chapter 3, but an example will illustrate the often dramatic reduction in manufacturing jobs in rural areas. Of the thousands of chair makers living in the scattered villages of the Chilterns in 1880, 30 years later there were only a handful, working in factories concentrated in High Wycombe (Saville 1957). Cairncross (1949) has argued that, as rural–urban migration in the nineteenth century was greater in the more prosperous farming areas surrounding towns, the attraction, or 'pull', of alternative jobs and higher wages must have been more important than the 'push' from the decline of farm jobs and the low wages in farming. This view is substantiated in recent studies such as that by Drudy and Wallace (1971), which compare young people's aspirations with the types of jobs available in rural areas. Two-thirds of their sample thought they could obtain their preferred type of job within 24 miles of home, but only 18 per cent were willing to travel this distance daily. The expectation at an early age that career aspirations cannot be met locally contributes to a lack of commitment to the home area and to the acceptance of out-migration as the inevitable solution.

Economic factors may be fundamental to rural out-migration but they are not the sole explanations. This is illustrated by the results of two surveys of the motivations of out-migrants (table 4.1). Direct comparison of the results of the two surveys is not possible because of the different methods of classification that have been used. But it can be seen that, while occupational and income motives are dominant in the Welsh borderland, employment reasons are less important in the Herefordshire survey. The other motives that seem to be important are social, community, housing and family reasons.

Perhaps the underlying feature of the social motivation is the decline in services in rural areas. This is linked to population decline in what is usually portrayed as a vicious circle of cause and effect: as services decline people react by out-migrating, which leads to further fall in demand and a consequent further reduction in service provision (Bracey 1970). This view is substantiated by a study of population loss in Somerset between 1931 and 1951 (Bracey 1958). Areas losing population were generally less well provided with public utilities (such as piped water and sewerage) than

Table 4.1   Motives for out-migration from the Welsh Borderland and Herefordshire

Welsh Borderland, 1958–68		Herefordshire, 1966–71	
Reason for moving	%	Reason for moving	%
Occupational	32	Employment	34
Income	29	Housing	28
Social	19	Marriage	12
Community	12	Retirement	9
Personal	8	Relatives/friends	11
		Other	7
Total	100		100

Sources: Welsh Borderland after Lewis (1969); Herefordshire after Dunn (1979)

expanding villages. In practice, it seems that it is not decline itself, but a fall in population to below critical threshold levels that is important in affecting service provision (Winter 1971). A study of the rural North East showed that critical thresholds may be as low as 120 persons, below which there is a precipitous fall-off in all services (Edwards 1964). Elsewhere, it has been shown that the closure of village schools can often trigger a rapid decline in rural services (Lee 1960).

The concept of the 'vicious circle' theory is, of course, underlain by people's expectations of what constitutes acceptable levels of service provision. With general improvements in standards of living, expectations have risen, so that young people are no longer prepared to do without the basic utilities or to accept a limited range of shops and services (Thomas 1972). Although some uneven distribution of utilities and services can be attributed to market forces, others result from decisions taken by public agencies, such as health authorities, or by local planning authorities (see chapters 5 and 8).

Changing housing requirements also affect rural migration and the family life-cycle is an important factor in residential mobility (Rossi 1955; Morgan 1976). Studies of rural migration have largely neglected these factors although Dunn (1979) has shown that a substantial amount of short-distance movement in rural areas can be attributed to changing housing needs. Movements between tenures, whether from tied cottages to council houses or from council houses to owner-occupation, is a particularly important reason for movements between villages (Dunn *et al.*

1981). There are however differences between short-distance and long-distance migration, because in the latter economic motives are more likely to be important (House and Knight 1965).

Finally, a number of other social and community reasons may contribute to out-migration. The sheer isolation of some rural areas, for example the Scottish Islands, may be important (Dunn 1976); there may also be more complex factors associated with the nature of the rural community. Mitchell's (1950) study of villages in the South West is particularly relevant because the considerable variations in population change rates that he noted did not appear to conform with any simple indices of accessibility. Instead, it seemed that the nature of social organization in the villages was critical. Villages that experienced population losses tended to be those that had 'closed, disintegrating societies', that is, those that had disharmonies in institutional life and where newcomers were regarded as 'foreigners'. By contrast, a sense of 'community' seemed to be absolutely essential if village populations were to be maintained at viable levels.

Who goes and who stays?

Out-migrants from rural areas are predominantly the younger members of the adult population. There is evidence that this trend existed in the nineteenth century (Hill 1925) as well as more recently. Saville (1957) observed that the bulk of rural out-migrants were aged 20–29, while Jones (1965) found in a study of mid-Wales that 38 per cent of all migrants were aged less than 25. Migration is certainly related to the family life-cycle: House (1965) discovered in the North East that migration peaked in the late twenties (when family commitments are fewest); there was then a lull for about 15 years, and migration again became more important when family ties had been reduced as children grew up.

There were also distinctive sex differences between migrants and non-migrants. The traditional view is that females are more likely to predominate among rural out-migrants for two main reasons: employment opportunities for women are even more restricted than those for men in rural areas, and women are more likely to move after marriage than are men (Hannan 1970). However, not all the evidence supports this view; both Hill and Saville found that, while women were more numerous among the youngest groups of migrants, men were more likely to be in the majority in the older groups. Even more interesting is the finding by Drudy and Drudy (1979) that there were no differences between male and female school-leavers regarding their expectation of migrating. Expectations may be frustrated, however, since constraints operate differently for men and women at various points in the family cycle and career structure.

Out-migration is also socially selective in terms of education and employment aspirations, which in turn reflect social class. The most useful evidence on this again comes from Drudy and Drudy's study of school-leavers in north Norfolk. Fewer than half of them wanted further education, while 29 per cent wanted training for skilled work, 9 per cent wanted vocational training and 15 per cent aspired to higher education. Aspirants to further or higher education may well have to migrate and, once the initial break with the home area has been made, there is always the possibility that young people will not return to their villages. Employment aspirations also differentiated the school-leavers; those who aspired to manual jobs were more likely to obtain them locally than were those who aspired to non-manual work, especially professional and managerial posts. It is therefore the more academically able who will have the education and occupational aspirations likely to lead to out-migration. This, in turn, may reduce community leadership and innovative capacity in the village.

Migration, however, is not a one-way process, and the stream of young out-migrants may cross a very different counter-stream of in-migrants to rural areas.

COUNTER-URBANIZATION

Flows of people from metropolitan to non-metropolitan areas have been observed in a number of developed countries in recent years, and the term 'counter-urbanization' has been applied to this process (Berry 1976; Bryant et al. 1982). Counter-urbanization in Britain has been measured in two major studies, by Hall et al. (1973) and Spence et al. (1982). The latter study, analysing population changes between 1951 and 1974, found that there was substantial and widespread decentralization throughout urban Britain. The conurbations had been losing population relative to the smaller 'free-standing' cities, and almost all the 'cores' of the metropolitan areas had experienced absolute or relative population shifts to their metropolitan rings. This is summarized in table 4.2 (see pp. 65–6 above for definitions). In the 1950s there was relative decentralization as population grew more rapidly in the rings than the cores, but by the 1960s there was absolute decentralization as a net loss of population was registered in the cores. This pattern became further exaggerated in the early 1970s when the cores lost population even more rapidly.

There is nothing new about the decentralization of population. Lawton (1977) has shown that many rural districts around London and the other major cities have had persistent population increases since 1921. This was

Table 4.2   Population change by 'urban' zone in Britain, 1951–74 (percentages)

	1951–61	*1961–71*	*1971–74*
Core	1.9	−2.7	−5.9
Metropolitan rings	13.6	17.5	8.6
Outer metropolitan rings	3.1	9.8	10.6

Source: Spence *et al.* (1982)

largely the result of the extension of commuting zones, a trend that has continued through the interwar and postwar periods. At first much of the increase in population was accounted for by suburbanization, that is, by contiguous physical expansion of the cities into the surrounding country-side. However, over a period of time, and partly encouraged by urban planning policies, commuter villages have grown up at greater distances from the cities. It is mainly as a result of these changes that there has been a decisive reversal in rural demographic patterns (see figure 4.1). Between 1939 and 1971 the population living in rural areas has increased from 7.3 to 10.6 million; in proportional terms, a rise from 17.6 to 21.8 per cent. Suburbanization, therefore, has become 'rurbanization', and physical urbanization has been replaced by functional urbanization of the country-side (Hall *et al.* 1973). This has been augmented by retirement migration, a topic that will be elaborated in the following section.

Rural population growth has had a distinctive regional pattern, which is, of course, the inverse of that observed for rural depopulation. The rural areas that gained population up to about 1970 were those in the South and East in the lowland areas of Britain. In particular, growth was most impressive in the accessible countryside, especially in rural south-east England (including most of Kent, Surrey, Hampshire, Berkshire, Oxford-shire, Buckinghamshire, Hertfordshire and Essex), although there were also important outliers in the South West, in Wiltshire and Dorset. However, as with the drift from the land, there are important sub-regional and local variations within this general pattern. For example, some of the larger key settlements in Devon and Warwickshire have experienced substantial growth while other smaller settlements have lost population (Cloke 1979).

The existence of this counter-urbanization trend, and its extension into the accessible countryside, has long been recognized, but many commen-tators were surprised by the population changes of the 1970s. There have

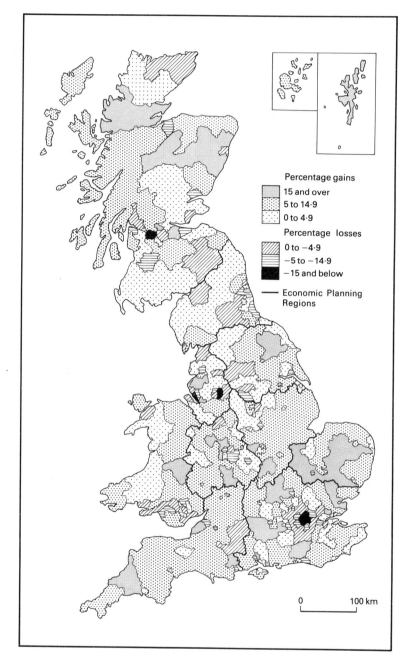

Percentage gains

☒ 15 and over
☒ 5 to 14·9
⸬ 0 to 4·9

Percentage losses

▨ 0 to −4·9
▤ −5 to −14·9
■ −15 and below

— Economic Planning Regions

0   100 km

FIGURE 4.2   Population change in Britain, 1971–81
Source: after Randolph and Robert (1981)

been substantial population losses in the more industrialized and urbanized regions, including the South East, North and North West, while the largest gains have been in the South West, East Anglia and the East Midlands. A district-level analysis reveals that population change is still greatest, and is even accelerating, in the conurbations (figure 4.2). During this period the population of inner London fell by 18 per cent, that of Glasgow by 22 per cent and of Manchester by 17 per cent. What is unexpected is the extent to which decline has extended beyond the conurbations into those adjacent districts that had previously grown so rapidly (Spence *et al.* 1982).

However, the really surprising feature of these population changes is the way in which growth now seems to have occurred in the more remote countryside. Large areas of western Scotland, mid- and North Wales and the upland zones of the North and South West of England have exhibited population gains, in some cases for the first time in over a century. Some of these gains have been quite spectacular; in Cornwall, for example, there was an increase of 50,000 on a base population of 380,000 (Robert and Randolph 1983). By contrast, almost the only areas of decline in Britain have been the conurbations and some of the older established industrial areas in South Wales, Scotland and the North of England. The list of the 13 largest relative population gains between 1971 and 1981 is dominated by new towns, but rural areas, some very remote, feature prominently (see table 4.3). If such population gains are repeated in the next few decades, the traditional demographic map of rural areas will be completely transformed. Already, it has been stated that 'the last vestiges of rural depopulation seem now to be rapidly disappearing' (Robert and Randolph 1983, p. 90).

A note of caution is necessary, however, for despite the apparent evidence of the 1970s, counter-urbanization is not an all-pervasive trend. Many parishes and villages have continued to lose population and will probably do so in the foreseeable future. Counter-urbanization, like out-migration, is a highly selective process.

Characteristics of rural in-migrants

There are at least four types of rural in-migrants, classified according to their reasons for movement: those using the countryside for recreation, for retirement, for employment, and for commuting.

First, there is a small, but in some areas important, group who see the countryside as a locale for recreation and therefore may sometimes purchase rural second homes. This group will be discussed further in chapter 5; here it is sufficient to note that they tend to be older people and those with higher incomes.

Table 4.3   Districts with largest relative population changes, 1971–81 (percentages)

Largest increases		Largest decreases	
District	population change	District	population change
Milton Keynes	85.2	Kensington and Chelsea	
Redditch	63.1	(London)	−26.3
Tamworth (Staffordshire)	59.6	Glasgow City (Strathclyde)	−22.3
Shetland Islands Area	54.2	Hammersmith and Fulham	
City of London (London)	38.8	(London)	−20.9
Gordon (Grampian)	38.2	Islington (London)	−20.9
Ross and Cromarty		Westminster (London)	−20.5
(Highland)	35.7	Lambeth (London)	−20.1
Cumbernauld and Kilsyth		Southwark (London)	−19.2
(Strathclyde)	35.3	Hackney (London)	−18.2
Badenoch and Strathspey		Manchester (Greater	
(Highland)	32.7	Manchester)	−17.4
Wimborne (Dorset)	32.4	Camden (London)	−17.0
Forest Heath (Suffolk)	31.1	Liverpool (Merseyside)	−16.4
Bracknell (Berkshire)	27.7	Wandsworth (London)	−15.4
Huntingdon		Haringey (London)	−15.4
(Cambridgeshire)	27.3		

Source: Randolph and Robert (1981)

A second group are those who retire to rural areas. There has been, over the course of this century, an increase in the number of elderly people, in the levels of pension available from private funds and the state, and in the number of people leaving work, voluntarily or through redundancy, before the accepted retirement age (which itself has been falling). Therefore there are now larger proportions of non-economically active persons in Britain than at any previous period in the twentieth century. Allon-Smith (1982) estimates that the proportion above pensionable age has increased from 7.8 to 16.0 per cent during this century. Some of the more wealthy groups, or those with better pensions, have greater means than ever before to choose where to live during their retirement (Warnes 1982). Although elderly persons, on the whole, are less geographically mobile than other age groups, the spatially selective nature of their migration gives them an important impact (Law and Warnes 1982). On the other hand, many elderly persons are 'trapped' locationally by their low earnings and position in the housing market, especially if they are not owner-occupiers.

There is also evidence that many who have the financial means to be mobile are actually committing themselves to post-retirement migration. Among the reasons are greater mobility before retirement, which enables them to acquaint themselves with alternative residential locations, and the financial advantages of moving from larger to smaller houses, perhaps in less expensive areas (Law and Warnes 1976). Apart from financial advantages, environmental preferences and the increasing amount of time available for leisure may also attract elderly migrants to non-metropolitan areas (Law and Warnes 1973). It is to be expected, therefore, that the major flows of elderly migrants will be either local (adjusting to changing housing needs) or from urban to rural areas, perhaps at an interregional scale. For longer-distance migration the destinations are likely to be places that are better known to tourists or are considered to be scenically more attractive. A major study of England and Wales using 1966 census data has shown that the pattern of out-migration is largely as expected (figure 4.3): the principal destinations are the South West, East Anglia, Wales and the outer South East, with the metropolitan London area being the source of most moves (Law and Warnes 1976). As a result the numbers of elderly persons living in these regions has increased substantially, especially in coastal locations. There has been a retirement migration to small inland towns in these regions for, as the authors of the study stress 'all of these are rural areas with attractive scenery which have been largely by-passed by industrial development of any scale' (Law and Warnes 1976, p. 470).

These migratory movements, adding to the numbers of ageing local residents, have led to quite phenomenal growth in the number of elderly persons living in specific areas (Allon-Smith 1982). At a regional level it has been demonstrated that, in 1971, over 30 per cent of the population in North Wales and Sussex was aged over 60, compared with the national mean of only 19 per cent (Law and Warnes 1975). However the most dramatic growth is observed at the local scale; in 1971, 159 of the 1,400 administrative divisions in England and Wales had a proportion of the elderly greater than one standard deviation above the national mean (Allon-Smith 1982). Most of these areas were urban centres on the coast or their immediate rural hinterlands, and the remainder were small inland towns. Size was one of their common characteristics: most were relatively small, and 81 had populations of fewer than 10,000. The top ranked places, all of which had more than 40 per cent retired in their populations, were Grange-over-Sands (Lancashire), Sidmouth, Budleigh Salterton and Seaton (Devon), Bexhill (Sussex), Southwold (Suffolk) and Frinton and Walton (Essex). The main concentrations of the elderly are therefore outside the metropolitan regions, and are more likely to be located in small towns than in villages or the open countryside – which tends to lack the

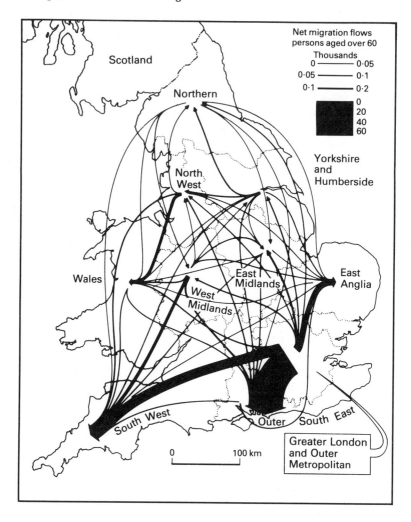

FIGURE 4.3   Net inter-regional migration flows of those aged 60 or over,
1961–66
Source: Law and Warnes (1976)

public transport and range of local services that are important to elderly
persons.

A third group of rural in-migrants comprises those who have moved
from metropolitan areas for employment reasons. These may include the
managers or key workers who have moved with a decentralizing firm,
although in some areas, notably Cornwall (Perry 1979), migration may

occur before employment is obtained. While some elements of this group are simply following the decentralization of jobs that has already occurred, others are moving for non-economic reasons, attracted by the quality of life in non-metropolitan zones. This group is likely to be fairly heterogeneous, both socially and demographically.

In the fourth group, in-migrants have moved out of cities in order to *live* in rural or semi-rural areas, but commute to urban jobs. There are a number of reasons to explain this, including the location of new housing beyond the existing built-up areas (Ambrose 1974), the desire for larger houses and gardens, improved mobility, and a preference for rural life. The advantages of village life are supposed to be friendliness and better surroundings (Clout 1972), although reality does not always match perceptions. Whatever the motives for rural residence, this group has profoundly transformed the social composition of many villages in the accessible countryside. In social terms it is a rather heterogeneous group, although it almost certainly excludes the lowest income groups, who may be caught in the housing and job 'traps' in inner-city areas (Department of the Environment 1977a). In addition, Pahl (1975) and others have shown that commuting may be a constraint rather then a preference, and that many higher income manual workers are 'reluctant commuters', who are only able to afford homes outside metropolitan areas.

The discussion in this chapter should not suggest that the entire rural populace is in constant flux. Most attention has been directed at the in-migrants and out-migrants to the exclusion of a core of more or less stable groups. Johnston (1967), in a study of Nidderdale, found that 51 per cent of the adult population had lived in the area at least 11 years. Others may come or go, but the entire life-cycle of many is lived within the confines of quite small areas.

SOCIAL CHANGE IN THE COUNTRYSIDE

Economic changes, the growth of commuting, and migration movements have all helped to modify the social structure of rural areas. In the same way that these changes have varied spatially – both regionally and at a local scale – so too have the modifications to social organizations themselves varied. There is no simple pattern or model of social change that can be applied to all villages, and there is no single continuum on which all rural communities can be placed (see chapter 1 above). In addition, attempts to interpret rural social change are hampered by the myths surrounding rural life, especially those that portray all rural communities as settings in which mutual aid and harmony of interests abound. Nevertheless, in spite of these difficulties it is possible to identify a number of central themes concerning rural social change.

The first of these is a fairly widespread concurrence about the demise of the traditional village community. Newby (1979) argues that in the mid-nineteenth century the majority of people living in villages relied on agriculture for a living, either directly or indirectly, so that each village comprised an 'occupational community'. Perhaps the main characteristics of this community were the senses of certainty and order in social life:

> Inevitably, the boundaries of what was and was not considered permissible in village life were much clearer in the nineteenth century, as they were in Victorian society generally. This conferred a sense of order on village life, a sense of 'place', in both a geographical and a social sense, which could be recognized and accepted as an immutable fact of life. For those villagers who accepted their 'place' this created a sense of psychological certainty and with it a not altogether unwelcome sense of security. [Newby 1979, p. 157]

Economic and social changes have combined to eliminate this occupational community, at least in lowland England, in all but a few very remote areas. The changes observed in the Sussex village of Ringmer between 1871 and 1971 are not atypical (Ambrose 1974). In 1871, 74 per cent of the village men were manual workers and most were engaged in agriculture, while the few women who worked outside the home were almost entirely 'in service'. By 1971 only one-third of the men worked manually and there was only one agricultural worker (in a survey of 150 households), while a large proportion of married and single women had jobs. As Ambrose emphasizes, the agricultural village had become the office workers' village.

Apart from the greater occupational variety, the greatest change in the village community has been the introduction of large numbers of new residents. This has sometimes led to social divisions between newcomers and locals, as mentioned in chapter 1, although the more remote rural areas are less affected by this influx than the accessible countryside. Much academic attention has been focused on the classification of the social groups comprising the new types of communities in rural areas. Four of the most frequently-used typologies are by Stamp, Pahl, Thorns and Ambrose.

1 Stamp (1949)
   (i) Primary rural population
   (ii) Secondary rural population
   (iii) Adventitious population

2 Pahl (1966)
   (i) Large property owners
   (ii) Salaried immigrants with some capital
   (iii) Spiralists
   (iv) Those with limited income and little capital
   (v) Retired
   (vi) Council house tenants
   (vii) Tied cottagers and other tenants
   (viii) Local tradesmen and owners of small businesses

3 Thorns (1968)
   (i) Professional and managerial
   (ii) Other white-collar workers
   (iii) Skilled and semi-skilled manual workers
   (iv) Farm workers and unskilled workers

4 Ambrose (1974)
   (i) Possess capital, can afford 'character' house and run two cars
   (ii) Can afford four-bedroom house and run a car
   (iii) Can afford two- or three-bedroom semi-detached house and run a car
   (iv) Can afford a two- or three-bedroom semi-detached house but not a car
   (v) Rent a council house and can run a car
   (vi) Rent a council house but cannot run a car
   (vii) Live in private rented accommodation

The earliest of these classifications is by Stamp, who divided the rural population into three groups. The primary population is directly dependent for its living on the land and includes farmers, farm workers and foresters; the secondary population exists to serve the primary population and includes the village shopkeeper, the smith and the doctor; by contrast, the adventitious population lives in the countryside by choice and includes newcomers such as elderly migrants and commuters. Saville (1957) considers that this is a useful analytical device, if rather imprecise. For example, it ignores the fact that a large proportion of the secondary population actually live in nearby towns rather than in the village. More importantly, the definition of the adventitious population stresses an element of choice in rural residence. This may have been true at one time, when the vast majority of commuters were middle-class, but it does not apply in the postwar period when large numbers of commuters have been 'reluctant' villagers, constrained by the availability of cheap housing to living in the countryside (Pahl 1965b).

Pahl (1966) instead suggested that eight distinctive social groups could be identified particularly with respect to housing, although these can have broader applications. The classification is further considered in the context of housing in chapter 5 but, essentially, Pahl proposed a two-dimensional model of stratification, with the two axes being income–housing tenure and newcomers–locals. This was made more complex by differentiation of those who intended to spend an appreciable period of time in the village (such as the retired and salaried immigrants), and those, such as career-oriented spiralists, who were merely passing through. The inclusion of the retired as a separate group added a socio-demographic element to the typology and, although the classification was two-dimensional, the two axes were not considered to be independent. Furthermore, Pahl has made it clear elsewhere (Pahl 1965b) that one of the axes is dominant; that class rather than commuting is more important in social change in the village.

Ambrose's (1974) typology has some similarities to Pahl's model because it also was specifically designed to analyse rural housing. Four income–capital groups were defined, each with access to different forms of housing, either in terms of tenure or in terms of the number of bedrooms available. These groups were then further sub-divided according to car ownership, important both in the access it allowed to jobs and services and in the flexibility it offered to migrants in the initial residential search process. This seems to be a particularly valuable approach to analysing the wider concept of access to resources in rural areas. Some families choose particular village locations because multiple-car ownership eases their problems of accessibility; others make the choice or are constrained to a particular area for economic reasons even though the ownership of just one car may cause difficulties for some members of the family; yet other households may be constrained even to particular houses in particular locations.

Thorn's (1968) classification is in many ways the most interesting for social geographers. This model was developed from a study of 11 villages in Nottinghamshire, where immigration had created a division between newcomers and locals. Thorns considered that the main social divisions were along class lines, and hence the four categories outlined are similar to those frequently identified in sociological studies (Worsley 1970). However, although there was a close association of life styles and values between the local and newcomer middle classes, there was a significant difference between the working-class farm workers and the other working-class groups. The farm workers were far more village orientated, were more likely to have been born and bred locally, and had lower incomes and poorer access to housing.

Thorns also elaborated a socio-temporal model of village communities, suggesting that there were three types of villages: those that have established structure (long-standing and with an accepted pattern of authority); those that are transitional, in which the higher-status group has lost its authority; and those that have been re-established, in which new leaders, mainly in-migrants, have filled the roles of authority. These types of villages can be located on the two axes of temporal and social change (figure 4.4). Following Mitchell's (1951) work, the villages may further be classified as being open or closed, and as being integrated or disintegrated (see previous section). Established villages are likely to be of type A, that is, closed and integrated; transitional villages will probably be of types C or D, that is, closed or open but disintegrated, while the re-established village is likely to be of type B, which is open and integrated. This offers an interesting insight into the nature of change in rural communities, and it is unfortunate that it has not been further researched.

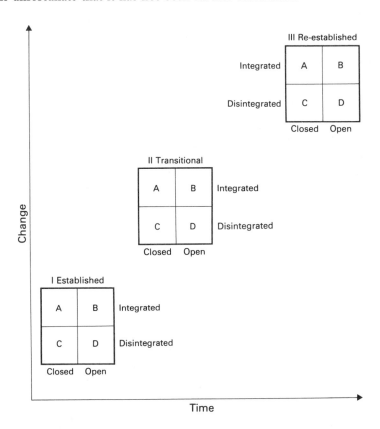

FIGURE 4.4   A socio-temporal typology of village structure
Source: Thorns (1968)

Consequences of social change in the village

The fundamental change is, arguably, social polarization (Harris 1973). Although polarization may include an element of newcomers-versus-locals, it is based essentially on social class, with the division occurring between the working class and the middle class. The former group is largely made up of locals while the latter mainly comprises newcomers, but the class dimension is paramount. These groups have different accessibility levels and are therefore subject to different life-style constraints (Pahl 1975). Since the working class is most affected by these constraints, it is more likely that a characteristically rural working class will develop than a distinctly rural middle class. The latter will be more likely to develop activity patterns typical of the middle class nationally (Thorns 1968).

The new social divisions in the rural community tend to cut across the old class divides of the former occupational community. The local working class may now be an 'encapsulated community', 'a village within the village, suspicious of and resistant to any intimate social contact with the commuters and the second home owners' (Newby 1979, p. 161).

Because of the way in which new housing has been developed in commuter villages, social polarization is likely to be reinforced by spatial segregation. Both new private housing estates and council estates are often peripherally located with respect to the existing village (Pahl 1965b; Blacksell and Gilg 1981). Sometimes working-class residents will live on peripheral council housing estates while older 'period' dwellings are taken over by the middle class. This is clearly the case in East Horsley, Surrey, where Connell (1974) has shown that spatial segregation was most clearly defined in the council estates, which were often morphologically distinct and separated by a considerable distance from the remainder of the village. By contrast, in the Devon village of Broadclyst, it is the middle-class estate of four-bedroomed detached dwellings that has been grafted on to an older core of smaller, less attractive houses.

One of the implications of spatial segregation seems to be that differences in housing quality will be reinforced further by the quality of the neighbourhood environment and facilities in each area (Ambrose 1974). In short, one group will be constrained to live in inferior housing with poorer immediate surroundings and will increasingly have fewer contacts with the other, wealthier, group in the village. Of course, no village has such a simple two-fold spatial organization, but the element of segregation is clearly evident in many rural areas.

The lack of social contact between the predominantly local working class and the predominantly newcomer middle class can be particularly marked. One of the most obvious symbols of this is in the public houses; if there is more than one pub, each tends to be patronized by different social classes, while a single pub will usually have socially segregated 'lounge' and 'public' bars (Newby 1979). This division extends across a whole range of social activities. In East Horsley, for example, the middle classes have organized several theatrical and musical groups, while the working class belong to the sports clubs, the Seniors' Club and the British Legion (Connell 1974). There are also differences in the schools that the children attend, in who recognizes whom as a neighbour, and in the use of village shops and other facilities. Some of these differences are outlined in the community studies reviewed by Frankenberg (1966).

The effect of middle-class newcomers on the level of services in a village is particularly important. On the one hand, their arrival may add to the demand for retailing and educational facilities, which may help to sustain the village shop or school; on the other, their children may attend other more distant schools and the newcomers may shop in the adjacent towns so that, if they have 'replaced' locals, there may be a downturn in demand, which could even precipitate the closure of these facilities. This is likely to enhance further any mistrust that exists between the two groups.

This is not to state that the middle class wants to exclude all the working class from the village. On the contrary, they may like to see farm workers around the village to mark it as being 'truly rural'. Newby (1979, p. 170) suggests that, in fact, 'what are demanded are pet farm workers who cause no trouble but who form part of the landscape along with the fields and the trees'. This probably excludes both the working-class commuters and the inhabitants of the council estates.

The two groups may also have very different sets of values, and this is well illustrated by Forsythe's (1980) study of the Orkney community of Stormay (a pseudonym). The values of the middle-class incomers are urban, and few migrants take active part in the traditional island activities. Even where migrants do join in, they tend to alter completely the nature of the events. For example, one migrant volunteered to organize the meal served at the annual Harvest Home, but he replaced the traditional supper of Orkney dishes with a meal that could have been served in any restaurant in the south of Scotland. The disparity in values also extends to social control and child-rearing. Orcadians, for example, apply informal means of familial control to under-age drinking, whereas newcomers wished to inform the police. Although the case of the Orkney community may be rather extreme, studies of villages in the more accessible countryside have also identified significant differences in the values of newcomers and locals, and the working and middle classes (Pahl 1965b; Thorns 1968). Upon such differences, the integration of all groups into the village community can sometimes founder (Dunn *et al.* 1981).

Different values can also lead these social groups into conflict. The two 'communities' are in competition for scarce resources in a number of instances, especially regarding housing, environment and land. Working-class residents may want a factory to be located in the village to provide local jobs, but the middle class, who wish only to consume (and not produce) in the area, may oppose this on conservationist grounds. Again, low-income local families may need council houses but the in-migrant middle class may oppose all new developments, having obtained their own foothold in the village. This conflict is clearly to be seen at the level of organized local politics (chapter 1), although the particular interests of the farming and landowning community add complexity to this. It is potentially an unequal conflict, as rural councils are dominated by various combinations of local and newcomer middle classes (Newby *et al.* 1978; Rose *et al.* 1978; Saunders *et al.* 1978; Rose *et al.* 1979). These groups operate sometimes in concert and at other times in opposition, but almost inevitably they seem to further their own interests at the expense of the rural working class. These conflicts over resources rarely come into the open; instead, rural political structures are characterized as being 'the non-politics of the status quo', a situation in which the effective control of local politics by farmers and landowners is matched by the acquiescence of the working class.

The transformation of rural communities, therefore, has led to new social divisions. In the most extreme cases this has meant that previously small, socially closely knit occupational communities, dominated by a squirearchy, have totally disappeared, or else survive only partly as encapsulated communities. In almost all villages however there has been some element of change, and usually there has been a set of related changes in which social polarization is accompanied by segregation and a shift of political power to a new ruling group, dominted by in-migrants.

5 Housing

Houses, particularly in Western society, confer upon their occupants much more than merely the roofs over their heads; they involve status and an expression of place in society. Housing requirements may alter as families move through life, and different types of financial commitments may be undertaken at different points in the life-cycle. In the countryside the type and quality of a family's housing is also affected by the accessibility of its location and by the social and financial circumstances of the family.

A COMPETITION FOR RURAL HOUSING?

The search for houses in both urban and rural areas can be regarded as an unequal competition between groups of people and between people within groups. This suggests that certain groups and individuals will be 'stronger' and better placed to obtain the housing they want, although this is something of an oversimplification since it implies that all are competing for the same types of house. The idea can be better focused by identifying the groups that are in potential competition in the countryside. We may think of them as competing for various tenures. Most such classifications should be treated with some caution, however, even if they help to identify the groups seeking accommodation within the rural housing market.

Numerous authors have attempted classifications, often not specifically with regard to housing but as part of a more general examination of social groupings in the countryside. Dunn *et al.* (1981) point out that a basic distinction can be made between those who can own (having the income and potential to be able to buy a house) and those who must rent. The theory of housing classes is based largely on subdivisions within these two main groups. Rex and Moore (1967) have provided the classic statement on this theme, suggesting seven categories:

1 the outright owners of large houses in desirable areas;
2 mortgage payers who 'own' their houses but on a mortgage;
3 council tenants in purpose-built council flats and houses;
4 council tenants in slums awaiting demolition;
5 tenants of private landlords;
6 resident landlords who take in lodgers to meet repayments;
7 lodgers in rooms.

It is, however, unrealistic to expect all of these to be visible in all locations, especially in rural areas where the balance of tenures differs considerably from the national picture. Rex and Moore's classification was based upon research in the Sparkbrook area of Birmingham, and it is more or less time-specific to the mid-1960s and applicable to medium- to large-sized cities. Also, it does not easily take into consideration key interests in housing such as absentee landlords letting as a business. The idea of housing classes does give a rudimentary sense of groupings of potential housing competitors, however, even if the categories may differ somewhat or be less clearly defined in rural areas.

Housing conversion from a Methodist chapel: a housing gain but a loss to the rural community (source: authors and A. Teed)

Fundamentally, many regard the 'conflict' over housing as an extension of the major divisions in society and argue that the allocation of housing is determined largely by the power that each group has come to possess in a society with a long history of class conflict (Haddon 1970; Duncan 1976; Mellor 1977). Rural social geographers take this view very seriously, as it stems directly from the political economy background outlined in chapter 1.

Some classifications of rural social groupings introduced in chapter 4 (pp. 90–1), particularly those by Pahl (1966) and Ambrose (1974), have a more direct relevance to rural housing. Pahl recognized that large-scale property owners, although few in number, can still exercise disproportionate political and managerial power in the rural environment, sometimes in a paternalistic manner (Newby *et al.* 1978). Pahl's 'salaried immigrants' frequently ally themselves with this group on housing matters. His 'spiralists' tend to own mainly modern village housing. They contrast with the 'reluctant commuters' of more limited means, forced to live in villages for the sake of buying at the cheaper end of the housing market. Another important group, the retired, can place significant demands on local facilities and services, but in housing terms they form a heterogeneous group since some have capital from the sale of housing in more expensive locations while others are in competition for cheaper housing, and especially for rural local authority houses and sheltered accommodation (Law and Warnes 1976; Phillips and Williams 1982a).

Council tenants, perhaps the 'fortunate few' in villages that do not have many local authority houses, are usually the more poorly paid rural workers and can include the homeless and ex-tied-cottagers rehoused under statutory obligations of councils. Tied cottagers (farm workers) and 'other tenants', such as those living in winter-lets or caravans, are another important rural group discussed by Pahl. These tenants can frequently be living in the least desirable and least secure of all housing in rural locations. Pahl's final group comprises local traders and small business owners. This is another mixed group including both owner-occupiers and those who rent their homes with their business. They may be better placed financially than many tenants, but their security of tenure can end with retirement.

This classification is a useful starting point for the study of rural housing. In addition, Ambrose's (1974) classification is interesting because of its emphasis on transport availability and tenure which distinguishes his seven groups outlined in chapter 4. Dunn *et al.* suggest that the transport element tends to dominate the classification, and in terms of opportunities available to the residents in any given location, their quality of life can be very much influenced by whether or not they can afford private transport.

Access to housing

A theme discussed in chapter 1 was the influence of managerialism and national policies at the local level which can have clear and direct influences on the housing market. A few examples illustrate this contention. If central government, as a matter of policy, curtails the building of new local authority houses then, within a very short time, there will be few council houses available locally for allocation. In a less obvious but equally influential manner, if a credit squeeze is applied as a macroeconomic policy, the resulting high interest rates will reduce the number of people able to take out mortgages. This will result in fewer sales of new houses in the owner-occupied sector and construction firms will then build fewer new houses. At a more general level, cut-backs in improvement grants and subsidies will retard any upgrading of local and national housing stocks.

Many centrally determined policies are implemented via the managers of housing; therefore it has become more accepted in recent years to adopt a managerialist stance in analysing access to housing. The majority of studies have been in urban areas and have focused on the activities of building societies and finance institutions in the private sector (Ford 1975;

Housing conversion from a railway station: one consequence of the Beeching and other cuts (source: authors and A. Teed)

Boddy 1976; P. R. Williams 1976, 1978; Short 1978), and on the activities of housing managers in the public sector (Gray 1976a, 1976b; Paris and Lambert 1979). Chapter 1 dealt in some detail with the more general aspects of managerialism. Here, it is necessary not only to highlight the diversity of 'managers' influencing housing but also the fact that key 'gatekeepers' tend to represent institutions or public bodies. Models of housing opportunity stressing choice on the part of the individual are essentially unrealistic, for constraints imposed by bank managers or building society officers may be much more important. The chances of mobility for a tenant in the local authority sector are often very slim, particularly if the managers in his authority do not operate a very efficient internal transfer scheme. For new applicants, different councils' rules and regulations on allocations may be more or less strictly enforced by local officials.

Most research has focused on the role of local authority managers (Gray 1976a; Phillips and Williams 1982a) and building society activities (P. R. Williams 1976, 1978; Boddy 1976, 1980). The latter can be very influential, since in 1981 they accounted for about four-fifths of home loans outstanding and made some two-thirds of net advances for house purchases (table 5.1). Therefore, if a building society prefers lending to white-collar workers wishing to buy modern houses, the chances of an agricultural worker being able to purchase an old terraced house or stone cottage could be slim. In addition, owing to the restrictions to fixed multiples of income for mortgages, the lower paid worker will be at a disadvantage. Individual societies may favour advances to people in salaried jobs, so hourly-paid workers can be discriminated against. Blanket embargoes such as the 'red-lining' of areas in which loans will not be advanced are

Table 5.1   Loans for house purchase, 1981

Institution	Net advances		Advances outstanding	
	£m	%	£m	%
Building societies	6,207	64	48,915	79
Local authorities	252	3	3,900	6
Banks	2,470	25	5,340	9
Insurance companies	239	2	2,346	4
Trustee savings banks	182	2	297	–
Other public sector	348	4	1,169	2
Total	9,698	100	61,967	100

Source: after Building Societies Association (1982)

probably rare in rural districts, but restrictions are sometimes placed on older cob, stone and thatched buildings so that many cheaper properties may not be mortgageable. Finally, the rules of 'new' providers of housing can also operate to exclude or favour certain areas or individuals. The Housing Corporation or their related housing associations may or may not favour schemes in rural areas (to date, they generally have not), and therefore their attitudes, rules and regulations can all influence the chances of a rural resident of obtaining adequate housing in the correct location.

In view of these constraints, it may be necessary to consider housing acquisition from the perspective of deprivation rather than choice. Shaw (1979b) has suggested one such model of housing deprivation in rural areas; he argues that poor housing, inappropriate housing or inaccessible housing is mainly a consequence of other types of deprivation which can act cumulatively, including opportunity deprivation (in terms of jobs, education, recreation and health) and mobility deprivation (in terms of poor transport and inaccessibility, which 'ration' opportunities). This is a useful concept although as Dunn *et al.* (1981) suggest, it does not emphasize sufficiently that poor rural housing is as much a symptom of deprivation as a consequence. Housing tenure, quality and location can be at least partly responsible for other handicaps, such as poor access to jobs, education and services, from which households may suffer. They suggest therefore that greater emphasis be given to housing tenure in evaluating relative deprivation. Their model (figure 5.1) sees family income as a key explanatory variable, as this will influence accessibility and mobility, and largely govern the tenure that can be entered. It is a useful model since it recognizes internal household characteristics and the requirements of other models such as life-cycle or space needs. It also indicates the links between accessibility and quality of life, and between housing tenure and housing conditions, and their eventual effects on the lives of occupants. In addition, the model can incorporate those rural families who are far from deprived and have high levels of mobility, high incomes and access to housing of a good standard.

HOUSING CONDITIONS IN RURAL AREAS

Two main aspects of housing condition are important: the overall quality of the rural housing stock; and the variations in quality within the tenure groups, a matter that is discussed in subsequent sections. In terms of housing standards and occupancy rates, conditions have improved considerably during the course of this century. Commentators such as Brock-

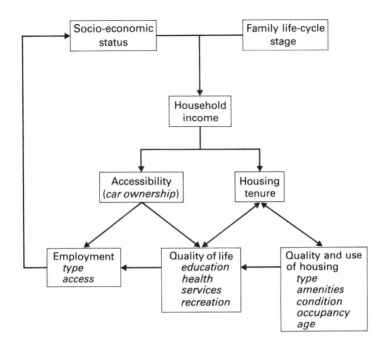

FIGURE 5.1 A model of rural housing opportunity
Source: Dunn *et al.* (1981)

way (1932) found appalling rural housing conditions in many areas of England between the wars: dwellings were in physically poor condition and insanitary, lacking water, electricity, ventilation or light. Since then the condition of housing in rural areas seems on average to have reached a higher standard than that in many urban areas, even where renovation or renewal policies have been conducted. Nevertheless the 1976 English House Condition Survey found that over 5 per cent of the rural housing stock was still unfit, and by 1981 this had risen to 6.7 per cent (Department of the Environment 1978, 1982).

The main safeguards in this area are the Housing Acts, supported by public health legislation, which is intended to ensure that no person should be allowed to live in a dwelling that is unfit for human habitation. The current definition of unfitness (under the Housing Act 1957) lists nine items in which a dwelling must be found to be 'reasonably suitable for occupation . . .'. These include general aspects such as state of repair, stability of foundations and freedom from dampness, and also quite specific matters of ventilation, natural lighting, waste disposal, sanitation and cooking facilities (Hadden 1979). In spite of statutory definitions, however, the designation of an 'unfit house' can still be a rather subjective matter, and standards in the past have been found to vary from one district to another. In addition, although not technically unfit, a house can still be very unsuitable for the needs of its occupants in terms of accommodation and access to jobs and services, aspects that are not generally the subject of legislation.

The Housing Act 1974 adds to the above criteria of 'unfitness' a list of certain 'standard amenities', the absence of which does not render a dwelling unfit but may make it eligible for improvement grants. These include quite basic facilities such as bath or shower, sink, WC, and hot and cold water supply. This indicates that, although technically 'fit', many dwellings may in reality have less than adequate amenities, such as outside toilets. In 1971 some 13.8 per cent of households in English rural districts lacked one or more basic amenity, and in certain rural districts (including some in Cornwall, Devon, Norfolk, Shropshire, Derbyshire and Durham), this was as high as 30 per cent. It seems clear that the poorest-quality rural housing persists where the traditional rural economy is still strongest and where urbanization levels are low (Dunn *et al.* 1981; Rogers 1983). As noted below, rural districts also tend to have far higher proportions of non-permanent mobile homes than do urban areas, and, while many of these are of high quality, some are in very poor condition.

During the 1960s considerable improvements were made in the condition of the housing stock both nationally and in rural areas. The early 1970s saw additional impetus being given to housing improvements by the designation, under the 1969 Housing Act, of General Improvement Areas (GIAs). This Act widened the scope of improvement grants, first introduced in 1949, and gave local authorities the power to declare general improvement areas within which grants covered up to 60 per cent of eligible expenses compared with 50 per cent elsewhere. However, with their emphasis on rehabilitation of stock and on area-wide environmental improvements, GIAs had a relatively limited impact, and only about 5 per cent of grants since 1969 have been issued within these areas. In some areas they have actually added to housing stress by contributing to gentrification, while areas with great social need or high levels of rented accommodation have sometimes been excluded (Lansley 1979).

As a result, the 1974 Housing Act introduced Housing Action Areas (HAAs), designed to give priority to the improvement of areas for which GIAs are not relevant, where poor physical condition of housing is combined with social stress and deprivation. New powers to purchase and to enforce improvements were given and grants of up to 75 per cent (90 per cent in hardship cases) became available. The policy was designed to improve communities both in social and housing terms during the five-year life of an HAA, and an overall aim was to remove heavy reliance on individual improvement and to enhance the environmental and physical quality of the areas.

The designation of HAAs and GIAs is essentially area-based however. As such, they may be more appropriate for urban areas, where most of the housing in any area tends to be of a similar age and type and the blanket effect of the area-based policy will at least have some logical basis (although even in inner cities problems do not necessarily come in a spatially concentrated form – see Smith 1979a). Rural areas do not display the same concentrations of poor housing and poor social conditions, and as a result very few HAAs or GIAs have been declared in them (Kirby 1977; Dunn *et al.* 1981). Therefore, grant-aided benefits and enforced improvements have not been as readily available to rural householders.

The 1976 English House Condition Survey found that some 28 per cent of all unfit dwellings in England but only 23 per cent of total stock were in rural areas, defined to include settlements of up to 1,000 dwellings. This provided something of a contrast to previous surveys, in which rural areas have shown up as having generally better housing than urban areas (Dunn *et al.* 1981). The 1981 English House Condition Survey (Department of the Environment 1982) supports the general urban–rural differences found in 1976, although slight changes in surveyors' classifications of

Table 5.2 Ratio of the proportion of sub-standard dwellings in each type of area to the average proportion in England as a whole, 1976 and 1981

	Conurbation	Provincial town	Rural
Unfit dwellings			
1976	1.06	0.87	1.13
1981	1.05	0.86	1.10
Dwellings lacking one or more amenities			
1976	1.19	0.98	0.80
1981	1.14	0.92	0.84
Repair cost over £7000			
1976	0.84	0.79	1.56
1981	0.91	0.79	1.49

Source: unpublished data from English House Condition Survey, 1981

district as rural, urban or conurbations make precise comparisons difficult. Instead, table 5.2 illustrates the proportions of dwellings affected (for
example, unfit) in each area and relates this to the average for the given
year for stock over all areas. This ratio shows that measures of housing
condition have remained quite stable between 1976 and 1981, with the rate
of improvement perhaps being slowed down by reduced grant availability
in the late 1970s, but that there are distinct differences between different
types of location in the incidence of poor housing. In general, dwellings in
rural areas and conurbations are about 25 per cent more likely to be in
poor condition than dwellings in provincial towns. The proportion of
dwellings lacking one or more of the basic amenities is highest in conurbations, but unfitness and disrepair (indicated by high repair costs) are more
common in rural areas.

Average over-occupancy and under-occupancy rates suggest an
additional rural problem: that in many locations the housing stock is not
being as 'efficiently' utilized as it could be. Only 4 per cent of housing
stock in English rural districts compared with 6 per cent of the total
English housing stock exceeded the official overcrowding index in 1971,
but almost 38 per cent of housing in rural districts was defined as 'under-
occupied'. Under-occupation of large dwellings, particularly by the
elderly, can be most undesirable, especially when rates, maintenance and
heating bills become too high for those on low incomes. However, because
of the low levels of provision of rural council houses and small owner-
occupied bungalows, especially purpose-built accommodation for the
elderly, people who want to move out of accommodation that is too large
may have nowhere to go locally. In addition, the relatively small number
of alternative dwellings available to families who have to live in specific
rural locations may mean that they have to take and retain whatever
dwelling is available, whether or not it is appropriate to their needs.

Poor housing can therefore assume many forms. Unfitness, substandard
amenities and under- or over-occupancy can all indicate 'bad' housing, but
in social terms location and accessibility are paramount. Accessibility as a
concept is discussed in chapter 6; here it is sufficient to mention its
implications for personal mobility. It is true that 'bad' housing is not solely
a rural problem, just as it is not exclusively urban. But is has been
identified as a cause for social concern by a number of recent researchers
on rural conditions (Larkin 1978a, 1978b, 1979; Dunn *et al.* 1981; Phillips
and Williams 1982a). In order to understand the nature of the rural
housing question, it is perhaps best to examine some of the features that
are specific to each tenure, although it is always necessary to be aware of
the many interlinkages among all tenures in the housing market, which
can in some ways render this an artificial exercise.

OWNER-OCCUPATION

The tenure of rural housing is of considerable interest to social geographers, since access to specific sectors is restricted for many persons and the variation in security of tenure has social implications relating to quality of life, welfare, accessibility and expenditure on housing. The significant features of rural tenure that differ from the national picture are: high proportions of owner-occupied housing, high levels of private rental, and generally low levels of council housing (table 5.3). National trends such as the predominance of private housing since the 1950s (figure 5.2) and the decline in private rental have of course affected rural areas also. The growth of home ownership even among the less well off in Britain has been said to have created a 'corps of working-class capitalists, a new type of property-owning bourgeoisie. . . .' (Dennis and Clout 1980, p. 153), even if there remains a strong private rental sector in rural areas and many owner-occupiers are already 'well-to-do'.

Owner-occupation has grown steadily, both nationally and in rural areas, since the 1950s. Over one-half of the houses in rural districts of England are owned by their occupiers, whether outright or on a mortgage. All of the major political parties since the Second World War have, to a greater or lesser degree, been in favour of extending home ownership. However, the national financial and economic climate prevailing at any given time has influenced the supply and demand for such housing, and

Table 5.3   Housing tenure in English rural districts, 1971 (percentages)

	Rural districts	England as a whole	
	1971	1971	1980
Owner-occupied	54.5	50.0	57.3
Local authority	21.1	28.0	29.2
Privately rented (unfurnished)	20.9	17.1	13.4
Privately rented (furnished)	3.3	4.7	
Other	0.2	0.2	0.1

Source: after Dunn *et al.* (1981) and Department of the Environment (1981)

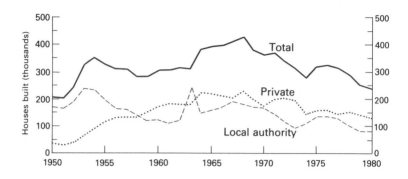

FIGURE 5.2   Dwellings completed, by tenure, 1950–80
Source: after Blacksell and Gilg (1981) and Department of the Environment (1981)

prices have altered at different rates (almost always increasing) during this period.

An important feature of owner-occupancy in rural areas is that the stock of housing is relatively limited in any given location and hence choice is restricted. This has come about partly because of low rates of building in the past (owing to a relatively small effective demand) and partly because of stringent planning controls, which have restricted the rate of growth of new housing particularly in national parks and other scenically attractive areas (see chapter 7). The net result is that prices are often higher for houses in attractive and accessible villages, and much of the new housing built tends to be of a more expensive kind which maintains this feature.

Various authors have suggested reasons for the building of expensive new homes. First, planners are often blamed, because they may frequently specify the styles and building materials with which new houses should be built, 'in keeping' with existing structures (Blacksell and Gilg 1981). Clark (1982a, 1982b) cites the example of the Lake District, where planning board regulations concerning slate roofs can add £2,000 to the price of a house. Second, although land is cheaper in rural than in urban locations, planning policies may have helped to increase its price considerably by limiting the amounts of building land available. However, planning should not always be indicted as a cause of problems, since the planning process has fostered generally higher standards in all housing, particularly in technical matters and, perhaps, site layout.

Even if all rural houses are not prohibitively priced, they can be expensive relative to the income levels of local inhabitants, and this can be the key factor that determines whether an individual family can afford to purchase a home. As discussed in chapters 2 and 3, many rural occupations have low incomes. Furthermore, in many more isolated and smaller settlements a wife may be unable to work regularly owing to a lack of jobs or transport; therefore the total mortgage that a would-be home buyer can obtain will be based on a multiple of the husband's income alone. Finally, the nature of rural employment can also militate against successful mortgage applications because of building societies' lending preferences for 'white-collar' occupations.

Owner-occupancy has probably been subject to less direct legislative activity than have the two other main tenures. However, some legislation has influenced this sector since the 1960s, such as the GIA and HAA grants discussed previously, and legislation ostensibly directed at other tenures has often had repercussions for this sector. For example, the encouragement of council house sales by Conservative governments under the terms of the Housing (Finance) Act 1972 and subsequently by the Housing Act 1980 has boosted owner-occupation. The Housing (Finance) Act shifted the balance further in favour of house purchase rather than rental when it imposed 'fair' (usually higher) rents on most council tenants. As Duclaud-Williams (1978) suggests, the operation of rent rebates and other principles embodied in the Act tended at that time to swing the balance further in favour of home buyers and away from the two rented sectors.

The Labour Government's 1977 Green Paper, *Housing Policy: a Consultative Document*, had a slightly different emphasis. Although it welcomed the extension of home ownership, it also recognized the problems of families who could not or would not take on the responsibility of home purchase (Department of the Environment 1977b). As a result, it saw the need to continue strong support for local authority housing provision. This view did not receive much support from the Conservative government that entered office in 1979. Its policy was to restrict public expenditure in fields such as housing and to extend home ownership for council house tenants with their Right-to-Buy legislation in the Housing Act 1980. In addition, during the early 1980s funds for housing improvement were very much subjected to central government control and were issued in a rather unpredictable fashion, which made the planning of local grants very difficult and variable.

It is clear that housing remains very much, as Berry (1974) described it, a 'political football', with different political parties favouring varying policies to each tenure. The overall result can often be disillusionment for the householder and frustration for housing professionals.

Second homes

The phenomenon of second homes in rural areas has been quite widely researched, although there is debate as to their definition (Dower 1977; Davies and O'Farrell 1981) and little agreement as to whether they constitute a 'curse or a blessing' (Coppock 1977). In parts of Britain, particularly in parts of Wales, second home ownership has been fiercely contested by some locals, but it is hard to judge whether such opposition is justified. Opponents of second homes argue that outsiders, being wealthier, can outbid locals for any specific property, thereby stimulating out-migration. In addition, social disruption and discontent are said to be fostered by temporary visitors, and ghost communities may be created out-of-season. Protagonists of second homes suggest that outsiders are actually saving homes for which there is no local demand, preventing dereliction, paying rates that would otherwise go unpaid and supporting local shops, services and craftsmen (albeit seasonally). These arguments doubtless have different real weight in different locations, depending on whether there is pressure on the local housing stock. The emotional contribution is difficult to evaluate in any circumstances.

The number of second homes in existence is surprisingly uncertain, partly because of problems of definition and partly owing to a reticence on the part of owners to advertise themselves in view of the possible local opposition. In Britain, the proportion of second homes per capita is still very low compared with North America and some European countries: Bielckus *et al.* (1972) estimated some 350,000 in England and Wales in the early 1970s, of which 180,000 were caravans. Sarre (1981) points to the quite marked fluctuations in numbers throughout the 1970s (although he recognizes the data limitations) which reached a peak in 1972 and a low in 1975, climbing back to about 155,000 in 1979 (table 5.4). Steady but slow growth in numbers is predicted for the 1980s.

Table 5.4   Numbers of second homes in Britain, 1968–79

Year	No. of 2nd homes	Year	No. of 2nd homes
1968	101,100	1974	109,800
1969	136,800	1975	74,800
1970	187,400	1976	117,500
1971	185,400	1977	100,400
1972	194,300	1978	146,300
1973	143,100	1979	154,700

Source: after Sarre (1981) (based on Audits of Great Britain data)

It seems, therefore, that second homes comprise, on average, no more than 1 per cent of British housing stock. Naturally, there tend to be strong regional and local concentrations; in some parts of North Wales second homes can comprise up to 50 per cent of housing stock in small areas (Bollom 1978). In a recent Lake District survey, only 48 per cent of house purchasers were local, with more than half the purchases being for holiday accommodation, second homes or retirement (Shucksmith 1981). In the Lake District too, Clark (1982a, 1982b) cites an estimate of 11 per cent of stock being in use as second homes in the mid-1970s, with figures of over 30 per cent in some parishes.

Within the South West of England a wide distribution of second homes was found; 10 per cent of the total building stock in the extreme north-west of Cornwall were used for this purpose but the figure was between 1 and 5 per cent in most districts (South West Economic Planning Council 1975). The tendency of second homes to be clustered in specific pleasant rural locations is probably the characteristic that exaggerates their significance. There is no general evidence as yet to link second home ownership with house price increases (de Vane 1975), but in local instances this has undoubtedly happened on a property-for-property basis, and it is easy to be convinced that dire housing consequences can come about for the 'traditional' rural population.

Occasionally, housing policies in local areas have attempted to restrict the sale of houses to local inhabitants. This is usually effective only with new houses or with council houses resold by their tenants. In the Lake District National Park, an experiment was conducted after 1974 to attempt to restrict second homes purchases of new houses (Clark 1982a, 1982b). The estimate of 11 per cent of stock in use as second or holiday homes was felt to be an underestimate, and it was suspected that the real figure was nearer 26 per cent by 1980. The policy was to restrict planning permissions for new house building to about 70 dwellings per annum. Permission for building would be given only if the occupier of a new house would live in it for at least six months per year and was a person employed or to be employed locally. This was a form of positive discrimination in favour of locals. The resale of the houses was also to be only to them. The powers involved were under Section 52 of the 1971 Town and Country Planning Act: however, subsequent intervention in late 1981 by the Secretary of State for the Environment appears to have prevented planners from being able to specify the nature of occupiers of new housing. Although this policy may have been viewed as a 'reasonable' intervention in the free market for private housing, there might in any case have been problems of enforcement of restrictions on resale.

LOCAL AUTHORITY HOUSING

In Britain local authority (council) housing has become the second largest sector of the housing market, holding considerable social significance in local areas. This is because a major aim of public sector housing policy has been to provide a good standard of accommodation usually for the less well-to-do who cannot or do not wish to buy their own homes. It can also be a tool of social and economic policies to help the aged, the homeless, single–parent families and the handicapped to obtain housing, as well as to provide flexibility in the attraction of key workers. In some urban areas it can comprise as much as 40 per cent of the stock and up to 100 per cent of houses over considerable tracts.

As it is publicly owned, this sector is subject to direct government influence and, frequently, political direction. For practical purposes, it is the local authorities that finance, build and administer these houses, but central government directives, legislation and grants have had direct influence on building rates, rents, finance and sales. From time to time there have been limits to the amount that councils can spend per house (the 'cost yardstick') and minimum standards have been established since the 1967 recommendations of the Parker Morris Committee. The cost yardstick system related the total approved cost of a development to the number of people it was intended to house. In the past, 'yardstick-plus' costs have been permitted, mainly in expensive urban locations but also in some rural locations in recognition of their higher building costs.

In general Parker Morris standards and yardstick limits made the development of small numbers of houses in rural locations very uneconomical, and, in response to this and other criticisms, their discontinuation was announced in January 1980; instead, cost estimates and project details were to be submitted directly for Department of the Environment approval. This has had the effect of making local authority housing even more subject to central scrutiny, and the current system of central government constraints has severely limited new council house provision in rural areas since 1980, particularly as the new proposals may see more expensive building in rural areas as inappropriate.

Numbers of council houses have, in any case, always been lower in rural than in urban areas. They comprise some 21 per cent of rural housing stock on average, and Shucksmith (1981) indicates that, during 1968–73, in England and Wales there were usually more than double the number of local authority houses being built per 1,000 population in urban than in rural districts. At a local scale, table 5.5 shows differences in tenure within Devon, an example of a predominantly rural county. The urban districts

Table 5.5 Household tenure by districts in Devon, 1971 and 1981 (percentages)

District	Owner-occupied	Council-rented	Privately rented and other tenures
East Devon	70.2 (61)*	15.7 (17)*	14.1 (22)*
Exeter	59.9 (55)	24.2 (25)	15.9 (20)
North Devon	66.1 (61)	17.4 (16)	16.5 (23)
Plymouth	54.6 (45)	27.0 (30)	18.4 (25)
South Hams	63.7 (55)	18.9 (19)	17.4 (26)
Teignbridge	66.9 (60)	16.7 (17)	16.4 (23)
Mid-Devon (Tiverton)	57.4 (49)	26.1 (27)	16.5 (24)
Torbay	72.6 (66)	11.3 (12)	16.1 (22)
Torridge	67.1 (61)	16.9 (16)	16.0 (23)
West Devon	67.5 (58)	14.4 (15)	18.1 (27)
Devon	63.4 (56)	19.9 (21)	16.7 (23)
England and Wales	(50)	(28)	(22)

* 1971 figures in parentheses
Sources: 1971 Census and 1981 Census, County Report

of Exeter and Plymouth and the partly urbanized Tiverton District have far higher proportions of council-rented accommodation than the rural districts. Only Torbay, with its high proportion of elderly and retired persons in owner-occupied accommodation, is more poorly provided. The very rural West Devon, Torridge, Teignbridge and South Hams Districts have percentages at least ten points below the national level of council house provision. In particular, the continued growth of owner-occupancy is emphasized here with the comparison of the 1971 and 1981 figures.

Why has the rate of council house provision been so much lower in rural areas? Reasons are not clear-cut, but various aspects of rural social life have been suggested. Attitudes appear to be somewhat unfavourable to 'welfare state' provision; Newby (1979) suggests that influential local interests (farmers and landowners) have been keen to minimize local council house building in order to keep down rates – and through key positions on councils have been able to realize this objective. In addition, farmers can maintain a greater degree of social control over agricultural workers living in tied accommodation. A declining agricultural workforce may also have helped to convince local interests there was no real demand for rural council housing. Although care must be taken in generalizing too much from Newby's research in East Anglia, these contentions might well hold true for other rural areas of Britain.

Financial reasons could be of more general importance. Housing subsidies in the past have sometimes favoured rural areas, but Shucksmith believes that the higher building costs have not been matched, and that 'it is clear that central government policies have played a major role in frustrating council housing in rural areas, both through the overall financial allocation to rural areas, and through the constraints imposed on individual developments. . . .' (Shucksmith 1981, p. 37).

Can a case be made for the continued provision of such housing? A number of authors maintain that a definite need does exist. Larkin (1978b) cites evidence to show that poor people in rural areas are frequently less well housed than their urban counterparts. Waiting lists also tend to be longer, and these are not complete indices of need since council allocation rules often exclude certain persons from them. In addition, tied accommodation, winter-lets and caravans are all sources of potential demand for council housing in rural areas. Shucksmith (1981) found waiting lists of over 1,200 and a housing stock of only 2,169 in the Lake District National Park, while Phillips and Williams (1982a) found a waiting list of about 1,000 and a stock of some 4,500 dwellings in South Hams, Devon.

Many of these applicants are living in very poor existing accommodation. Niner (1975) estimated from census data that some 250 applicants to Copeland Borough Council would be without a fixed bath or shower. Phillips and Williams (1982b) found that over 10 per cent of the 1,000 applicants in South Devon were living in bedsitters or caravans, while about one in five were sharing a kitchen, bathroom or WC; 5 per cent were living in accommodation that lacked at least one of these facilities, and some even lacked mains electricity or water. All these data indicate a considerable need for rural council houses, and authors such as Shucksmith, Newby and Larkin argue that need and demand for council housing outstrip the supply and any foreseeable increase in supply.

Figure 5.3 indicates the characteristics of council housing and its management which must be considered when analysing any given rural area. The first main factor concerns the distribution of the housing stock. It is sad but true that existing houses are often poorly located with respect to current jobs and services. Even if there are relatively good overall stocks of rural council houses, they may be concentrated mainly into a few larger settlements, and persons who need to work in the more remote or smaller settlements can be severely disadvantaged. Shucksmith (1981) highlights the fact that the pressure in district councils has been to build (if at all) in larger settlements rather than in isolated locations. Planning policies of concentration have fostered this, sometimes to facilitate the provision of

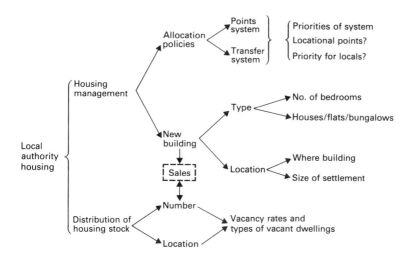

FIGURE 5.3   Local authority housing in rural areas: analytical variables

amenities and services to housing. Government subsidies were also, in effect, greater for higher-density development (subject to Parker Morris minimum standards), and all these factors have combined to militate against the building of few dwellings and small estates in isolated locations.

Evidence to support this general contention has been found in Warwickshire and Devon, where it appears that new building has been concentrated mainly in the major settlements of the hierarchy. In Devon, in particular, both private and public sector new housing has been predominantly in the larger settlements, especially those within commuting distance of the main urban centres (Cloke 1979). At the district scale in South Devon, 531 of the 734 completions of local authority dwellings between 1976 and 1979 were in the three main towns of Kingsbridge, Totnes and Ivybridge and only 51 completions were in parishes outside the seven main settlements (Phillips and Williams 1982a).

All this evidence tends to support the contention that there will be relatively few new council houses available for allocation in the more remote areas where housing need and accessibility problems may be most acute.

Management of council housing in rural areas

Distributional factors tend to make more difficult the task of housing management, the second main aspect displayed in figure 5.3. The management of housing stock can have wide-ranging social implications, and, in their interpretation and execution of national and local housing policies, local authority housing officers may become key figures in social policy in one of the key areas of people's lives. It is the managers of local authority stock who determine who is allocated to which houses and where; who can enter the waiting list and how long they have to wait and, crucially, who can transfer within this sector. Therefore an examination of housing management must consider the following: pointing schemes or other forms of assessment of applicants; allocation and transfer policies; building policies and sales policies (Phillips and Williams 1982a, 1982c).

Allocation of housing is frequently carried out by quasi-objective schemes to allocate 'points' to each applicant. Some rural districts, however, still lack separate housing departments staffed by professionally trained housing managers, and in extreme instances allocations have been carried out on a more or less *ad hoc* basis by local councillors. Where points schemes do exist, they are usually based on criteria such as family size and existing housing space, lack of a separate home or facilities, medical need, separation of families, length of local residence, and a number of discretionary points. Only in a very few cases are points awarded explicitly to recognize the need to reside in specific rural locations, which is a sad reflection on the past role of allocation policy. Some authorities now, such as South Hams, have awarded extra points for persons who live in, or need to live in, certain rural parishes which have small local authority housing stocks. These can give people who have to live in certain remote locations a slightly better chance of obtaining appropriate accommodation.

Many local authorities in addition to 'pointing' applicants, place them in queues for accommodation, based on type of dwelling required and location. The different relative lengths of queues can be very important in determining the time spent on the waiting list. Again, taking South Hams as an example, applicants are placed in queues for one of five housing sub-districts and also in one of five groups according to family size, marital status and number of children. Although some of the groups would clearly not be competing with others for the same kind of housing (for example, families with two or more children versus single applicants), there are potentially 25 different queues. Applicants do not necessarily know the relative lengths of queues or their chances of obtaining housing in one sub-district rather than another. Queues vary, being shortest, for instance, for three-bedroom houses and much longer for 'specialist' accommodation for the elderly (a common rural problem). Applicants clearly have a better chance of obtaining accommodation quickly if willing to accept a dwelling in one of the main settlements, and this in turn may be detrimental and cause long journeys to work.

Important management decisions relate to the levels of priority accorded to different groups for accommodation. There are statutory duties to house certain categories of homeless persons and some tied cottagers (these will be discussed later). In many small rural districts these obligations can effectively pre-empt almost all 'voids' (vacancies) occurring during the year and leave very few opportunities for housing applicants from the general waiting list. In addition, applicants with high numbers of points awarded for medical reasons may be favourably treated. When an applicant comes into a priority category or reaches the head of a queue and is offered housing, he or she then has to decide whether to accept the offer if it does not accord with the original preference. Usually a limited number of offers can be rejected but there is no guarantee that a subsequent offer will be an improvement, so in many rural districts applicants may have to make the best of either inappropriate housing or housing not ideally located with regard to their workplaces or existing patterns of use of facilities.

Once within the council sector, tenants may find their circumstances changing: families may increase or decrease and places of work or school attendance may change, so that many tenants apply to transfer accommodation. There was a transfer waiting list of over 500 applicants in early 1980 in South Hams, and many of these, if moved, would release houses for families, especially if they were elderly persons waiting to go into purpose-built flats. The small stock in rural areas frequently makes it very difficult for councils to meet transfer requests, even though these may lead to more efficient utilization of their resources. Phillips and Williams (1982d) suggest a 'positive' approach to transfer management in the rural sector in which housing visitors 'scout' tenants and try to suggest ways in which a small (and diminishing) stock can be better used both in terms of persons per dwelling and of the tenants' patterns of spatial behaviour. The Scottish Development Department (1980) also suggest that all allocation schemes should be sensitive to transfer requests, especially where these will release housing that is in considerable demand by other groups. This is one way in which rural housing departments can attempt to overcome certain of their problems, and it seems that at least some councils are adopting such procedures of 'positive' transfer management.

Council house sales

A final aspect of housing management is the sale of houses to tenants (figure 5.3). This has caused much debate and emotion. Opponents of sales see them as reducing a vital social resource built up at the ratepayers' expense, while proponents see sales to long-standing tenants as almost a recourse to 'natural justice', although there are also the political overtones of the desire of Conservative politicians to build up a property-owning base to their vote. In rural areas, with the small stocks identified earlier, the issue of sales can be particularly emotive. District councils at present will rarely be able to afford to replace such houses, and, if all or most of the houses in a small village are sold, then the council's ability to meet housing need locally is effectively negated. The additional fear has been that properties sold in attractive rural settings may eventually become 'second homes' for rich urban dwellers.

The sale of council houses to tenants is not, however, new. It has been occurring for many years and has been embodied in legislation such as the Housing Acts of 1935 and 1957, although numbers of sales have fluctuated considerably according to the political complexions of the government of the day. In the year 1972 alone, for example, 60,000 dwellings were sold with the encouragement of the Conservative administration (Hughes 1981). Even Labour Party policy has been to permit sales, provided they do not disadvantage the community or impair housing authorities' abilities to meet their obligations, which can be difficult to prove in practice.

The Housing Act 1980 introduced a new aspect to sales (Hughes 1981; Smith 1981). Whereas ministerial consent was previously required, now certain 'secure tenants' have the right to buy their houses (flats, initially excluded from purchase but available for long lease, were later included). Local authorities will now be unable to prevent the exercise of the 'Right-to-Buy'. Not even all Conservative politicians were happy with the implications of the notion of compulsory sales, particularly as they might affect rural areas, and certain safeguards have had to be incorporated. Basically, however, secure tenants of three years' standing can buy their houses at discounts ranging from 33 per cent of market price to a maximum of 50 per cent.

Section 19 of the Act did protect rural areas from the immediate profiteering resale of houses in attractive areas, for example in small rural estates or in lone rural settings. In national parks or Areas of Outstanding Natural Beauty (AONBs), or in areas designated by the Secretary of State as 'rural', the sale contains a covenant limiting the freedom of the purchasing tenant and his successors to resell the dwelling; houses can be resold only to 'locals' who fulfil certain criteria, such as living or working in the designated rural area for the previous three years; or, for ten years after the original purchase, the tenant has first to offer to resell to the council (Liell 1981).

In addition to the national parks, AONBs and certain areas in rural Wales, a number of rural authorities have applied for designation as 'rural' to benefit from such protection. Not all have been successful (and some have been only partly designated), but the list has grown since 1980 (figure 5.4). A major problem is that, even in very rural districts, much of the council's stock will frequently be in the largest settlements, which in many cases have not been included under the rural designation. These settlements can still be attractive, and the larger part of authorities' stock can therefore remain unprotected. In South Hams, for example, the towns of Totnes, Kingsbridge, Ivybridge and Dartmouth have not been designated 'rural', and they contain more than half the council's stock, with many houses located not on large estates but in pleasant settings. The same may be said of a number of other rural districts designated under Section 19 of the Housing Act 1980, ostensibly protected but in reality having quite large proportions of their stocks vulnerable.

The major implications of these sales of rural council houses will be an eventual reduction in the ability of authorities to meet even their statutory obligations, let alone to use housing as a tool of social policy (Phillips and Williams 1981). However, at present it must not be assumed that sales always produce immediate problems. Many of the tenants buying would have remained in the same houses, so there would not have been 'voids' for allocation in any case. It is in the long term that the ability of councils to transfer tenants and to optimize the use of stock will be lost.

PRIVATELY RENTED HOUSING

Accommodation rented from private landlords has always represented the most heterogeneous sector of the housing market in terms of quality and type of dwelling. In rural areas it assumes a greater significance, comprising, in 1971, 24 per cent of the total housing stock compared with 21 per cent nationally, although this proportion is falling quite rapidly everywhere. A full range of types of rented accommodation is also found: in addition to houses, bungalows, flats and bedsitters of all ages, there are some types of dwelling not as commonly seen in urban areas – caravans and mobile homes, winter-lets and tied accommodation.

The privately rented sector has traditionally been enumerated according to whether it is let furnished or unfurnished, with the latter usually providing somewhat greater security of tenure. However, owing to the very mixed nature of rented housing, we shall concentrate on the more distinctively rural aspects, namely winter-lets, caravans/mobile homes and tied accommodation.

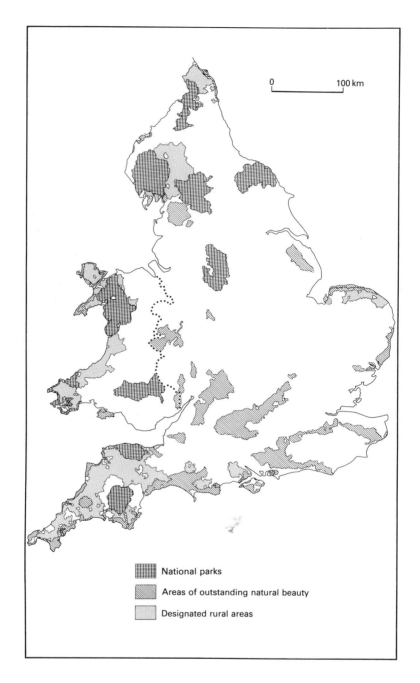

FIGURE 5.4   Designated 'rural areas' (Housing Act 1980), national parks and
Areas of Outstanding Natural Beauty
Source: Phillips and Williams (1983)

Winter-lets

The term is self-explanatory and covers mainly those second homes that have been called 'holiday investment properties' (Davies and O'Farrell 1981). Countryside cottages, seaside flats or even terraced houses in villages are the usual type of properties involved. The short-term lets often suit people such as students when the off-season coincides with their term, but for families the disruption of having to move out for the summer is frustrating. For many, the only alternative rural accommodation may be in a caravan, seasonally almost as expensive as a holiday investment home.

The Housing (Homeless Persons) Act 1977 can sometimes assist these families. However, local authorities have adopted varying interpretations of the law. A number of classes of homeless persons has been created by a rather cumbersome section 4 of the Act, and local authorities, differing in their interpretation of the Act, have accordingly treated residents of winter-lets differently. West Dorset District Council, for instance, was refusing to house people evicted from winter-lets unless they qualified for housing prior to entering such accommodation, even though in this case they would presumably have sought council accommodation in the first place (Larkin 1979). Persons with 'priority need', which includes having children who are also homeless, actual or threatened homelessness through emergency such as fire or flood, old age, illness, physical or mental handicap or pregnancy, can expect to have accommodation provided, at least while enquiries proceed. If not in priority need, particularly if considered for the purposes of the Act to have become 'intentionally homeless', persons may receive only advice and 'appropriate assistance', leaving much to an authority's discretion.

There is little detailed work on homelessness in rural areas, largely because of the diffuse nature of the problem. Most homeless persons and families have the common feature of poverty although a variety of personal and other reasons may underlie their homelessness. Winter-lets can be one possible cause of homelessness, although the reasons for occupants being in seasonal accommodation in the first place are very difficult to evaluate, and only now is the law being clarified in the courts. Hughes (1981) cites recent cases, some of which are in rural areas such as the West Country, in which the homeless tenants from winter-lets have not always been rehoused.

The 1977 Act adds another housing responsibility to local authorities, and the government unfortunately refused to allocate any new resources to implement it, in spite of repeated requests for aid. Greater resources are needed to meet these obligations but they have not been forthcoming. In rural Devon, for instance, South Hams District Council's lettings to homeless persons increased from 16.2 per cent of all lettings in 1976–77 to

29.7 per cent in 1979–80. This probably represents a combination of the requirements of the Housing (Homeless Persons) Act 1977 and the Rent (Agriculture) Act 1976, which added some agricultural workers to the authority's responsibilities.

In many districts it is impossible to distinguish exactly the contribution of winter-lets to homelessness, but they must add a considerable degree of uncertainty to housing demand in any given rural location, particularly in attractive holiday areas. Indeed, Larkin (1979) cites cases of families in Dorset who have followed the pattern of moving out of winter-lets into summer caravans for over ten years without local authorities taking responsibility for their permanent rehousing. Winter-lets are not intrinsically bad, but they are 'symptoms rather than causes of insecure housing, chiefly because many authorities ignore the needs of people who have to resort to them for want of a better choice. . . .' (Larkin 1979, p. 76).

Caravans

As noted earlier, estimates of the number of second homes in the United Kingdom indicate that about one-half of them are caravans or mobile homes. In many areas, these comprise both second home dwellers and those households least well established in the housing market. A popular view is to regard the latter mainly as young families outbid for rural property, perhaps by the second home buyers. In size and quality, caravans range considerably from lightweight mobile vans on holiday sites to those in sometimes quite plush mobile home establishments in which prices can often be from £10,000 to £20,000 (as much as many built-homes in the locality).

The range of quality from very good to squalid is of significance, because at one end of the range many authorities view mobile homes as being more or less equivalent to permanent dwellings, while some of the poorer, less well serviced, caravans cannot be regarded as permanent homes. In addition, although many residents own their mobile homes or caravans, sites are usually only rented, and local authorities and site owners remain as landlords and sometimes as notoriously poor ones.

Caravans can serve the function of temporary housing for homeless persons, but too often regulations on their seasonal use are ignored even by local authorities to avoid the creation of homeless families who would have to be rehoused (Larkin 1979). They can function as first homes for some young families, and Dunn *et al.* (1981) emphasize the role of caravans as transitional on the way to more permanent accommodation. Sadly, however, they can become the 'true ghettoes of the rural poor . . .' (Larkin 1979, p. 75) since they can be subject to little planning control and have easier access than other rural housing tenures. They can become long-stay expedients both for families and for housing authorities wishing to dump tenants, particularly problem families hard to house elsewhere.

Rural England has significantly higher proportions of 'non-permanent buildings' than does urban England: 1.3 per cent of the stock in rural districts compared with 0.5 per cent in urban districts. Their spatial distribution in some rural districts has been noted by Dunn *et al.* (1981) and by the Department of the Environment (1977c) in their review of mobile homes. Berkshire and Lancashire have rural concentrations, while Larkin (1979) notes that south Oxfordshire has more than 10 per cent of all its 'permanent' dwellings in the form of caravans. They are also to be found near to towns and some holiday resorts in South East England where many of the perhaps 70,000 residential caravans are located. All in all, in 1975 it was estimated that some 145,000 persons lived in a mobile home of some type. Although they may be regarded as suitable accommodation by some people, especially retired couples able to afford good-quality mobile homes, relatively poor facilities and frequently isolated locations make them less than ideal for the majority of inhabitants.

Tied accommodation

Although there are many forms of accommodation 'tied' to employment, the agricultural tied cottage is of prime interest (Shelter 1974; Schifferes 1980). Its quality, in terms of amenities and physical condition, has been found to be generally poorer than that of other rural rented accommodation, which itself is often poor (Fletcher 1969), and it can be very variable, depending as it does on the individual farmer's upkeep. Agricultural tied cottages formed the largest category of this type of housing in 1974, when there were an estimated 100,000 dwellings (Shelter 1974). The proportion of farm workers who live in tied accommodation also requires comment; estimates range from just over one-half to 70 per cent (Shelter 1974; Irving and Hilgendorf 1975); Gasson (1975) suggested the existence of 73,000 tied agricultural cottages in England and Wales. According to the parliamentary debates on the Rent (Agriculture) Act 1976 (discussed below), of the 223,000 men employed in agriculture, presumably full-time and part-time, 70,000 were housed in tied cottages in England and Wales, with a further 20,000 cottages occupied by retired farm workers.

Some interesting research has been conducted on the regional distribution of these cottages. Irving and Hilgendorf's (1975) data (table 5.6) broadly support Gasson, who found, using a rather finer regionaliz-ation, that the parts of England with the highest proportions of full-time agricultural workers in tied accommodation were the South West and the

Table 5.6   Numbers of farm workers living in tied cottages, 1974

MAFF* regions	Sample figures		Population estimates	
	%	Total	%	Total
South Eastern	68	123	66	25,205
South Western	55	121	57	25,958
Northern	54	28	54	6,073
West Midlands	53	85	50	17,248
Eastern	45	130	41	25,027
East Midlands	43	80	44	17,113
Wales	33	21	29	4,236
Yorks and Lancs	29	56	25	12,399
England & Wales	50	644	49	133,259
Scotland	67	159	69	23,666
Total	54	803	52	156,925

*MAFF = Ministry of Agriculture, Fisheries and Food
Source: after Irving and Hilgendorf (1975)

South East. In most surveys, Scotland is also shown as having a very high proportion of workers living in tied accommodation – over 80 per cent in a number of counties. Only in Wales, Yorkshire and Lancashire do tied cottages house fewer than one-third of agricultural workers.

The regional distribution is important, but at a local scale it is the location of tied cottages that is crucial. Key farm workers such as foremen and stockmen need to be close at hand to the farm and in these locations there are often very few other dwellings available. It is true that, without the farming job, the need to live on or near to the farm would be removed, but tied cottages can reinforce ties of dependency and can create considerable problems for employees wishing to change or to leave jobs (Newby 1979). Legislation in the 1970s attempted to improve matters, but the only way realistically to overcome the problem is to provide more local authority dwellings near farms since owner-occupancy is beyond the means of virtually all agricultural employees. As Shelter (1974) point out, one way of abolishing much tied accommodation would be to eradicate the need for it, which is based on housing shortage. As long as the housing shortage exists, tied housing will continue to be offered and accepted.

The Rent (Agriculture) Act 1976 made some attempts to introduce greater security of tenure for tied cottagers. It was explicitly 'an act to afford security of tenure for agricultural workers housed by their employers, and their successors; . . . to impose duties on housing authorities as respects agricultural workers and their successors. . . .' (Rent (Agriculture) Act 1976, introduction). There was, however, scope for considerable flexibility of interpretation of many aspects of this Act, as with the Housing (Homeless Persons) Act 1977, and minor points required clarification under the Rent (Agriculture) Amendment Act 1977. Nevertheless, the main provision of the Act did improve the legal protection of tied cottagers, since previously protection had varied for different categories of tenants. In most earlier cases, the occupant of tied accommodation had not enjoyed full protection against eviction under the Rent Acts since no money was paid, the accommodation usually being provided rent-free as part of remuneration. Tied cottagers received protection under the Rent Act 1957 only in so far as they were 'tenants' who were entitled to four weeks' notice to quit and could not be evicted without prior warning. The Protection from Eviction Act 1977 gave some additional protection since the courts could delay eviction.

However, the term 'security of tenure' is in fact a legal misnomer when applied to the majority of tied cottagers (Clements 1978). To receive protection under the 1976 Act, an agricultural employee has to achieve the legal status of 'qualifying worker', which requires that the person has worked at least 91 out of the preceding 104 weeks whole-time in agriculture. Previously, if dismissed a qualifying worker would normally have lost his home, but the Act now provides security of tenure that extends to a surviving spouse and, under certain circumstances, to some other family members. The tied cottager can then become a 'statutory tenant', obliged to pay a weekly rent and paying for services and rates. Farmers however are entitled to obtain vacant possession of a house occupied by a former employee in order to provide accommodation for a present or prospective agricultural employee. The local authority should then provide suitable accommodation for the present occupier 'in the interests of efficient agriculture'. To prevent collusion between employer and employee, the local authority is not obliged to do this when the tied cottager is still employed by the farmer (who could otherwise obtain a council house for the tenant by threatening to terminate his employment).

The Act gives protection, if sometimes uncertain protection, to most full-time workers living in agricultural tied cottages. But hardships can still be experienced by non-qualifying workers such as part-timers. In addition, in the case of dismissed workers, some local housing departments will try to assess the merits of the dismissal before rehousing, and the clause 'in the interests of efficient agriculture' is far from clear. Clements (1978) goes so far as to suggest that this Act may precipitate the demise of agricultural tied cottages. While the Act was being debated there was apparently a thinning of numbers, and subsequently some employers may have offered only limited-period or part-time employment to prevent employees from achieving the crucial 'qualifying worker' status. Rather than let their cottages become occupied by potential sitting tenants, some farmers may prefer to let them to anyone but their own employees. Legislation may therefore have done relatively little to help tied cottagers or to improve low cost agricultural housing.

ALTERNATIVE TENURES

In rural areas, as in urban areas, some alternatives have been developing to the three main tenure groups. Although as yet they have made relatively little contribution to the overall rural housing scene, their existence and growth seems assured.

Probably the most important 'alternative' tenure – that provided by *housing associations* – is really a supplement to the existing owner-occupied and public rented sectors. Their development was stimulated since 1964 with the establishment of the Housing Corporation which provides overall regulation of their affairs. To some, they represent the 'third arm' of housing policy, although in their first 20 years their activity was mainly in urban areas. They represent a potentially very important method of providing good rented or cheap owner-occupier housing in rural areas since they are an established medium for obtaining finance and for managing schemes. They have also been associated with a variety of approaches such as self-build schemes, renovations and housing trusts.

Housing associations attempt to provide housing at fair rents either for community needs or for special groups such as retired rural workers, the elderly or the handicapped, both through building and through acquisition of existing properties (Clark 1981). Most exist under the scrutiny of the Housing Corporation, which is a source of funding, although they are often able to obtain local authority finance, sometimes for joint ventures. As a result, they frequently delegate to local authorities the right to nominate perhaps 50 to 70 per cent of their tenants if the authorities have provided finance. In addition, they will be registered as charities or as 'societies' under the Industrial and Provident Societies Act. Housing associations received a major boost from the Housing Act 1974 when a new once-and-for-all capital grant became payable at the outset of each scheme (Baker 1976; Lansley 1979).

A few of these associations have been providing homes in rural locations, and although individually their impact has not been great, collectively it is growing. Clark cites the example of the Newcastle-based North Eastern Housing Association, which has built some 3,000 homes in rural areas within that region. Local councils set the rents and nominate the tenants in this case and the Association has been willing to build relatively small-scale developments (sometimes fewer than ten houses) suitable for village settings. The National Agricultural Centre Housing Association is an example of an organization that more specifically intends to provide rural housing. However, financial uncertainty, a low priority attached until recently to rural schemes by the Housing Corporation and problems associated with its national-scale administration, coupled with some rural planning restrictions, have meant that only a very small number of the schemes of this and other organizations have come to fruition.

Nevertheless, a few moderately successful rural schemes have appeared. Particularly hopeful was the sanction in 1978 by the Housing Corporation of up to 200 units per annum in the Special Investment Areas, where the Development Commission (the parent body of COSIRA) is involved in providing advance factories for job creation. As a result, a housing association presence has been achieved in a number of relatively small villages. However, as the majority of schemes proposed was to have been in small towns where there was already a relatively good provision of council houses, they have often not been implemented. Recent reports indicate that only 100 houses rather than the projected 200 per annum have been provided which suggests a rather slow take-off (Gilg 1981, p. 110).

To date, many housing associations' rural ventures have not met with marked success. Uncertainties of planning, finance and building, along with flagging enthusiasm, have often proved too much for local initiatives. Certainly there is evidence that their distribution is very patchy and not always related to known housing need (figure 5.5). Partly to overcome this, the Housing Corporation now favours local groups linking to existing national or regional associations rather than starting their own associations. However, larger-scale organizations tend to be less sensitive to local requirements and to have greater inertia and administrative encumbrances (Richmond 1983). National associations also tend to sponsor larger schemes in the more important settlements rather than in areas of isolated housing need. However, a hopeful sign is a recent indication from the Housing Corporation that it would be interested in funding well conceived schemes in country areas where numbers of people may be small but needs acute. In particular, they feel they may be able to develop new forms of equity-sharing in rural areas to provide, say, sheltered housing for the elderly owner-occupier (Clark 1981).

Other alternative schemes in rural areas include conjoint ventures

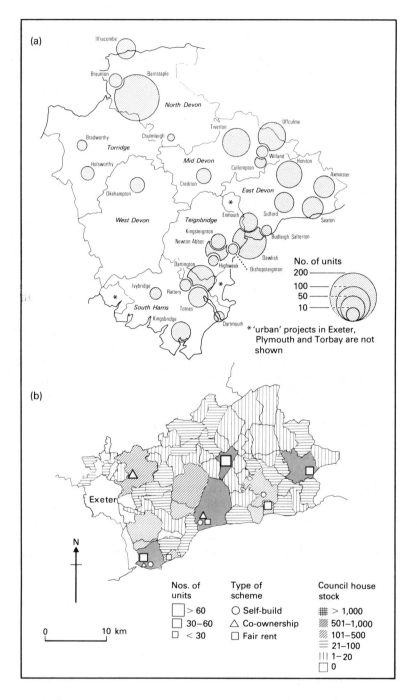

FIGURE 5.5 Housing association projects (a) in Devon, by size and location, and (b) in East Devon, showing the location of existing local authority dwellings
Source: Richmond (1983)

between local authorities and private developers, and self-build schemes. The *joint venture approach* involves a transfer of land direct to new owners from the council, with private developers building the houses and the land profiteering element eliminated. 'Starter schemes' or 'shell-housing', ready plastered-out but not finished, have often been built on this basis, for example in Ribble Valley District, some Devon districts and in Suffolk Coastal District. A number of the schemes have attempted to control speculative resale by using Section 19 of the Housing Act 1980 to restrict resale in rural areas. By and large, it appears that building societies and other financial 'gatekeepers' are willing to advance money on houses built to NHBC standards, although this may exclude 'shell' homes.

Under a *self-build scheme*, a group of seven or more persons can form a housing association to use their own labour to build homes for separate owner-occupation. Since the members provide their labour free, houses can be built cheaply and the members can register as a friendly society with the National Federation of Housing Associations (rather than the Housing Corporation). Such schemes depend on local enthusiasm, skills and initiative, although some work may be performed by contractors. Finance can be available from the Housing Corporation, building societies and local authorities, from whom land can also sometimes be acquired at a reasonable price if councils want to dispose of some building land unwanted because of reductions in their own building programmes – perhaps at prices below market value if restrictions on resale are accepted.

Examples of self-build schemes in rural areas exist in West and East Sussex, Bordon (Hampshire), East Cornwall, Chesterton (North Oxfordshire) and Somerfield (Gloucestershire). They can be particularly appropriate to smaller villages since they can be small-scale and use small plots of land, and as a result they are more likely to receive planning permission. However, self-build schemes are really possible only where a number of energetic persons, usually young, coincide. Strains are imposed on the self-builders' families and main jobs, and as a result these schemes are not suitable for all persons and rarely for the elderly. Therefore it is fitting to remember that such houses are no substitute for fair rent housing from local authorities or housing associations (Clark 1981).

Issues raised in this chapter touch upon many related questions discussed elsewhere. Housing can be a tool of social policy; in fact it can be argued that it *must* be, since it is a crucial element in people's lives and fair access to housing is essential to achieving social justice (Burke 1981). Housing and statutory planning should be closely related in terms of both general strategic planning and physical planning within settlements. Unfortunately, they have not always been mutually supportive. To some extent this has been exacerbated by trends in rural transport, and these form the subject matter of the following chapter.

6 Transport and Accessibility

ACCESSIBILITY AND MOBILITY

Transport availability and costs assume a greater importance in rural areas than in urban areas. Travel times and distances are usually greater and services and facilities less conveniently situated. Rural areas are often considered 'inaccessible' not only because of locational factors but also because of poor transport provision. However, this generalization hides the fact that many areas of the countryside are actually traversed by good main roads, even though some areas do lie well away from major transport networks. There are also important differences in levels of mobility *between* rural residents. This chapter intends to highlight three important themes: accessibility in the countryside, transport costs and availability, and the ways in which various sub-groups are affected by them.

Accessibility has long been recognized as a 'slippery notion'. In crude terms, an 'accessible' thing or place is one that is 'get-at-able' (Gould 1969; Moseley 1979a). However, there are great differences between physical, social and economic accessibility. 'A well-paid job, a pretty girl or a desirable residence may each be located only five minutes away and yet be effectively inaccessible because one's inadequate skills, social talents or incomes effectively place them out of bounds. . . .' (Moseley 1979a, p. 56). These *social* dimensions of accessibility may be very important to the quality of life, but rural residents usually face problems of accessibility because of spatial separation; theirs is a problem of *physical accessibility*, which requires that an individual must be able to command the transport facilities needed to reach the requisite supply points at appropriate times. The two concepts of social and physical accessibility are related, as social benefits often accrue from physical accessibility. This will be seen in chapter 8, particularly in relation to accessibility to cultural, educational, information and social services, the improvement of which can enhance the quality of life for rural residents.

Moseley cites two definitions of physical accessibility which have strong common themes; 'the ease with which people can reach distant but necessary services . . .' (Daly 1975, p. 75) and 'the ability of people to reach destinations at which they carry out a given activity . . .' (Mitchell and Town 1976, p. 3). These provide links with the concept of *mobility*, which itself has at least two important facets. The most basic of these relates to personal physical mobility, which can be impaired by physical handicap or old age. But mobility can also be achieved through having access to transport in order to get from place to place. *Personal mobility* has been defined as 'the capacity that a person possesses for getting around . . .' (Hillman *et al.* 1973, p. 2), and this clearly incorporates both facets of the term.

Mobility therefore relates to people's ability to move and to reach desired goals. It depends on matters such as physical attributes and abilities of individuals, their monetary resources, the availability of mechanized means of transport and the appropriate infrastructure; but it does not depend on the opportunities that may or may not present themselves as a result of moving: accessibility alone incorporates this feature (Moseley 1979a). Here, therefore, it is assumed for simplicity's sake that mobility is equated with transport availability (in terms of provision, costs and time). Accessibility to other services and facilities forms the subject of chapter 8.

Any attempt by geographers to define 'accessible' or 'inaccessible' places is an approximation. To say that a certain village enjoys a certain level of accessibility is to summarize much too crudely the position of the middle-class person in a two-car household and the elderly person without a car because, as Moseley (1979a) so correctly points out, these neighbours are effectively living in different worlds in terms of mobility. Therefore the spatial dimensions of accessibility and mobility have complex but very important social overtones.

Travel involves a number of costs to the individual, including financial expenditure, time and effort spent. Therefore, the availability, speed and pricing structure of various modes of transport must be taken into account when travel and mobility are analysed. The time that an individual has (literally, his time budget) is a valuable commodity, and travel by a faster mode of transport can allow more time and leisure to enjoy services once reached. It is the conjunction of travel time, costs and opening hours (availability) of services that combine to render rural residents more or less isolated or inaccessible, and this question of poor spatial and temporal synchronization of services and public transport (in particular) will be developed in chapter 8. To begin with, however, it is necessary to review the different modes of transport available in rural Britain.

PRIVATE TRANSPORT

For the majority of people living in rural areas, the private motor car has come to be the main, or vastly preferred, mode of transport. It enables individuals to overcome some of the accessibility/mobility problems outlined above; they can come and go largely as they please, use the services they wish and enjoy a wide range of social, business and leisure contacts, conditioned only by the time that is available for driving from place to place and the running costs of the vehicle. Because of the decline of public transport, it is often no longer possible for those who do not have access to personal transport (their own or shared) to commute daily to and from rural settlements; these people and places may effectively be isolated.

Therefore, the main factor identifying rural people who are disadvantaged in terms of access or transport is the lack of a car (Moseley 1979a). This is exacerbated by the fact that, where car ownership levels are highest, demand for, and therefore provision of, public transport, will usually be the lowest (Whitby and Willis 1978). This has serious implications for people in rural areas who cannot afford to run a car or are physically unable to do so. Whitby and Willis further suggest that the demand for private transport will continue to grow in spite of oil price increases, and that losses arising from over-pricing of oil are disproportionately borne by rural residents. Equally important are the increasing closures of small independent petrol stations, many of which are in rural areas, which can mean higher petrol prices and less petrol availability.

Car ownership rates are higher in rural areas than the national average. The General Household Survey indicates that, nationally, about 58 per cent of households had at least one car in 1980 (Central Statistical Office 1982) but that around 70 per cent of rural households have at least one car. In rural Lincolnshire, Clark and Unwin (1981) found that 77 per cent of respondents in a survey had regular access to private transport. It is therefore not very surprising that rural public transport provision is lower than in many urban areas, where demand will be higher because of lower rates of car ownership.

Two of the main determinants of car ownership rates are undoubtedly income and age of household, and these have important implications in different rural areas. Moseley cites a University of East Anglia Survey in rural Norfolk which indicated that, in 1975, only 8 per cent of households with an income of more than £2,000 per annum had no car, although even families with much lower incomes attempted to run cars in rural areas (Moseley *et al.* 1977; Moseley 1979a). This would suggest that many poorer households must make enormous sacrifices in other areas of spend-

Private transport is essential for bulk buying at rural supermarkets (source: authors and A. Teed)

ing in order to maintain a car, perhaps to the extent of going without adequate food and buying clothes at jumble sales (Brown and Winyard 1975; Winyard 1978). But if they wish to visit shops, get their children to schools and use other services they have little choice – even if the price of petrol means that journeys have to be kept to the minimum. With regard to age, in rural Lincolnshire 13 per cent of those aged over 60 were found to have no access to any kind of private transport compared with only 5 per cent in the population as a whole (Clark and Unwin 1981). This would seem to indicate that car availability can be directly related to age.

However, absolute levels of car *ownership* do not necessarily indicate true levels of mobility, since this is governed by car *availability*. In the past car ownership has been assumed to give equal 'mobility' to all members of a household. This is not strictly so, however, since if the husband takes the car for work, the remainder of the family (which could include one or more members attempting to reach work or services themselves) are effectively marooned until he returns (Moseley 1979a; Phillips 1981). While 73 per cent of economically active heads of households in the General Household Survey of 1980 had one or more cars, the fact remains that three in five adults even in car-owning households do not drive, and many more do not have a car available for use during the daytime (Hillman and Whalley 1977).

The spatial behaviour of those rural residents without the use of cars in car-owning households may more accurately be compared with that of behaviour in non-car-owning households. Their work, patterns of social contacts and service use will all tend to be governed by the distance they can walk or the availability of convenient public transport. Age, employment and social status all influence the possession of driving licences. Those under 17 years of age will not be eligible; also very few women over the age of 65 (possibly only 4 per cent) and only 7 per cent of women in skilled and unskilled manual occupations have their own cars. Hillman *et al.* (1973) also found, in a rural parish in Oxfordshire, that pensioners and women were far less likely to have driving licences.

The social implications of differing levels of car availability are very important. As governments increasingly demand cost-effective public transport, poorly used routes are likely to have their services curtailed. Infrequent services will be used even less, and, as levels of car ownership grow in rural areas, so demand will continue to fall until the services may eventually be withdrawn. This vicious circle tends to leave a 'rump' of inhabitants who are unable to run a car, many of whom could be defined as the 'transport poor' (this term will be discussed below). Numerous figures can be cited to support the view that specific types and ages of households tend to be thus affected, but perhaps the most telling is that 90 per cent of single-person households over the age of 60 years do not have a car (table 6.1). The majority of writers and researchers agree that this has serious personal, community, planning and service implications (Age Concern 1973; Pulling and Speakman 1974; Munton and Clout 1975; Wibberley 1978; Moseley 1979a; Hillman and Whalley 1980).

PUBLIC TRANSPORT

A major question is how far public transport can substitute for, or fill the vacuum left by, the absence of private transport. It will rarely be as convenient, and rarely as cheap (see table 6.2), as private transport. The relative costs of bus, coach and rail fares since 1975 have all increased more rapidly than the costs of running a private car or motorcycle. With a base of 100 in 1975, the relative costs in 1980 of bus and coach stage fares were 237 while the costs of motoring had reached only 193, roughly the same level as the Retail Prices Index. In relative terms, people forced to rely on public transport pay more than car users for their mobility. Can public transport, therefore, even if available, fill the gap, in view of the low incomes of many of the elderly and rural poor?

In addition, public transport is much more subject to direct government policy and to the influence of political decisions. Although private transport is also subject to government policy, it will be affected more slowly. For instance, road fund licence charges and petrol prices tend to creep up gradually, whereas decisions in the sphere of public transport can effect substantial changes almost immediately. Routes may be closed, reducing accessibility, or subsidies may be removed, increasing fares for users at a stroke. Public transport has been subject to numerous policy changes, especially since the 1960s (Banister 1983).

Table 6.1   Availability of a car or van, by socio-economic group of head of household and household type, 1980 (percentages)

Socio-economic group of head of household	No. of cars available to household			
	None	*1*	*2*	*3 or more*
Economically active heads				
Professional	9	55	29	7
Employers and managers	6	50	36	8
Intermediate non-manual	18	63	16	3
Junior non-manual	36	50	12	2
Skilled manual and own account non-professional	25	59	14	2
Semi-skilled manual and personal service	49	43	7	1
Unskilled manual	71	27	2	–
Total	27	53	17	3
Economically inactive heads	70	26	3	–
Household type				
2 adults aged 16–59	26	58	16	1
Large family	30	51	15	3
2 adults, 1 or both aged 60+	49	46	5	–
1 adult aged 60+	90	10	–	–

Source: Central Statistical Office (1982)

Table 6.2　Passenger transport costs 1961–80 (1975 = 100)

Cost to the consumer of:	1961	1966	1971	1975	1976	1979	1980
Railway fare	31	40	57	100	129	184	225
Bus and coach stage service fares	30	40	61	100	125	189	237
New and second-hand cars	56	48	61	100	117	185	209
Motor vehicle-motor bike running costs	35	41	53	100	111	157	193
Retail Price Index	38	45	59	100	117	166	196

Source: Central Statistical Office (1982)

Monetary inflation, falling demand and rising fuel and running costs have all made public transport much more expensive to provide in rural areas. The revenue required to support bus services in Gwynedd, for example, rose by almost three times between 1974/75 and 1978/79, yet the £700,000 subsidy in the last year was worth considerably less to operators at that time than earlier subsidies had been. Rural counties such as Gwynedd suffer particularly since they often have very low density settlements, rugged terrain and relatively poor roads. Sparsity of population in some rural counties of Britain can create considerable problems for bus operators. For example, routes will frequently be made economical only if adults are taken on the school transport services. However, school children pay only about two-thirds of the adult fare and for only 200 days of the year, and for the remainder of the time adult passengers may not be numerous enough to cover operating costs. Apart from these 'peak' hours, there is often a considerable surplus capacity, with buses and drivers perhaps being inefficiently used.

Public opinion sometimes erroneously accuses the partly empty, off-peak buses of being run inefficiently. However, since drivers' wages are already being paid for full shifts, Dobbs (1979) argues that the extra costs of providing more off-peak buses on low demand routes is not very great. Buses that would otherwise sit unproductively in garages could be turned out to provide services for doctors' surgeries, shopping and social trips. Nevertheless, it is apparently particularly difficult to convince councillors of the justification and effectiveness of these services, which could be life-lines to a minority of rural inhabitants. Therefore public transport policy for rural areas requires very careful evaluation, not only in terms of economic viability but also in terms of the social impact of reducing services.

Generalizations about public transport decline almost certainly obscure the complexity of the picture in any local area, and there is very little precise, comparative information on local or even regional variations in the rates of increase, decrease or changing fortunes of different modes or routes at different dates. Also generally unknown is the extent to which decline is due to the abandonment of routes or to the reduction of frequencies. Therefore warnings should be sounded about the uncritical interpretation of data indicating supposed 'decline'.

Bus services

The 'stage carriage bus service', or public omnibus, is the service usually referred to when rural transport is under discussion. Such services are flexible, in that they can be routed wherever roads are suitable, and with a frequency to suit demand. In addition, a range of bus sizes is available from the mini-bus to the large double-decker. Furthermore, the considerable infrastructural investment of railways is not needed, or, at least, such

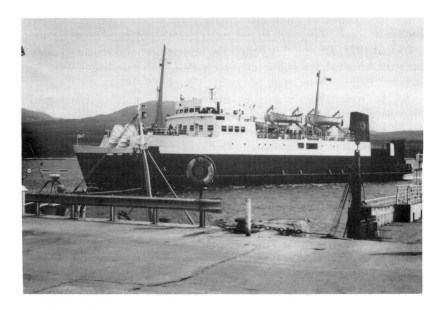

Public transport is in decline, but this ferry still provides an essential link to the Isle of Islay in the Scottish Highlands (source: D. G. Lockhart)

fixed costs are not all charged directly to bus companies. At the same time, where demand is low, services can be withdrawn easily, and this has been the most characteristic trend in recent years. Moseley (1979a) shows that in many counties, including Norfolk, Oxford, Leicestershire, Warwickshire and Northamptonshire, between 20 and 35 per cent of the parishes had fewer than six buses per week in 1976. The picture is very variable but, as might be expected, larger settlements tend to have better services. Much of rural Britain has a non-existent or very rudimentary bus service, and about one-quarter of all the rural parishes of lowland England have fewer than one bus daily. Clearly it is not possible to rely on this form of public transport for commuting to work or for visits to local towns for access to a range of services. Clark and Unwin (1981), in a study of 50 contiguous and rather remote parishes in rural Lincolnshire, found that 16 had no bus service at all and many others had a service that would not permit visits to towns of long enough duration to attend a variety of services.

National-scale data, which should be treated with caution, illustrate that the number of passenger-kilometres travelled by private vehicles increased from 60,000 million to 380,000 million per annum between 1951 and 1977, while the number of passenger-kilometres travelled by public service road vehicles declined from 80,000 million to 50,000 million. This trend has been even more marked for rural areas; figure 6.1 shows a decline of some 29 per cent in passenger journeys by rural buses between 1965 and 1975. During this period the vehicle fleet size remained almost constant, although it was less intensively used, with a decline of 9 per cent in vehicle miles (Association of County Councils 1979).

At the regional scale a much more varied picture of bus services emerges. In rural Wales, for example, taking 1938–39 as the year of the 'peak' network, considerable decline may be seen in route mileage in the first decade up to 1949, although this did not occur at a constant rate and varied considerably in the north and south of Wales, and according to the specific operating companies considered. The net loss of route mileage by one mainly rural operator (Gosville's, of mid- and North Wales) was 24 per cent between 1938 and 1979, but this was mitigated by re-adoption of some routes by other operators, leaving a net loss of 13 per cent to the public transport system. The interchange of routes between operators complicates analysis, but operators in South Wales also appear to have made a net loss of some 12 per cent of mileage since 1939. Nutley (1982), analysing these data, suggests that decline may have proceeded mainly by frequency reductions which have not gone as far as complete closures. A number of very different trends were to be seen in a sample of frequencies on bus routes, ranging from consistent decline over the period since 1939

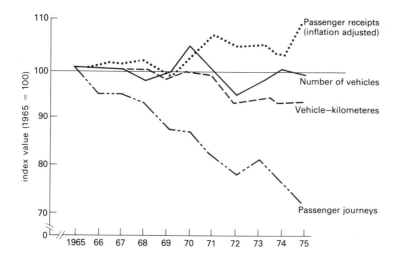

FIGURE 6.1 Trends in country bus services, 1965-75
Source: after Association of County Councils (1979)

to slight increase in recent years on a few routes. However, for the Gosville Company the general picture was of increase from 1939 to 1949, then a period of stability, followed by decline in service frequency of just over 15 per cent during the 1970s. The company's mid-Wales network, the most rural area it served, showed the greatest decline in the 1970s – 35 per cent – which supports the contention discussed later that these are the types of areas that now typically have the poorest effective public transport provision.

Some authors suggest that the decline in bus transport is not so extreme. However, even if bus networks have not declined as markedly as has, say, the rail network, frequency of services has usually declined and fares have increased. Route mileage alone is not a very useful index of service quality since a reduction in frequency in one area can constitute a more serious deterioration in service than a complete closure of a very lightly used route elsewhere (Moseley *et al.* 1977).

Bus use rates do seem to vary. In particular, fare increases appear to lead to high losses of passengers, particularly at off-peak periods. Although the levels of 'resistance' vary, such passenger losses on rural routes can be very damaging (Holding 1979). Relatively few rural residents appear to rely solely on public transport, perhaps because it is not regarded nowadays as a worthwhile alternative – Moseley *et al.* (1977)

found that only one-third of respondents in a large survey of transport availability in Norfolk had used a bus or train in the preceding month. The Department of the Environment (1971a, 1971b) also found low rural rates of regular use (about 6 per cent using public transport on most days). It is these few people who are probably very dependent on public transport, and, if it becomes too expensive or infrequent, they may find themselves unable to live in the rural community. The young and the old are obviously vulnerable in this respect (Hall 1975). Frequency is one important aspect of bus services, while costs, convenience, reliability and network pattern are others. Surveys have generally found that what consumers want are more frequent services with lower fares and more convenient routes (Hislop 1975; Moseley 1979a).

It appears that many bus services were considered to be relatively marginal in cost terms even during years of peak usage in the 1930s and early 1950s. The 1968 Transport Act (which established the National Bus Company) recognized this, and brought the county councils into the provision of bus services to enable subsidies to be made for socially necessary but loss-making services (Moseley 1979a). There is, of course, considerable debate as to the degree to which profitable routes should subsidize (in conjunction with the rates) the non-profitable routes.

One area of reasonably firm public support remains the school bus. The guaranteed customers (even if at cut-price) twice daily during term-time can assist the financial success of many rural bus routes, which can sometimes also be used by adults to travel to nearby centres. A slight staggering of schools' starting and finishing times sometimes leads to a more efficient use of buses (although the service may then be less convenient to other users). However, when children's fares are below the full adult fare this can cause difficulties for operators (Dobbs 1979), and the economic and social costs of getting children from more remote rural settlements to school remains an outstanding problem in many localities. The questions of access and transport to schools for rural children are discussed further in chapter 8.

The Transport Act 1980 has attempted to encourage private operators to enter passenger transport under the philosophy that more competition will lead to better services. This Act was important in that it eased restrictions in the field of public service transport, but critics felt that it would weaken the protection necessary for essentially unprofitable bus routes, mainly those in rural areas. Advocates of the Act claimed that it would update the restrictive licensing system which had its basis in the 1930 Road Traffic Act, which itself discouraged newcomers from entering the industry for reasons of safety and standards. In the event, in a number of rural areas small-scale operators have managed to provide services at cheaper costs than have been managed by larger national firms, mainly because of lower overheads. Some small subsidies are still paid on non-profit-making routes, and companies such as Red Rover Buses of Ayles-bury, Buckinghamshire, now operate a limited number of routes in local areas to meet local needs. The Aylesbury firm runs about a dozen routes in rural areas, and similar firms sometimes use a variety of sizes of buses and vehicles. There are still critics, however, who believe that only the more profitable routes will be retained in this system; that it places too great a reliance upon operators identifying socially important routes, and seeking and obtaining subsidies to maintain them; and that a piecemeal system will result. The Conservative Government believed, however, that what they thought to be excessive subsidization would be stemmed and resources would be better employed. These views are not mutually exclusive, though the dangers to low-use but socially important rural routes could still exist.

At the local level, there has been a considerable range of approaches to public transport provision. In 1976 the government argued that, although it would set the 'broad lines of transport policies', local communities would make their own decisions within the context of the national policy. The range of attitudes is illustrated by strategies that state, at one extreme, that 'all people should be provided with access to public transport services for three return trips a day to the nearest market town, providing for a journey to work in the morning, a mid-day shopping journey and a journey home in the evening . . .', and suggest, at the other extreme, that all 'deep' rural areas should have a public transport service to a local centre on at least two days a week or that all sizeable villages should be served by public transport on one day a week (Adams *et al.* 1977, p. 3). Clearly, the life chances of many rural residents would be considerably influenced by the policy adopted.

Train services

Railways are not really flexible enough to be able to serve isolated com-munities in rural areas. Many lines were laid only where a considerable volume of traffic (passenger and goods) was assured. However, some rural communities did become quite reliant on rail for outside contacts, in particular the rural mining settlements in Wales and the North of England, commuter villages in the South East and some more isolated estuarine settlements in the South West. In addition, many rural areas were traversed by the rail network, which gave them an additional lifeline and a link with main centres. As Thomas (1963) wrote, people were affected by trains to some extent even in the most remote parts of England during the latter half of the nineteenth and early years of the twentieth centuries. By the time of the First World War, an enormous number of quite small villages and hamlets had their own wayside station or halt, and at its peak Britain's railway system was (to Thomas) 'almost absurdly dense'.

The major reason given for the closure of railway lines and stations was that the 1950s modernization plan for the railways had had little effect on stemming an ever-rising deficit in running costs. The Transport Act 1962 broke up the British Transport Commission established under the Transport Act 1947. Instead of attempting to integrate and co-ordinate internal transport services as a whole, individual boards, such as the British Railways Board, the London Transport Board and the British Docks Board, were to have as much individual responsibility as possible, especially in commercial terms. This reorganization in 1962 was largely a result of the pressing need of the railways for financial readjustment. Dr Richard Beeching had been brought in in 1961 with the prime mandate of improving commercial viability. The result of major surveys during late 1961 and most of 1962 appeared as *'The Reshaping of British Railways'*, known as the Beeching Report (British Railways Board 1963).

This Report was, of course, the subject of much debate, particularly concerning the validity of some data used to support its contentions. Nevertheless, perhaps the most startling statistic contained in it was that some one-third of the rail route mileage carried only about 1 per cent of the freight and passenger traffic, while one-half of the route mileage accounted for only 4 to 5 per cent of total traffic. From a commercial viewpoint, this was clearly intolerable, although socially these may have been lines in very remote areas where rail was an important link. The most unprofitable services were singled out as 'stopping trains', which made enormous losses and cost almost twice as much to run as revenue received from them. The majority were in rural areas and the traffic densities were so low that there was no prospect of making them pay. Therefore, the Beeching proposals were quite drastic, although arguably there was no commercial alternative to closing numerous uneconomic lines. It was suggested that 400 passenger services be withdrawn or modified and 2,000 stations and 5,000 route miles closed to passenger traffic. It was recognized that this would inevitably deprive many parts of Britain, especially Wales and Scotland, of passenger services altogether (Aldcroft 1968).

The Beeching proposals have been criticized for the lack of serious consideration given to the possibility of retaining many unprofitable passenger services, and the case for closure was presented in a way that prejudged the final decision. Some of the Report's data were criticized, and it was argued that the specific social effects of closures were not fully appreciated even if some of the wider social and economic repercussions had been noted. In the end, many of the Report's recommendations were implemented quite speedily. By 1966 the route mileage had been reduced by 4,500 miles and over 2,000 stations closed, a reduction of 44 per cent on the 1962 figure.

On the positive side, steam traction became almost a thing of the past; by the end of 1966, 96 per cent of total coaching train miles were operated by diesel or electric trains. Also, standards of service on many main line routes were improved considerably, particularly the inter-urban routes. The irony was that the economic returns expected from the reforms were hardly gained at all, and the railways were really no nearer paying their way by the end of 1966 than they had been in 1962. The Labour Government outlined its 'New Deal' for transport in 1966; its 1967 development plans aimed to retain some 11,000 route miles of the 13,500 left in existence against Beeching's original plan for an eventual reduction to some 8,000 miles. Emphasis was to be placed on retaining commuter and rural services and routes deemed to be of value in spite of costs. These policy recommendations formed the basis of the 1967 Transport Bill.

The Beeching proposals for the railways (figure 6.2) can be compared with the 1982–83 rail network (figure 6.3) although, as with bus services, the network itself may not be as crucial as the frequency and cost of train journeys. What is evident is that, in spite of variations in the rate of reduction of rural services and the different attitudes of various governments to the public subsidy of railways, the pattern of rural services is now very much as Dr Beeching seems to have wanted. The cuts in services appear to have been most severe in Wales, the South West and parts of the Midlands. Services in Scotland, Lancashire and Yorkshire, while not unscathed, seem to have survived more successfully.

Numerous examples of rail closures in specific rural areas can be identified. Norfolk, for example, lost 70 per cent of its rail network during the 1960s, but some closures had come about even before the 1963 Beeching Report, having been underway ever since postwar nationalization of the railways (Moseley 1979a). Many lines in North Wales have been closed since the late 1940s, although the 1960s were also years of decline: figure 6.4 illustrates the railways closed to passengers in that region between 1948 and 1976 (Halsall 1979). The tragedy is that, although many small settlements never had a railway station, the inter-small-town rail network has been destroyed nationally and the service is now effectively inter-city, so that 'the rural branch line is a thing of the past . . .' (Moseley 1979a, p. 23). Some of the options for the future of British Rail outlined in the 1983 Serpell Report would, if adopted, leave the network effectively only inter-main-cities, and would make the decline of rural railways almost complete.

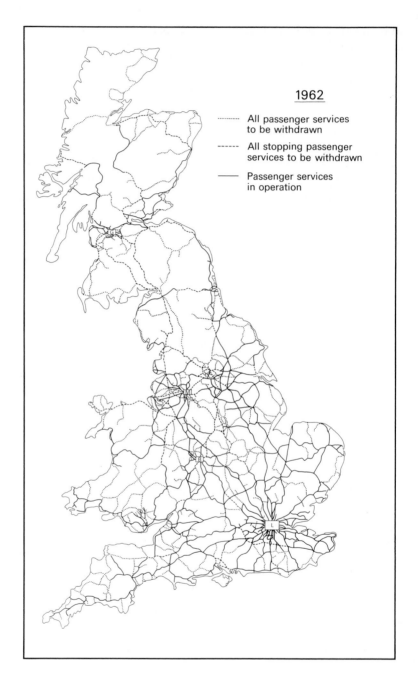

FIGURE 6.2   British Rail proposed routes for withdrawal post–1962
Source: after British Railways Board (1963)

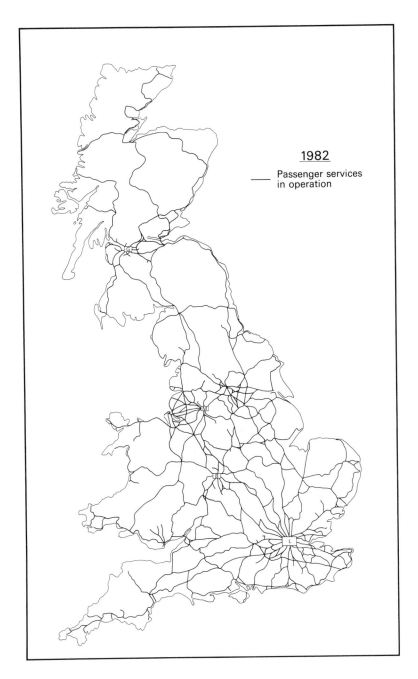

1982

—— Passenger services
in operation

FIGURE 6.3 British Rail passenger routes in operation, 1982–83
Source: based on British Railways Board Timetable, 1982–83

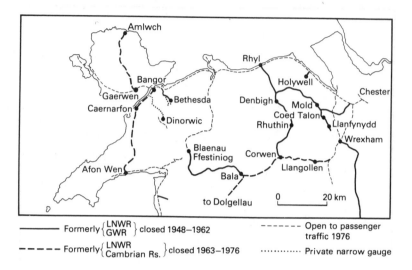

FIGURE 6.4   Local rail closures: North Wales passenger services withdrawn, 1948–76
Source: after Halsall (1979)

One solution to the problems caused by the withdrawal of rail transport in rural areas has been to replace these services with buses. Improved bus services with co-ordinated timetables were widely suggested in the 1976 Green Paper on Transport Policy and in the response of British Railways' Board to this, *Opportunity for Change*. It was felt that this would enable more rail services to be withdrawn in rural areas without 'undue hardship' (an ill-defined term) being caused to the communities currently served by rail. However, there is now a wider awareness of the need for greater attention to be paid to changing public attitudes and to the financially unquantifiable effects and social costs of closures to residents (Hillman and Whalley 1980). Some of these are discussed in the conclusions to this chapter.

TELECOMMUNICATIONS

Telecommunication links provide a type of 'mobility' that is becoming more and more important in terms of business and leisure contacts as telephone ownership and possession of home television computer links grow. To some extent, the deficiencies in private and public transport can be offset by the use of a phone. Trips that are solely for information or for social contact can be replaced by verbal contact via the telephone and the outcome can be satisfactory for the rural resident, although not as rewarding in terms of personal contact.

However, unequal access is again a feature. Moseley (1979a) found that only about one-half of Norfolk's rural households had a telephone and the figure was lower for more inaccessible places. In addition, the lower-income households are far less likely to have a telephone – and at the same time are less likely to have a car. These households, already disadvantaged in terms of personal mobility, can thus be further disadvantaged. They will suffer still more communication deprivation if 'uneconomical' public telephones are withdrawn from villages; yet, sadly, in the early 1980s many rural public telephone boxes are being removed by British Telecommunications, in spite of campaigns to retain them, because they are not felt to be economically viable.

The increasing range of new and improved telecommunications services can have potentially profound effects on future travel and home-based employment opportunities, because certain types of jobs do not need face-to-face contact and may be carried out from home by the linking of the telephone to home computers or the use of other teleconferencing, text-handling or information-retrieval systems. Much regular ordering by retailers or other rural service points can be done by telephone or other systems based on remote computer linkages and improved 'information technology'. However, evidence suggests that non-business travel is also important and can cover 67 per cent of all movement (Clark and Unwin 1981); if this were to be substantially reduced by remote linkages by telephone or other means, the consequences for continued viability of still more rural public transport routes could be serious, especially where comparatively minor variations in demand can be critical.

The telephone can reduce the need for personal contacts both at a local and a non-local scale. Some 24 per cent of daily contacts in rural Lincolnshire were by phone, a proportion that rose to 28 per cent for non-local contacts for information. It is such non-local visits that raise the most serious problems of accessibility and are of the greatest importance to rural transport policy-makers (Clark and Unwin 1981). The elderly, the semi-skilled and unskilled, emphasizing their relative isolation, make relatively fewer non-local visits compared with those who have access to private transport or who have phones. However, journeys for information and for social contacts form a substantial part of daily activity for all people, and the telephone could become a substitute for at least some journeys and reduce the need for direct personal contact.

On the other hand, it is possible that, instead of substituting for transport interactions, telecommunications will broaden people's activities and actually stimulate further activities and trips (Tyler 1979; Clark and Unwin 1981). As a result the telephone might, ironically, accentuate and compound the rural accessibility problem. Those who have regular access to private transport may find their social activities increasing, while the relatively immobile may experience an increase in their wishes to make social visits which cannot readily be satisfied. Therefore modern communications can increase some people's awareness of their isolation and spatial immobility (and, presumably, their frustrated opportunities).

ALTERNATIVES IN RURAL TRANSPORT

In addition to the means of transport already discussed (private car, rail and bus), some additional or innovative methods of 'getting about' have been introduced in rural areas of Britain. They will not suit all areas, and it should be stressed that, from a social viewpoint, an adequate travel network and frequent service is the most desirable solution, given that not everyone can be 'personally mobile'. Alternatives to this usually provide only a palliative for the rural transport problem.

Moseley (1979b) suggests a few alternatives: these should be borne in mind when access to services is discussed in chapter 8, because there are also innovations in service type and provision aimed at improving accessibility. Many of the alternatives depend on the use of buses in, for example, off-peak excursion services (say, twice monthly), which can be run quite cheaply to large towns in view of marginal pricing and maximizing use of vehicles. Mini-bus services have been experimented with in a number of areas, although the savings over larger buses are not always felt to be great and, frequently, mini-buses will be too small to cope with maximum demand over part of the route (Dobbs 1979). In the Snowdon National Park a local Sherpa bus service was started experimentally in 1976 as a means of getting visitors into and out of the Park and reducing the volume of private cars (Mulligan 1979). The use of postal transport to act concurrently as post-buses has been hailed as an important and efficient way of reaching small settlements. However, the Post Office requirement that the mail delivery and collection must take priority has inevitably meant that circuitous routes and awkward timings have developed, rendering the post-bus unattractive to many potential customers (Moseley 1979b). Dobbs (1979) cites a proposed service in Anglesey that would take 70 minutes by post-bus compared with 27 minutes by conventional bus. Clearly, even with cheaper fares this would be unattractive for all but the most impecunious rural resident.

School buses have sometimes been used by adults, although not frequently – again, sometimes owing to routes and timing. Car-sharing has received a recent boost since the petrol price increases; owners are able to share petrol costs without endangering their insurance policies as long as sharing is on a non-profit basis. However, it is unfortunately true that many unconventional forms of service can be relatively inconvenient for users and tend to have a romantic, if empirically unsound, appeal. They generally present ways of extending rather than replacing conventional public transport (Dobbs 1979).

Some more drastic solutions than those discussed above have been proposed, although, as Moseley (1979b) argues, they are based on a number of myths about rural mobility. The first is that rising car ownership will eventually solve the transport problem. This is true to an extent, but many individuals either cannot run a car or will not always be able to run one. The second myth concerns the attitude that, if rural residents do not like their locations, they can move. In fact, many people are effectively tied to rural areas because of their own or their spouse's occupation, and residential choice is not free as envisaged in the theoretical residential decision-making models. Third, the myth persists that private enterprise, unfettered by legal constraints, could fill the void in transport provision, but the risk is that only profitable routes will be maintained. This links with the final 'myth', that rural bus services are very little used. As discussed earlier, the emphasis must be on the residual rural population, even if in a minority, who are, and will always be, dependent on public transport. These myths, suggests Moseley, have underlain the widely found reluctance in rural Britain to promote the provision of a co-ordinated, efficient system of public transport. Perhaps changing levels of transport provision can be regarded as part and parcel of rural change as a whole, as discussed in chapter 1.

SOCIAL CONSEQUENCES: ISOLATED PLACES AND ISOLATED PERSONS

This chapter has provided evidence of the increasing isolation of some rural communities, particularly in terms of public transport provision. However, the extent of the loss or deprivation of public transport should not be exaggerated. For example, Nutley (1979), when using transport coverage as a basic and simple indicator of accessibility, found that only 15 out of 365 sample settlements in the Highlands and Islands of Scotland were totally deprived of public transport in 1977. In the national context this is a good record, and shows no significant decline from the 1960s. Rural Wales (excluding the urbanized south and north-east) provides a contrast with the Scottish Highlands, as here a large number of parishes were without any public transport at all. Although their population was only about 5 per cent of the total of rural Wales, some districts fared relatively worse than others, particularly in Powys (Brecknock, Montgomery and Radnor) and parts of West Wales (Preseli and south Pembrokeshire). In Radnor and Montgomery, about 13 per cent of the scattered population was totally without public transport in the late 1970s (Nutley 1980).

As mentioned earlier, and as will be referred to again in later chapters, it is important to recognize that the mere presence of a public transport service is not a good index of its usefulness. The option of using public transport for travel to work or to use services may be very limited. The presence or absence of public transport that can get people to work, that may be thought of as a service available between 8 and 9 am and 5 and 6 pm from Mondays to Fridays, is a much more realistic indicator of accessibility. Nutley (1980) formed an overwhelming impression of vast areas of rural Wales with no public transport suitable for journeys to work (figure 6.5). The whole of Radnor, most of Brecknock and much of Montgomery lacked this facility, and it was estimated that 14.5 per cent of the population of rural Wales was without effective public transport to work. This, of course, illustrates powerfully the lack of choice facing rural dwellers, imposing the need to work within walking distance (if there is any) and enforcing car ownership, lift-sharing or migration. It is hardly surprising that journey-to-work surveys in rural Wales have found that the very high proportions of between 48 and 84 per cent of trips are made by car (Nutley 1980).

Ultimately, however, there is still the problem of the individuals who rely on a poor frequency of public transport and this can be the most significant feature of isolation. Individuals may not have access to private transport to substitute for inadequate public provision; they may not be able to obtain a lift when necessary and they may not possess a telephone or the resources to obtain a car or phone. These people will often be very isolated and their social and spatial contacts will be very much determined by what is available in the local community.

The 'transport poor'?

Several groups now constitute what can evocatively be called the 'transport poor' (Wibberley 1978). These are pensioners, others on low incomes, the unemployed, children, housewives and disabled persons. Transport deprivation is a real form of poverty and often exists with other forms of poverty (see chapter 10). Evidence is not hard to find to support these assertions. In a large survey of almost 800 respondents in the Cotswolds, 38 per cent of elderly persons were found to have total dependence on public transport and a further 21 per cent had at least partial dependence. Similar proportions were seen among social classes 4 and 5

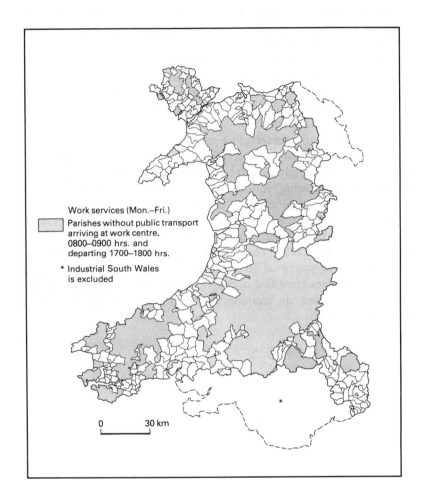

Work services (Mon.–Fri.)
Parishes without public transport
arriving at work centre,
0800–0900 hrs. and
departing 1700–1800 hrs.

* Industrial South Wales
is excluded

0   30 km

FIGURE 6.5   Accessibility of parishes in rural Wales to centres of work by
public transport
Source: Nutley (1980)

with 34 per cent totally dependent and 26 per cent at least partly dependent on public transport (Smith and Gant 1981).

It is misleading to assert that only *areas* are isolated, since the 'transport poor' are individuals who will be isolated in relative terms no matter how rural or urban their location may be (Coles 1978). Instead, it is sometimes useful to envisage a three-fold classification of constraints on transport availability for households. First, there are capability constraints, such as age, health, income, possession of a driving licence, and car ownership.

Second, there are 'coupling constraints', which reflect individuals' commitments to engage in specific activities at specific times (work, school, or appointments) which may be at odds with the timing of public transport services. Finally, there are 'authority constraints'; for example, free school transport may not be available to children living within a certain distance of school; or opening hours may be mis-matched with the timings of public transport, rendering the services effectively inaccessible to users dependent on public transport.

Mobility deprivation is therefore real and can afflict many persons and groups in more or less rural areas. Community isolation undoubtedly results, and a commonly perceived feeling in rural areas bereft of public transport is one of being 'cut-off' from the services and facilities outlined in chapter 8. Geographical and transport remoteness make areas less accessible to friends, relatives, some tourists and businessmen. This can induce a feeling of insularity and reduce opportunities for residents (Hillman and Whalley 1980). The loss of opportunities can be particularly damaging to the young or to the needy and can exacerbate the rural population changes identified in chapter 4. The effects on communities of mobility deprivation can therefore be either visible or intangible: rarely are they negligible.

7 Planning within the Countryside

THE GROWTH OF STATUTORY PLANNING

The concept of planning encompasses a wide range of activities that affect the living conditions of those in particular areas. We have already mentioned some of the agencies that 'plan' the countryside: these include the EEC, whose prices affect the types of crops grown (chapter 2), the Development Commission, which locates factories in rural areas (chapter 3), and local authority housing departments, which develop and manage village stocks of council houses (chapter 5). The full range of such agencies is considerable, as Gilg's (1978) survey of countryside planning illustrates.

In different ways, all the planning bodies affect land use and social activities in rural areas. Many of these activities have been discussed elsewhere in this book, so the scope of this chapter is limited mainly to analysing the role of local authorities, which exercise specific statutory planning powers *within* the countryside.

As there are several excellent histories of the development of town and country planning legislation (Ashworth 1954; Cherry 1974a, 1974b; Sheail 1981), we shall give only a brief review here. Individual property owners in cities have long had to conform to legal controls, but planning as a more widespread activity dates only from the mid-twentieth century (Hall 1982). An outstanding feature of the interwar period was the sprawl of suburbia into the surrounding countryside, especially in the South East. Except for measures such as the Ribbon Development Act 1935 and the Green Belt Act 1938, introduced too late to be effective, little was done to control this urban sprawl. During the Second World War, three influential reports were published which were to shape the evolution of statutory planning: the Barlow Report, in 1940, which advocated controlled industrial decentralization from the conurbations; the Scott Report, in 1942, which argued for a system of planning controls to protect the agricultural use of the countryside; and the Uthwatt Report, also in 1942, which recommended nationalization of undeveloped land to secure for the community the value added to land by the planning system. These were complemented by the Dower and Hobhouse Reports of 1945 and 1947, recommending the creation of national parks.

The two most important outcomes of these official inquiries and reports were the Distribution of Industry Act 1945, which introduced controls over new and expanded factories, and the Town and Country Planning Act 1947, which introduced a system of development plans and development controls for land use in England and Wales. Local authorities were to prepare detailed land use plans for their areas against which individual planning applications for new or extended dwellings or for changes in land use were to be evaluated. In time, the system came to be criticized for being too narrowly focused on land use (to the exclusion of social planning), as well as for being slow and inflexible.

Following the Planning Advisory Group's Report in 1965, a new two-tier system of planning was adopted under the Town and Country Planning Act 1968. In England and Wales, counties were to prepare structure plans to establish general social and economic development plans with 'key diagrams' and 'written statements'. The structure plans then provided a framework for local plans, which were to be more detailed strategies prepared at district level. The local plans could take one of three forms: district plans as overall plans; action area plans for smaller areas undergoing more intensive change; and subject plans for particular issues such as conservation. The format for statutory planning has also changed, so that there is now greater public participation in the identification and evaluation of key issues, more formal examination in public and the presentation of several alternative planning options rather than a single final plan. In practice, there has been considerable disappointment with the new system of planning, partly because of the lack of guidelines provided by central government and partly because of the slowness and cumbersomeness of the new procedures (Barrass 1979; Shaw and Williams 1982a).

Although there have been considerable changes in the machinery of statutory planning and in the scope of the development/structure plans, the powers available to planners have altered little. These powers are enshrined as development control procedures which enable local authorities to reject, approve, or approve with conditions, applications for planning permission for new buildings, extensions to existing buildings and changes in land use. There have been some adjustments to the extent of these powers; in particular, the Local Government Planning and Land Act 1980 relaxed the controls and shifted more responsibility from the counties to the district (Catchpole 1982). These development controls do give the planners an influential role in local development, even though the powers are mainly negative, comprising the ability to refuse rather than to initiate development. Occasionally they can be used in a more positive manner, and both the addition of 'conditions' to planning permissions and informal discussions between planners and developers allow the former to exercise a more decisive influence on new developments (Blacksell and Gilg 1981). There is still, however, a gap between social and physical planning; structure plans may set broad social and economic objectives, but the powers available to the planners relate largely to land use control over specific development proposals.

Statutory planning has influenced the evolving social geography of postwar Britain in two main ways. The first concerns the general control exercised over development and especially the resolution of land use conflicts in the countryside. This includes control over new housing and industry, or arbitration between urban expansion and rural conservation. The second major influence of statutory planning in rural areas has involved settlement policy, and is clearly related to general land use control. In rural areas of both growth and decline, selected or key settlement policies have been adopted as the planning 'solution' to a number of social and economic problems (Cloke 1979). The importance of such policies is the way in which they redistribute resources and accessibility within the countryside.

CONTROL OF DEVELOPMENT IN RURAL AREAS

The first real planning act, the Housing Town Planning [etc.] Act 1909, was followed by two other important measures during the interwar years; the Housing Town Planning [etc.] Act 1919, which encouraged adjacent districts to co-ordinate their plans, and the Town and Country Planning Act 1932, which sought to encourage local action to regulate activities in both the town and county (Sheail 1981). These powers were permissive, and in most of Britain urban sprawl and ribbon development continued more or less unabated. It was in response to this that the Scott Committee on Land Utilization in Rural Areas urged that agricultural use should have priority in any conflicts over rural land use. This influenced the spirit and the formulation of the Town and Country Planning Act 1947, so that the main tasks of country planning were viewed as being the exclusion of urban sprawl from rural areas. The countryside was also viewed as having a 'natural' beauty which was self-perpetuating and under threat only from urban growth (Robinson 1976). These aims were to be advanced through the twin application of development plans and development control powers.

The essence of these planning powers lay in *development control*, because no persons, industries or non-statutory organizations could undertake development without planning permission. However, there was a number of exceptions that were particularly significant in rural areas. The most important concern agriculture, government departments, including the large areas owned by the Ministry of Defence, and Crown lands. In particular, vast tracts of agricultural land and agricultural buildings are excluded from the obligation to obtain planning permission (Gilg 1978). Apart from these exemptions, planning controls operate in rural areas in the same way as in urban areas. Therefore, although farmers and foresters can change land use and erect new non-residential buildings, private individuals have to apply for planning permission for industrial or residential developments. In practice, development plans have zoned most of the open countryside for agriculture, so that spatial restraints have been applied to development.

In addition, some areas are considered to have special value, either for amenity, for beauty or for scientific interest, and are protected by further restrictions on development. This also applies to rural areas that are under immediate pressure from urban expansion. There are now a number of types of specially protected areas including national parks, Areas of Outstanding Natural Beauty (AONBs), nature reserves, Heritage Coasts, green belts, Areas of Great Landscape Value, country parks, forest parks, and Sites of Special Scientific Interest. It has been estimated that more than one-third of the land area of the United Kingdom is covered by these additional restraints. Figure 7.1 shows the distribution of such zones in England and Wales. It can be seen that both more remote areas and parts of the more accessible countryside are included. In these areas development is not normally permitted and will be approved only if there are exceptional circumstances, although in practice these guidelines are not always adhered to (Davidson and Wibberley 1977).

Green belts and national parks

The most intense physical pressures on rural areas have, of course, been in the urban fringes. The expansion of towns and cities has increased the demand for development land for housing, industry, retailing and other activities. Land in the urban fringe is also at a premium for recreation, whether for rambling or for sports and recreation grounds. In some areas urban pressure on the periphery creates additional problems because expansion may be into areas of considerable landscape value. This is true, for example, of some of the towns located near the Downs in Sussex or the Pennines in northern England. Urban growth in the interwar period was characterized above all else by the suburban expansion of towns and cities, frequently at unprecedentedly low densities. These changes placed enor-

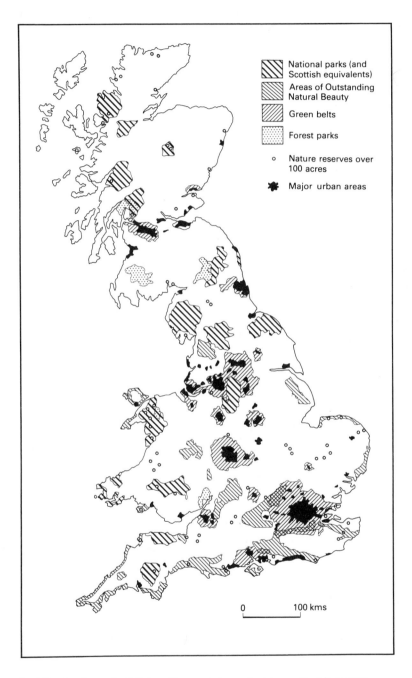

National parks (and
Scottish equivalents)

Areas of Outstanding
Natural Beauty

Green belts

Forest parks

○ Nature reserves over
100 acres

✳ Major urban areas

0   100 kms

FIGURE 7.1   Areas in Britain with special constraints on development

mous pressure on agriculture in some areas, especially because of land speculation (Low 1973; Rettig 1976). As a result of the growing competition and conflict between different land uses, and because of the spirit of 'anti-urbanism' in debates over the countryside, special attention has been directed to planning in these urban fringe areas.

Green belts have been the major instrument of planning in fringe areas, having long been advocated by leading planning theorists such as Unwin and Howard. The latter viewed the 'green belts' around towns as an integral part of urban life, to be conserved for recreation and for meeting local demands for food. The first such green belt was introduced in 1938, when an Act of Parliament allowed a zone to be established around London. However, the influential Greater London Plan of 1944, proposed by Abercrombie, advocated an enlarged green belt for London, mainly as a 'sanitary zone' around the city, to prevent further urban encroachment. This was the spirit that influenced the Ministry of Housing and Local Government in 1955 to urge a more widespread adoption of green belts. Three reasons were given for this policy: to check further growth of large built-up areas; to prevent neighbouring towns from physically coalescing, and to preserve the special character of some historic towns (Elson 1981). More recently, it has been shown that the aim of preservation has been somewhat relaxed, and some attention has been given to non-agricultural uses of green belts, particularly for recreation (Hebbert and Gault 1978).

In terms of the aims set out in 1955, it can be said that green belt policies have been fairly successful. They have physically contained the growth of some cities, prevented coalescence of others, and have helped to retain the character of some historic centres, such as Cambridge and York (Davidson and Wibberley 1977). However, it has also to be pointed out that many intrusive land uses have occurred in green belts. Furthermore, as many of these zones already contained substantial built-up areas prior to designation, green belts frequently contain a mixture of land uses and rarely form zones of attractive or continuous open landscape (Thomas 1970, 1974). It has also been argued that green belts have been used as instruments of preservation rather than conservation, and that insufficient attention has been devoted to positive planning, and to provision for recreational use. In response to such criticisms, many feel that a more flexible approach to green belts is required. Policies should aim to create and improve accessible landscapes, and not just to preserve all land around cities, irrespective of quality. At the same time, the Secretary of State has revealed his attitude to developments in his response to structure plan policies; in many cases, while approving the general outline of the structure plans, he has also given more emphasis to permitting further development in rural areas and has substantially reduced the proposed limits for some green belts (Elson 1981). Therefore, both the extent and the functions of green belts may be expected to change in the near future, and this change may also have social implications.

The other major type of area with special development constraints is *national parks*. Following the Dower and Hobhouse Reports, the National Parks and Access to the Countryside Act 1949 was passed and the National Parks Commission set up to designate suitable extensive areas of land of national scenic importance as 'national parks'. Twelve areas were identified and ten were designated as national parks in England and Wales between 1950 and 1955 (Bell 1975). The majority are in the upland regions of the North and West (figure 7.1). They comprise some 13,600 km², approximately 9 per cent of the land surface of England and Wales (there are no national parks, as such, in Scotland). Unlike national parks in some other countries, these are not supposed to be wilderness or isolated areas. Instead, they are inhabited and the economic and social activities of the rural communities are expected to continue more or less normally. Indeed, it is the 'cultural environment' of farms, farm landscapes and villages that is often the most attractive feature of these areas (Whitby and Willis 1978).

The 1949 Act established four goals for the national parks: (1) the characteristic landscape beauty was to be strictly preserved; (2) there was to be access and facilities for public open-air enjoyment; (3) wildlife and buildings and places of architectural and historic interest were to be suitably protected; and (4) established farming use was to be effectively maintained. While it was generally agreed that these broad aims were appropriate, there were considerable difficulties in their detailed implementation, often arising from conflicts over land use. The Countryside Commission, which replaced the National Parks Commission in 1968, established the National Parks Policies Review Committee to examine the policies in operation, and their 1977 Sandford Report stated the aims of national park policies as being the preservation and enhancement of natural beauty, and the provision of access and facilities for enjoyment by the public. Where the two aims were in conflict, the former was to take precedence.

Implementation of these broad guidelines is left to the national parks boards or committees. These are dominated by the local authority within whose boundaries the park lies; for example, Devon administers the Dartmoor National Park. Where the park straddles a county boundary, two joint-planning boards were established, and these have operated successfully in both the Peak and Lake District regions. Since 1974 each park authority has been required to prepare a five-year management plan for its area (see, for example, Dartmoor National Park Authority 1977 and Peak Park Joint Planning Board 1978). These plans have tended to emphasize multiple land use management so that recreation, conservation and the needs of the local community can be met (Hookway 1978). However, the powers of the authorities are not very extensive, for although they have the right to buy land within the parks they largely lack the means to do so, and ownership, therefore, is predominantly in private hands. As a result, policy aims have to be secured by and large through the normal development control procedures (Whitby and Willis 1978). The structure plans have also had an input into national park planning. In most cases they provide general guidelines; the Peak District and Lake District National Parks are unusual in having structure plans covering solely or mainly their areas.

In retrospect, it is clear that three main problems have faced the national parks, to which suitable solutions are still being sought. First, there has been an enormous increase in the pressure on the parks. This has stemmed partly from the growth in the demand for recreation and the fact that they are accessible to the metropolitan areas, especially given the improvements in road transport and the increase in car ownership (chapters 6 and 9). However, there have also been economic pressures to allow developments within the national parks, including mineral workings in the Yorkshire region and oil refining in Pembrokeshire. Furthermore, many of these developments have actually been proposed by government departments or statutory bodies; examples include the Fylingdales Moor Defence Station on the North Yorkshire Moors and nuclear power stations in Snowdonia. In practice, therefore, a number of substantial developments have been allowed in the parks, often against the wishes of their management boards or committees.

Secondly, a continuing and, in some ways, irresolvable problem is how to balance the twin aims of conservation and recreation since, despite the Sandford recommendations, it has not always been clear where the emphasis should be (Cripps 1980). It is interesting that a number of individuals on the Sandford Review Committee felt that there was a need to establish a new type of national park zone; these were to be 'inner' National Heritage Areas, where the claims of conservation were to have clear priority. This recommendation was not accepted, however, and the authorities still have to balance the need to provide access to the parks with the need to preserve them from the increased pressure that results. Another strategy involves the creation of country parks which have the main function of recreation. These should have the capacity for absorbing large numbers of people from nearby towns. The emphasis is on accessibility and the provision of facilities. It is intended that the country parks should reduce pressure on the more remote areas and reduce damage to the countryside caused by recreation. By 1981, there were 167 country parks in England and Wales, of which 28 were managed by private owners such as the National Trust (Countryside Commission 1982).

Third, as the powers of the national park authorities are limited to the normal development control procedures, agriculture is excluded, although it contributes so much to the valued cultural landscapes of the parks. One approach to this problem has been to establish management agreements in which landowners voluntarily agree to manage their lands in specified ways receiving in return some financial compensation (Blacksell and Gilg 1981). More recently, Exmoor National Park has decided on a more active policy of land purchase as the only sure way of conserving existing agricultural landscapes.

It is rather peculiar that no national parks exist in Scotland. Although the Ramsay Committee had suggested them in 1945, they were never established. Therefore there was a lack of clear guidance on land use in Scotland until the Countryside Commission for Scotland was established under the Countryside (Scotland) Act 1967. The most significant achievement of this body was to identify 40 national scenic areas in Scotland having outstanding landscape value. These covered more than 12 per cent of the land area. Extra development control powers applied to these areas, and all substantial developments now have to be referred to the Countryside Commission for Scotland. However, there have not yet been any plans for positive management of these areas (Blacksell and Gilg 1981).

Other protective designations

Although national parks and green belts are probably the most important elements in the 'special protection' of the countryside, there are a number of other instruments. Foremost among these are the *Areas of Outstanding Natural Beauty* (AONBs) which, along with the parks, had been proposed by both the Dower and the Hobhouse Reports. These were to be more densely populated and smaller areas than the national parks, but areas still requiring special protection. By the late 1970s the Countryside Commission had designated 33 AONBs in England and Wales, occupying more than 9 per cent of the total land surface. As can be seen from figure 7.1, these cover a number of coastal zones as well as upland areas that lie outside the parks, such as the Quantocks, Cotswolds, Chilterns and Sussex Downs. ANOBs have been designated since 1956, the most recent in 1983. This is in contrast to the national parks, since none have been added to the original ten. They are the direct administrative responsibility of the local authorities, and are covered only by normal development control. There are exchequer grants available to finance improvement schemes, but these are limited in extent, and little effective work seems to have been accomplished.

The British coastline, which has been under greater developmental pressure than almost any other part of the country, has been the subject of particular interest for conservationists. Large stretches of coastline are inside AONBs and national parks, but since 1973 other stretches of high-quality undeveloped coastline have been designated as *Heritage Coasts*. These are usually agreed jointly by the Countryside Commission and local authorities, and it is intended that strict development control should be applied within them. By the late 1970s over 30 stretches, extending over 1,100 km, had been designated, including large parts of the coastline of north Northumberland, north Anglesey and Cornwall (Countryside Commission 1982). By contrast, and usually in inland locations, the Foresty Commission has since the 1930s designated *forest parks*, which are open for recreation. However, these are limited in number and apply to only a small proportion of all Forestry Commission lands (Hall 1974).

Another agency with responsibilities for 'protecting' the countryside is the Nature Conservancy Council (NCC), established in 1949 and covering Scotland as well as England and Wales. One of its roles is the designation of *national nature reserves*, areas of land that are managed in order to preserve their flora and fauna. The NCC has the power either to acquire land or to enter into agreements with its owners which may involve some financial assistance from the Council. Over 150 reserves have been established. Although most are quite small, they cover over 120,000 ha. In addition to these national nature reserves, local planning authorities, in consultation with the Council, may also establish *local nature reserves*.

Finally the NCC is also entitled to designate *Sites of Special Scientific Interest*, where they deem that this is necessary in view of the flora, fauna, geology or physiography of the area. By the late-1970s, over 4,000 such sites had been designated. There is only limited additional protection for these areas, but all development proposals have to go to the NCC for comment. If an important site is threatened the only real recourse open to the Council is to step in and purchase the land, as in the widely publicized case of the Ribble Estuary Marshes where drainage plans had been proposed. However, the funds for this came from a special central government grant and the NCC normally lacks the finance for such intervention.

It can be seen that there is a wide range of statutory and semi-public bodies exercising a variety of controls over development in particular areas of the countryside. However, their powers are essentially limited to development control procedures, which are often usurped when 'national interests' are at stake; furthermore, most agricultural activities are excluded (Shoard 1980; Green 1981). The fundamental weakness of these bodies is that they do not usually own the land they are trying to control, so that the most effective preservation of landscapes may well stem from private landowning bodies that have an interest in conservation. The outstanding example of such a body is the National Trust, which owns more than 200,000 ha of land in England and Wales (there is also a National Trust for Scotland). However, even they may have to submit to 'national interests' on occasion, as was evident in the case of Bradenham. Many Trust members object to the lease of inalienable Trust land in this area to the Ministry of Defence, but the National Executive Committee argued that the lease had to be granted as the case would probably have been lost on appeal.

Evaluation of control powers

Ultimately, control over development depends on the statutory powers of the local authority. The important question is whether town and country planning has successfully constrained development in rural areas. A broad answer to this is provided by Best's research using agricultural returns (Best and Champion 1970; Best 1976, 1977). Best argues that in the early 1920s there was a conversion of land from rural to urban uses at a rate of 9,100 ha per annum, but that this increased to a level of around 21,000 ha during the 1930s. Since 1945 conversion rates have fallen to a lower level, of about 15,000–17,000 ha, and this is considered to be the direct result of stricter planning controls. This conclusion is supported by an investigation into the effectiveness of urban containment policies in England and Wales (Hall *et al.* 1973). However, both the research projects mentioned were dependent on aggregate published statistics, and although they provide useful overviews, they measure the impact of planning only indirectly.

The above-mentioned studies are complemented by others that actually consider the planning process itself. The first and landmark study was undertaken by Gregory (1970) in Seisdon District, located within the West Midlands Green Belt. Gregory analysed all the planning applications in the area between 1957 and 1966, and showed that development permission had been refused for 83 per cent of the 3,000 ha for which applications had been made. Here, at least, the policies of special restraint seem to have been effective. Blacksell and Gilg (1981), however, in a more comprehensive evaluation of development control in Devon, are rather less sanguine in their conclusions. They observe that application rates were greatest in an area such as east Devon, which is also mostly protected. In such a zone the refusal rate was a high as 40 per cent compared with only 20 per cent in mid-Devon, which has little protection. Nevertheless, in absolute terms, large numbers of applications are being approved even in protected rural

Table 7.1   Decisions on development applications in Devon, 1964–73

	Approved: no conditions		Approved: with conditions		Refused	
	No.	%	No.	%	No.	%
East Devon	138	12.9	502	46.8	433	40.3
South-east Dartmoor	42	5.8	286	39.5	396	54.7
Mid-Devon	22	6.7	240	73.2	66	20.1
Western Exmoor	5	3.3	82	54.7	63	42.0
Total	207	9.1	1110	48.8	958	42.1

Source: Blacksell and Gilg (1981)

areas. The difference between the Devon national parks is also interesting. In eastern Dartmoor, which is under strong developmental pressure, the refusal rate was 55 per cent, while in western Exmoor, an area of population decline, the refusal rate was only 42 per cent (table 7.1).

These figures on their own do not really provide a full assessment of the effectiveness of planning. The simple existence of development control powers, and the likelihood of having applications refused in an area such as Dartmoor, has probably reduced the number of applications for planning permission. Therefore, the designation of specially protected areas is perhaps quite effective as a deterrent.

However, it should be noted that Blacksell and Gilg (1981, p. 143) consider that 'in many respects, whether or not an application is granted or refused is less important than the safeguards that are attached to any permission.' In the Devon case studies, it appears that only 9 per cent of all the applications were granted without conditions, and in the two national park study areas the figures were 6 and 3 per cent. As an example of the conditions applied to one new scheme within the Dartmoor area, there were strict guidelines on using approved natural slate for the roofing, for the position of the gable on an outbuilding and even for the lining materials to be used for proposed trout-breeding pools. It is interesting to ponder how the values of planners are formulated with respect to determining aesthetic criteria for decision-making. This can have considerable impact on the built environment but, with some minor exceptions, it is still an under-researched area (Harrison 1972).

SELECTED SETTLEMENT POLICIES

Development plans and development control have been concerned predominantly with restricting development in particular parts of the countryside. Settlement policies have a complementary role, in that they affect the distribution of employment, services and housing within rural areas. At the simplest level, it can be argued that the concentration of growth in a small number of settlements will ease pressure on, and help to preserve, the remainder of the countryside. However, settlement policy is broader in scope than this, for it can also incorporate elements of positive social and economic planning. Selected or key settlements may be service centres; they may also be associated with public investment in facilities such as schools and council housing, and designated for residential expansion or for industrial growth (Woodruffe 1976). They may also be used in pressurized rural areas as a strategy for concentrating growth in order to relieve congestion in other villages, while in more remote regions they may be used to 'intercept' or reduce out-migration. Cloke (1977b, p. 19) provides probably the most useful definition: 'the key settlement itself is planned for comprehensive growth in terms of housing, services and often employment . . .', while 'the key settlement policy incorporated an overview of the settlement pattern as a whole and lays special emphasis on the relationship between the key settlement and other settlements served by it. . . '. This may be rather a purist definition, but it does direct attention to the role of key settlements within the wider settlement system.

A number of arguments is usually advanced in favour of a selected or key settlement policy for rural areas rather than a strategy of dispersed growth. One argument is environmental, stressing the protection of valued landscapes through a policy of spatially limited growth. Another stresses the fact that minimum population thresholds are necessary to maintain particular services and that, therefore, the most effective way of reducing or halting rural service decline is to concentrate growth and development in a limited number of locations (Green 1971). However, as discussed in Chapter 8, it can be difficult to establish the precise levels of these thresholds in practice.

Cost, or more precisely the economies of scale in service and housing provision, is another major argument proposed in favour of a selected settlement policy. Thorburn (1971) considered that important economies of scale could be achieved in the provision of public utilities, transport, education and retailing. Research in Norfolk revealed that the costs of providing electricity, water supply, telecommunications and education were up to 50 per cent higher in dispersed than in concentrated developments (Shaw 1976; Moseley 1978). Some have questioned whether small villages can be afforded, and most economic evidence in the 1970s suggested a negative answer. Furthermore, the real difficulty is not only that costs seem to be higher in areas of sparse population, but they are also likely to increase as depopulation occurs.

Another argument used to advocate key settlement policies is that they favour employment growth. Concentration of employment in a few locations will reduce infrastructural costs and may increase the external economies of scale available to firms and provide support for growth centre strategies for economic development, although it is by no means clear at what scale these advantages become significant (Moseley 1974). There is also uncertainty about whether the economic benefits of industrial growth centres will spread to the surrounding areas or will be restricted to the centre. In practice, it seems that 'spread' effects are limited to the journey-to-work catchment areas (Moseley 1973), and the 'key' in rural areas therefore is the availability of private and public transport. For a number of reasons, therefore, planners may recommend that growth should be channelled into selected settlements. Such designations may be comprehensive in that the key villages are usually designated as the loci for growth in employment, services and housing.

The actual definition of key settlements, the hierarchies of settlement types and the nomenclature adopted for these vary enormously among counties. Two examples will illustrate the policies that have been adopted by different authorities. Probably the best-known, and perhaps the most notorious, selected settlement policy is that adopted in County Durham, where there were special difficulties in planning for the dispersed villages that had grown up in the coalfield (Barr 1969; Blowers 1972). All the villages in Durham were classified into one of four categories, as follows:

A Substantial investment is envisaged as population is expected to increase.
B Population is expected to remain constant and investment should be sufficient to cater for the present population.
C Population is expected to fall, and investment should be reduced in recognition of this.
D Considerable loss of population is expected and there should be no further investment.

In effect, the policy proposed that D category villages should be allowed to wither away; as houses became uninhabitable they would not be replaced. As might be expected, such a policy aroused enormous controversy and opposition, and was later modified.

Not all selected settlement policies propose such a stark categorization of villages. Angus District in the Tayside Region is an area of general population loss especially in the glens and the highlands, but some pressure for commuter housing exists in the south near Dundee. All rural settlements in the areas were classified according to their size, existing facilities and the scope for further development. On this basis each village was placed in one of five categories (see figure 7.2):

Key centres	Outside the catchment area of a burgh; basic services available; some growth potential; some encouragement to industry.
Dormitory centres	Within the catchment area of a burgh; basic services available; some growth potential and encouragement to industry.
Intermediate centres	Limited basic services, suitable for in-fill housing development only.
Remote centres	Located in highland glens; unsuited to large-scale growth; limited development related to recreation, agriculture or forestry.
Other rural communities	Unsuitable for development except for agricultural or forestry workers' housing.

This policy was formulated in 1976, and the range of locational, growth and service features that it incorporates illustrates the increased sophistication that now characterizes selected settlement policies (Lockhart 1982).

When it comes to implementing key settlement policies, local authorities have considerable resources at their disposal. Development control provides the negative instrument with which growth in non-key settlements can be prevented. However, there are also some positive powers available, because the county and district councils control the provision of educational facilities, social services, libraries, council housing and road improvements, all of which can be directed to the key settlements. In addition, infrastructure such as water, drains and electricity are controlled by public bodies, as is some of the provision for industrial developments and transport. Therefore, powers do exist to enable a controlled reshaping of the settlement geography of rural areas.

There is a number of general commentaries on key settlements, but few detailed analyses of how effectively these policies have been implemented. Cloke's (1979) work on 'pressurized' Warwickshire and 'remote' Devon is the most comprehensive study so far completed. Although such a classification is rather crude, especially in the case of Devon, the contrast between the two study areas is interesting. Cloke assessed population change, housing development and service provision in the key and non-key settlements within these two counties. In Warwickshire the policy had not been able to limit growth to the selected villages in the more pressu-

FIGURE 7.2   Proposed rural settlement plan for Angus District, 1982
Source: after Lockhart (1982)

rized parts of the county. Public sector housing development had followed the guidelines more closely than the private sector, but even so there had been substantial investment in some non-key villages. Devon, too, had succeeded only partially in terms of the policy aims. Population and housing growth in the more pressurized areas had been channelled into the key settlements, but the selected villages in the more remote areas were simply too small to function as foci for growth. That the policies have been more successful in the pressurized areas should not be surprising; the most powerful planning instrument available is still development control and this, of course, can be effective only in areas of growth.

These general conclusions have been further qualified by Blacksell and Gilg's (1981) detailed analysis of planning applications in parts of Devon, where there were large numbers of applications and approvals for residential developments outside the selected settlements. In a Dartmoor study area, key settlements attracted only 22 per cent of outline planning permission compared with 34 per cent in non-key villages. In mid-Devon results were even more surprising: the key settlements attracted 8 per cent of permissions, the non-key villages had 51 per cent, and the remaining 41 per cent were in the 'open' countryside. These mostly involved piecemeal or rounding-off development in existing settlements or small groups of houses, but it nevertheless indicates a surprising flexibility in the application of policy even in those areas where one would expect the policy to be strongly applied.

Notwithstanding these observations on the effectiveness of policy implementation, the entire approach to selected settlements has been heavily criticized in recent years. The first criticism is that, although key settlement policies are theoretically sound, they have been poorly implemented in practice. Cloke (1980a, p. 98) suggests that this may be because the concept of 'key settlements has been a cosmetic justification for a policy created merely out of economic expediency and administrative pragmatism'. In other words, the title 'key settlement policy' has often been lent to programmes devised only on very narrow cost or administrative criteria. Furthermore, many key settlement policies have not been properly implemented because there has been a lack of co-ordination among the relevant planning agencies (Cloke 1980b). Education and housing departments, water and electricity boards have often failed to follow policy guidelines or to co-ordinate their work. A clear example of this is provided by Glyn-Jones (1979) in a study of Hatherleigh in Devon. In spite of the fact that the village was designated as a key settlement, there has been a sharp fall in new housing because of a failure to provide the necessary improvement to the sewerage system.

It is possible to sympathize with these arguments, but there are more fundamental criticisms of key settlement policies. One problem is that key settlements have been seen as panacea for all rural problems, irrespective of social and regional context. For example, Thorburn (1971) considers that settlement policies have been applied in 'blanket fashion' to villages, ignoring their individual characters. Dunn (1976) underlines this point and argues that, in some rural areas in Britain, the largest settlements would not qualify as service centres according to some threshold criteria. This seems to have been a particular problem in the more remote areas, whether in Devon or in the Scottish Highlands (Varwell 1973; Cloke 1979).

Even the argument that key settlements offer economies of scale has not remained unscathed. The most devastating attack comes from Gilder (1979), who has provided empirical evidence on the costs of educational, sewerage, public transport and health facilities in rural areas. In terms of internal economies of scale, these were significant only for sewerage and primary education. More interestingly, he found that 'economies of scale are insignificant in villages having a population of up to 2,000 and that the unit costs in these villages are not significantly higher than in a town of 29,000 . . .' (Gilder 1979, p. 252). These findings are confirmed by more impressionable evidence from the Scottish Highlands (Greaves 1979). Many commentators would now agree that the marginal costs of making fuller use of existing facilities outweigh the economies of scale to be obtained from their concentration. Indeed, economies of scale are likely to vary so much between different services that they cannot all be served by a single settlement policy. Therefore perhaps support should be given to the idea of 'functional interdependence', in which different facilities are located in different villages within a cluster of settlements (McLaughlin 1976).

Key settlements have also been criticized on social grounds, a point that will be elaborated in the next section. The criticisms outlined above have not been completely ignored by the planners, since, although the new structure plans still exhibit a keen adherence to key settlement policies (National Council of Social Service 1979; Shaw and Williams 1981), alternative settlement policies have also been considered. For example, the idea of functional dispersal among a group of villages has been adopted in the structure plans for North Yorkshire, Gloucestershire and Cumbria, and a more flexible approach to allowing housing development outside key settlements has also been adopted by many counties (Derounian 1980; J. M. Shaw 1982). There does seem to be a greater sensitivity to community needs and to the dangers of 'blanket' application of general policy.

SOCIAL CONSEQUENCES OF STATUTORY PLANNING

Although the total amount of resources devoted to the needs of the rural population is arguably the prime factor affecting standards of living, statutory planning has played an important role in influencing the distribution of resources and employment within the countryside; including the availability of shops, houses and services. There has been a greater social and economic input in structure plans than in development plans, but there is little agreement as to the scope of social planning (R. Williams 1976). The most important powers available to planners are development controls, which operate predominantly at the level of the built environment.

Although planning has a number of wider social implications for rural areas, many of these have been unintentional side-effects of physical planning policies. The policy of constraint, whether in AONBs, national parks or other areas of valued landscapes, is a case in point. These areas were designated to conserve valued landscapes and to make them more accessible to the general public (or at least to those who own cars). The restrictions that have been placed on development in these areas have partly secured these conservationist goals. At the same time, they can conflict with the needs of the local community; although houses, factories, swimming pools and supermarkets may appear ugly or aberrant land-uses to the outsider, to the local community they may be essential ingredients in improving the quality of life. The Sandford Report on the national parks explicitly recognized these conflicts and called upon central government to alleviate some of the special problems of such local communities. The argument was advanced that a form of welfare payment should perhaps be made available to those who happen to have been born in national parks (as opposed to those who chose to move there) if job and housing opportunities have been restricted by conservationist planning policies. In practice, of course, it would be very difficult to implement a policy of this nature.

The example of the national parks illustrates some of the consequences of negative development control planning, but positive planning may also have serious implications for local communities. The key settlement policies are a case in point. These were designed partly to ensure the survival of a minimum level of service provision in rural areas, and, in the face of the continued decline of rural services, such a policy may have been necessary in some locations. However, this strategy appears to have contributed to a more rapid decline in services (and sometimes to population losses) in more remote areas outside the selected settlements (Hancock 1976; McLaughlin 1976; Cloke 1979). Overall service provision may be stabilized, but a more uneven distribution may result. In theory, people living in the non-key settlements should be able to utilize the provision in selected centres. However, the decline of public transport and the far-from-universal availability of private transport militates aginst this in practice. The real losers are the 'transport poor' (chapter 6), and the reason for this is that official estimates of the costs of key settlement policies do not generally include the time and money costs of individuals. This is why commentators such as Shaw (1978) have argued in favour of a broader 'social cost accounting' approach to settlement policy. It may be impossible to quantify precisely the social costs to individuals of thwarted employment aspirations and extra-long journeys to shop, but a social cost accounting method would at least increase an awareness of these social consequences.

Apart from employment, the most serious implications of the policies of contraint are for housing. Restrictions on new building, both in general and to specific locations (usually key settlements), has two direct consequences. First, there will be an absolute lack of new housing available, especially in particular villages; second, prices of the available houses will consequently be greater. Together, these can give a 'further twist to the inflationary spiral' in rural house prices (Blacksell and Gilg 1981). Costs are, in fact, forced upwards both by the limitations on the supply of land and the restrictions on the densities of housing that may be constructed per hectare (Hall *et al*. 1973). There is now considerable evidence to show that prices are higher in areas of special restriction, such as AONBs and national parks, than in the surrounding region (Penfold 1974; Bennett 1976; Standing Conference of Rural Community Councils 1979; Shucksmith 1981). Hall *et al*. (1973) have also shown that urban containment policies have resulted in higher house prices as a result of the higher price of land, so that there has been a fall in the quality of new first-home, owner-occupier dwellings in town and country.

The consequences of these developments in rural housing are socially selective, and were discussed in chapter 5. As locals and lower income groups can be forced to move to other areas or to nearby key settlements where housing is available, the social composition of the community may change. In time, the future and viability of rural communities may be threatened (Standing Conference of Rural Community Councils 1978).

These trends pose a dilemma for the planners. If they permit the expansion of a village, it may be 'invaded' by newcomers who will change the social character of the community. On the other hand, if they restrict development, this may force up house prices and exclude lower-income local inhabitants anyway. Some councils have tried to tackle this difficulty through a policy of permitting only those new developments that will serve local needs. This strategy has been recommended in a number of structure plans for areas ranging from accessible Hertfordshire and Surrey to remote Cumbria and the Peak Park, although the Secretary of State has later modified some of these policies (D. Clark 1981; G. Clark 1982a).

Ultimately, the role of planning is limited by the restricted powers available and by a lack of co-ordination with other public and quasi-public agencies. Planning can prevent some poor features of development, but without controlling all the consequences, while other positive aspects of developments may be beyond their influence. As Shaw and Stockford (1979, p. 122) state, 'it is the problems of implementing 'socially-based' policies for rural areas through the medium of the statutory planning system which accounts for much of the gap between society's expectations of planning, and the results in practice'.

VILLAGE PLANNING

Although most research in settlement geography has been directed at settlement *systems*, or the distribution of villages, it is also important to consider village development or planning at the micro-scale of design or general layout. The intiative usually comes from the developer proposing an addition to an existing village, or from the local authority housing department wishing to construct a new council housing estate. The developer (public or private) or the architect takes the lead in suggesting densities, house styles, building materials, estate size and layout; planners play a fairly passive role, approving or refusing the planning application. In practice, developers will probably consult planners in advance in order to ascertain the type of development that is likely to be approved, but there is no obligation to do this. Planners can also give approval with conditions appended to the details of the scheme. Therefore successful schemes will reflect a combination of the 'good' design perceptions of both planners and architects, within the financial constraints imposed by the developer. The constraints are particularly important in the case of council housing, as changes in government financial yardsticks have led to considerable variations in the quality of housing built over time (Byrne 1976).

Green (1971) has summarized criticisms of village designs, suggesting that the new development tends to be dull and monotonous, that many layouts lack open spaces, and there is a lack of footpaths and loop roads to link new housing to schools, shops and buses. While all these points are important, the last-named is crucial as it influences the way in which new development is linked to the existing village core. Woodruffe (1976) suggests that new developments may be divided into four categories:

1 extensions of old village cores by consolidation with new perimeter developments;
2 in-fill sites; that is, consolidation of the existing close-knit character of villages;
3 establishment of definite edges to villages;
4 formation or retention of village greens together with the encouragement of social amenities.

The main debate within planning has focused on the first of these types of development. Sensitive infill or retention of village greens generally raises few criticisms, but the addition of perimeter development has often been highly contentious. The main criticism is that the development of peripheral estates (public or private) can create a dual village, in which the new housing is sometimes physically and socially isolated from the existing village core.

An example of this type of development has been analysed by Ambrose (1974) in Ringmer, Sussex. The village has a 'two-cell' structure, comprising the old core and a number of peripheral estates, which has

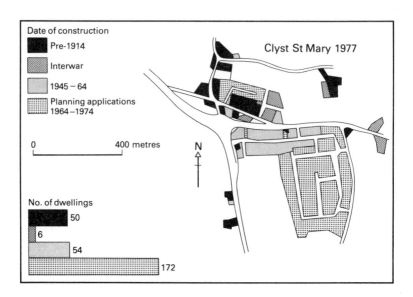

FIGURE 7.3   Development in Clyst St Mary, Devon: actual and proposed
Source: after Blacksell and Gilg (1981)

been socially and spatially divisive. The people living on the estates, especially the elderly, tended to be isolated, and a number of new residents felt lonely and insecure. These criticisms are echoed in a number of other studies. Martin (1976, p. 72) writes that village extensions in Hampshire and Cumbria were like 'a series of linked housing estates with the layouts encouraging a separate identity on each estate and going no way towards promoting a sense of 'community' between the newcomers and the established residents . . .' Another example is the village of Clyst St Mary in Devon (figure 7.3) where prior to 1914 there were only 50 houses, a number that hardly changed in the interwar years. However, since the 1950s some 226 new dwellings have been built. This new appendage is 'out of all proportion to the initial development and separated from its services, including a primary school, by a busy main road' (Blacksell and Gilg 1981, p. 186).

The tragedy of these kinds of development is that the opportunity may be lost of creating an integrated community, and of benefiting from the social advantages that can accrue from good design (Masser and Stroud 1965). It is not the designs that are important but their social impact; and it is not the *physical* distance between new and old that is of concern, but the *social* distance.

8 Services and Retailing

THE GEOGRAPHY OF RURAL SERVICES

Traditionally, geographers have been concerned with the locational aspects of services. In particular, classical Central Place Theory suggests that goods and services of a given type and quality (in a hierarchy of services) will be provided only when sufficient demand exists for them (the so-called 'threshold population') within the distance that people will be willing to travel to obtain them (the 'range'). Naturally, the more specialized goods and services will require larger catchment populations and will therefore tend to locate mainly in the larger centres. Nevertheless, the theory supposes that many frequently required services will locate in smaller settlements to serve local needs. Today, however, trends in distribution and management have tended to reduce locational flexibility and to increase levels of centralization. The size of service unit has often increased; for example, many village shops have been closing down in the face of price competition from larger stores and warehouses, while doctors have often combined in large health centres and solicitors in group practices or law centres. This trend, sometimes termed 'centrism', has been encouraged by the spatially selective approach to planning referred to in the previous chapter, which holds that many services are better provided from centres or at least in centralized locations (Low 1975). Manifestations of this can be seen in many rural locations in variants on key settlement strategies. It has also been encouraged by technological developments enabling centralized control and bulk buying, which tend to militate against the continuation of smaller service outlets.

The provision of services in rural areas has deteriorated steadily since the end of the Second World War. As Moseley (1979a) points out, the tendency has been for service outlets to become fewer, larger and more widely spaced. This reflects the economies of scale that can be enjoyed by many services: for example, it is generally cheaper to educate 100 children in one school than 25 in each of four schools, although this may be feasible only because of the substantial increases in personal mobility of most (but not all) households.

When considering service accessibility, it is useful to distinguish between locational accessibility (simply a measure of proximity) and effective accessibility, which depends on having the ability, mobility and time to reach and use a service (Ambrose 1977). Accessibility to jobs, services and amenities must be carefully qualified in terms of individuals' time budgets, discussed in chapter 6. 'Since most people's daily lives follow a variety of closely constrained and well-worn paths through time and space, it follows that effective accessibility to particular locations will depend not only on their physical proximity but also on whether they are free to make the journey in the first place . . .' (Knox 1982, p. 184). The study of time–space geography emphasizes that, to maximize utilization, service opening hours should coincide with the times at which a person can reach the facility in question because of other commitments and transport availability; that is, 'coupling constraints' should be minimized (Hägerstrand 1970; Carlstein, Parkes and Thrift 1978; Moseley 1979a). The daily prism (the effective range of a person during the day) of people in rural areas can be very limited. Consider the daily prism of the car-less suburban housewife, whose opportunities are restricted to those that can be reached on foot or by bus. Routine shopping becomes a chore, socializing is limited to the local neighbourhood, and, with children under school age, she is locked into a very limited physical space because of coupling constraints and societal expectations concerning her family role (Pred and Palm 1978). However, the car-less rural housewife can be in an even worse position, since services available within walking or bus distance can be very limited or even non-existent. It is useful to remember that many services are not offered all the time each day and that 'time-divisible' services are becoming increasingly common (and essential) in rural areas, including travelling shops, libraries, banks and doctors, which might serve isolated villages on one or two occasions per week. These can be invaluable in reducing coupling constraints and in extending the opportunities available within the prism of a rural resident.

VILLAGE SHOPS AND THE JOURNEY-TO-SHOP

A consistent trend in post war Britain as a whole has been the declining number of retail outlets. In the face of rationalization to achieve economies of scale, bulk purchasing, out-of-town shopping centres and similar related developments, shop numbers have declined in virtually all regions of Britain. Kirby (1974) documents the change in shop numbers between 1966 and 1971 as falling from 504,000 to some 485,000, a decline of about 3.8 per cent, although this varied from a 43.6 per cent decline in co–operatives to an 8.6 per cent decline in multiples and only a 0.3 per cent decline in independents. However, this does not represent a falling-off of retail trade, since during this time turnover for all shops increased by about 37 per cent. Apparently, therefore, more trade was being done by fewer, larger outlets. This trend of falling shop numbers has been especially important to smaller rural settlements, although exact data are hard to obtain to enumerate the trend. The regional subdivisions available to Kirby did not permit a fine locational analysis, but it appeared that Scotland, East Anglia and the North West of England had witnessed the largest decline in numbers of shops.

Mackay and Laing (1982), on behalf of the Scottish Consumer Council, surveyed 26 parishes in 'remote Scotland', defined as being a minimum of ten miles from an urban centre of 2,000 or more; 6 per cent of Scotland's population lived in such parishes. Their survey supports the above contentions, since the number of parishes containing a shop had fallen by 15 per cent between 1960 and 1970, and the number containing a sub-post office had decreased by the same amount. By 1980 these had fallen a further 36 per cent and 32 per cent respectively, so that over the 20-year period the numbers of remote parishes with shops and sub-post offices had been halved. Some of the implications of these findings of general service decline will be discussed in chapter 10.

Various authors have written about the 'demise' of the village shop and have emphasized its dire consequences for the non-mobile, especially the elderly and unemployed (Harman 1978; Standing Conference of Rural Community Councils 1978; Dawson and Kirby 1979). In rural Norfolk the number of shops has fallen substantially since 1945 – in one area of Norfolk, north-west of Norwich, the number was reduced from 227 to 140 between 1950 and 1964, a decline of 38 per cent (Moseley and Spencer 1978). Moreover, in spite of this rationalization, retail turnover per village establishment had fallen, which indicated that rural residents were shifting their business to larger centres in the county.

The survey examined four larger parishes with over 800 residents and 40 smaller parishes in two study areas in Norfolk. Table 8.1 illustrates the findings and suggests a correlation between population size and number of outlets, although clear 'thresholds' are not evident. The smaller parishes tended to lack fixed-location commercial outlets apart from general stores-cum-grocery shops, sub-post offices, pubs and garages, while some of the larger parishes had a number of more specialist shops such as hardware stores, drapers, butchers, fishmongers, bakers, chemists and even a wine

Table 8.1   Numbers of shops in parishes, by size of parish, in 44 Norfolk parishes

No. of shops	No. of parishes	Mean population, 1971	Population range
More than 3	4	1,293	836–1,538
2–3	11	480	208–722
1	15	361	103–715
0	14	204	92–321

Source: after Moseley *et al.* (1977)

Table 8.2   Shops and post offices in 44 Norfolk parishes

	No. of parishes with					
	Combined shop/PO	Separate shop/PO	Shop but no PO	PO but no shop	Neither	Total
Small parishes	24	2	0	4	10	40
Large parishes (> 800 population)	0	4	0	0	0	4
Total	24	6	0	4	10	44

Source: after Moseley *et al.* (1977)

merchant (table 8.2). Only 65 per cent of the smaller villages (those with fewer than 800 inhabitants) had at least one shop, while 75 per cent had a post office. However, almost 70 per cent of proprietors were over 45 years of age and there was a general feeling that the shops did not provide an adequate return on capital. As a result, many were pessimistic about their ability to sell or pass on the shop, which bodes ill for the continuation of retail provision even at current levels in these and similar villages.

Low levels of rural shop provision have also been found in South West England. The structure plans produced within this region and their reports of surveys contain valuable information on this theme. G. Shaw (1982), in an analysis of the structure plans of Devon, Dorset, Gloucester-

Table 8.3   Rural retail provision in Dorset (excluding SE area)

Facilities	No. of villages	%
More than one shop	33	12
PO and/or general store	116	41
Only part-time PO	8	3
No shops	124	44
Total	281	100

Source: G. Shaw (1982)

shire, Somerset and Wiltshire, found a disturbing decline in rural retailing. In Dorset (excluding the south-east, which produced its own plan) 44 per cent of all villages were without any form of shop in 1979, while only 12 per cent had more than one shop (table 8.3). This extreme picture can be compared with that of Devon, where only some 30 per cent of villages were without shops in 1975. In the West Wiltshire Structure Plan area, the proportion of villages without shops increased from 14 to 22 per cent between 1974 and 1978. Six larger villages in this area, with populations of between 1,200 and 1,500 persons, also suffered considerable decline in shop numbers, which suggests that village size is not the only factor involved. Indeed, villages in south and east Wiltshire often had declining shop numbers in spite of increases in population (sometimes of more than 25 per cent) between 1974 and 1978. Nevertheless, according to Shaw, the main tendency is for a lack of the dual services of a retail food shop and a post office to occur predominantly in villages of fewer than 300 people.

A sad picture of declining numbers of village shops is therefore substantiated in many parts of rural Britain. The inevitable consequence is a growing dependence on towns, while the lack of essential retailers imposes increasing economic and personal burdens on rural residents, forcing them to travel further and further to shop. In many parishes in mid- and north Devon, local residents travel on average between five and ten miles for essential goods. Surveys during the past five years have consistently indicated an increased tendency for long-distance shopping trips, especially for goods such as food and everyday purchases. Travel over long distances for such items can become a real problem for those who have to rely on inadequate public transport.

Somewhat surprisingly, studies have indicated that few shopping linkages develop between villages. Where shops are available, they tend to be used by people living in that village but rarely by people living in neighbouring shopless villages – the usual pattern is for people in those villages to travel to a much larger centre (G. Shaw 1982). It is therefore difficult for a shopkeeper to maintain the viability of his business by acquiring the patronage of customers from nearby villages, and one of the reasons may be that inter-village public transport is often much poorer even than public transport from village to town.

Many households, particularly the better-off, seem to bypass the village shop; research supports the suspicion that local shops tend to be used more by lower-income households (Thomas 1976). In the Norfolk study, 19 per cent of households rarely, or never, used their village shop where this existed. The mean household income of these respondents was £2,790, while the mean income of the 53 per cent of respondents who frequently used their village shop was £2,140. The main reasons cited for non-use of village shops were usually that prices were too high or that respondents preferred to shop where choice and range of goods was greater, especially if working elsewhere (Moseley and Spencer 1978). Age and the ability to drive appeared to be key variables; 51 per cent of female respondents with driving licences shopped in Norwich (the main nearby town) or in small towns, as opposed to their villages, while only 32 per cent of non-drivers and 30 per cent of elderly respondents did so. The two last-named groups were very dependent on village shops, and hence had to accept the higher prices and the more limited range of goods available.

Even where village shops do still exist there are limitations of type and range of goods available. Combined post offices and shops can usually offer only a restricted selection of goods and many village residents feel that being unable to obtain the range and selection of goods available to the rest of the population is a form of deprivation through location. This problem is particularly acute with regard to the more specialist shops, such as pharmacies, boutiques or hairdressers, and the 'professional' and financial services such as banks, insurance offices and solicitors. A visit to the last-named, usually an exceptional event, will frequently necessitate a day off work while it is often almost impossible for rural employees to attend a bank during opening hours. As a result, many have to cash cheques in the village shop or go to town on a Saturday morning to a building society. Personal time-budgets can be as important as service availability in influencing the type of service that a working rural resident is able to attend – and, indeed, the variety of activities that may be undertaken.

Recently, considerable interest has developed in the relative cost of goods in rural shops. The Price Commission (1975) found that, although

Post office and general store, often the only surviving retail provision in villages
(source: authors and A. Teed)

overall food prices were somewhat higher in the outlying areas of Britain
than in the more central areas, these differences tended to be relatively
small except in places such as northern Scotland and the Scottish Islands;
the average level of prices in rural Scotland has been estimated as being
between 8–10 per cent higher than in Scottish cities (Mackay and Laing
1982). Indeed country-wide, substantial differences have been noted for
individual prices, and Winyard (1978) goes so far as to suggest that food
prices are significantly higher in the country, which is ironic since much
fresh food is produced in these areas. The social importance of such price
differences is considerable, particularly for the many rural residents who
are on low wages or are retired. In addition, many low-income rural
families need to spend a relatively greater proportion of their money on
transport than do urban households in order to get to the shops, and on top of
that rural transport is often more expensive (Thomas and Winyard 1979).

High transport costs have been identified as one cause of expensive
goods in rural shops. Indeed, the effects of increased taxation on petrol
have been held to be disproportionately severe in rural areas where cars are
more essential, and petrol price rises in the 1970s and 1980s have caused
much rural discontent. Furthermore, because of relatively low profit

margins and suppliers' refusals to deliver to smaller outlets, and stricter regulations regarding conditions of storage, many petrol stations have closed in rural localities. Nationally, over 10,000 petrol stations have closed over the past ten years according to the Motor Traders' Association, which predicts that the 1982 figure of 24,000 petrol stations in Britain will fall to 17,500 by 1985. The majority of closures have been, and will be, among independent garages which supply many rural areas.

Other reasons for the higher cost of goods in rural shops relate to the small volume of business such areas afford to traders and, to some extent, the lack of competition. In areas where cash-and-carry or discount stores operate, prices will tend to be kept down, although this may also have the effect of forcing marginal retailers out of business. Changing consumer behaviour, especially by car owners, has led to bulk buying and freezer storage of many goods, with mobile consumers in rural areas often developing patterns of weekly or monthly shopping at cheaper, larger centres (G. Shaw 1982). Whether such behaviour is a cause or an effect of higher prices in rural shops is hard to establish, but the trend is certainly on the increase, which will often mean that the only customers in the expensive and ailing village shops are the less affluent or immobile. When a shop does close it will rarely re-open, and the village will have lost a function that tends to enhance the feeling of community, as well as an essential service to an important minority of residents.

What is the answer to declining rural shopping provision? Britain, unlike many other countries in Western Europe, lacks a national framework of policies towards retailing. Although structure plans have often noted retailing as a key area of concern, little has been done to alleviate the decline. In addition, in spite of pressure since the 1930s, Dawson (1980) notes that successive governments have ignored matters such as aid for small shops or the provision of training programmes for shopkeepers. Indeed, it can be argued that successive changes in con-sumer, taxation and employment legislation have imposed such a burden on small-scale retailers that the job has become unattractive. On the positive side, attempts to encourage patronage of village shops and services such as a 'use it or lose it' campaign by community councils may offer psychological and practical support.

However, some form of positive planning is needed for retailing in a rural environment. Structure plans have not had this effect, although they have often focused attention on the problems of rural retailing (Shaw and Williams 1980). At present they provide the only viable means of attacking these problems at an appropriate scale, but policies must become positive rather than passive. G. Shaw (1982) suggests that training and advice for existing shopkeepers, aid such as that available to rural industry and the promotion of new sites and premises are all required. In particular, dual-role shops could be encouraged so that garages and post offices, for example, may survive by running small shops.

Of particular interest are mobile services, which will be discussed below when medical and welfare services are considered. With the exception of milk deliveries, the availability of these services has declined since the 1960s. Today, many rural localities can no longer obtain daily deliveries of newspapers or regular deliveries of bread and groceries. Fewer than 50 per cent of Dorset villages in 1979 had regular grocery deliveries and this can disadvantage many social groups. Only by rigorous action, timely subsidy and positive transport planning can the decline in rural shops be halted and adequate retail provision be re-established in the village.

PROFESSIONAL SERVICES

These services include a medley of facilities such as banks, building societies, accountants, solicitors and insurance brokers, as well as the police and fire services. Rural residents are at something of a disadvantage when it comes to acquiring professional opinions, particularly legal and financial advice (investment, accountancy and insurance). In the first place they will usually have to make a more positive decision to seek out such advice. In addition, whereas the urban resident will usually have a range of these services nearby from which to choose, the rural resident will usually have no choice, assuming the service is available. While urban residents will often have access to services such as law centres there has only recently been interest in extending these on a mobile or visiting basis into some rural localities.

Some lawyers have recognized the need for good professional advice in rural areas, and in certain areas such as the South West law centres are encouraging a wider spread of legal services into more remote areas. These centres offer free legal advice by qualified staff, and often the type of 'welfare' advice not readily available from private solicitors' practices. The Royal Commission on Legal Services (1979) noted the concentration of solicitors in larger settlements and agreed that private law firms could be expected to locate near those institutions with which they have most dealings. 'It would be unusual, if not eccentric, for them to actively seek out legal problems in sparsely populated areas. Yet this is precisely what is needed if rural problems are to find legal solutions . . .' (Economides 1982, p. 50). It is to be hoped that future legal centres in rural districts will be funded by the government and local authorities as they have been in many urban locations, particularly those offering 'proactive' legal services, which seek out legal problems, especially those of a welfare nature, rather

Mobile services offer one solution to the problem of supplying rural communities (source: authors and A. Teed)

than simply providing 'reactive' legal advice once crises occur. In particular, a system of 'satellite' law centres in villages to which lawyers travel at regular intervals from a regional centre might be a valuable intermediate stage (Economides 1982).

Mackay and Laing (1982) did not, in fact, find much dissatisfaction with financial services in their survey of remote parishes. Out of 26 parishes, 13 were served by mobile banks (one run from the bank manager's car). Also, a number of villages in England and Wales have banks with limited opening days or restricted hours. Legal services were more of a problem in the Scottish survey, but not a great one when compared with the lack of public transport and poor range of shops. One parish did have a lawyer's weekly surgery and also a branch office of an insurance agent. No significant change in service provision was envisaged in the future. Perhaps the surprisingly high levels of satisfaction relate to this knowledge and to the acceptance that out-of-the ordinary arrangements will nearly always have to be made to reach services of these types. Perhaps there are also generally lower expectations regarding specialist services; whether this is a reflection of a form of rural deprivation is discussed further in chapter 10.

EDUCATION AND ACCESS TO SCHOOLS

Education services in Britain are provided mainly by the state (the so-called 'maintained' sector). The main basis for the current education service is the Education Act 1944, with a series of subsequent minor amendments. Compulsory education is provided for all pupils aged between 5 and who 16, if need be in specialist schools; and continuing education is provided in secondary schools for pupils over 16 who (usually) wish to prepare for public examinations. Pre-school education is usually offered 'where possible', and courses of higher and further education are generally supported by the public sector. In addition careers guidance, adult education, school transport, school meals and out-of-hours recreation and community education can be supported by the education services. Therefore, the range of activities that is provided for the community goes beyond pure teaching, and schools and colleges have become essential focal points of many localities.

Education services are the largest of the county services in Britain accounting in the non-metropolitan counties for between 60 and 70 per cent of expenditure. Although schools are only one part of the service, they are the largest part, and considerable interest has focused on the question of school sizes and costs. There is, as yet, no clear agreement as to what constitutes the minimum size of viable school in economic terms, let alone in educational terms. Indeed, it has been pointed out that many urban schools have more than 30 pupils per teacher while some rural schools have as few as 10 pupils per teacher, so that it could be argued that the latter are in fact being subsidized by other parts of the service.

The minimum 'economic' size is probably a one-form entry primary school with 210 pupils. Costs per pupil can be shown to rise quite sharply in schools with below 100 pupils but particularly for schools with fewer than 50 pupils (figure 8.1). Primary schools, being smaller in scale, are more frequently affected than secondary schools, and evidence of increased costs in small schools has been found in studies in West Suffolk (Gilder 1979), in Cumbria and in Salop (Association of County Councils 1979). Often the cost per pupil in a small school is over twice or even three times the average in larger schools. As a policy guideline, a minimum size of 60 pupils for primary schools with three teachers was suggested by the 1967 Gittins Report on Primary Education in Wales. However, this has been opposed by proponents of even smaller establishments, and in practice it seems that only schools with falling rolls and having fewer than 40 pupils are in real danger of closure or 'rationalization' (Martin 1976). In the largely rural county of Gloucestershire, about one-sixth of the 290 primary schools had rolls of fewer than 50 pupils and over one-third had

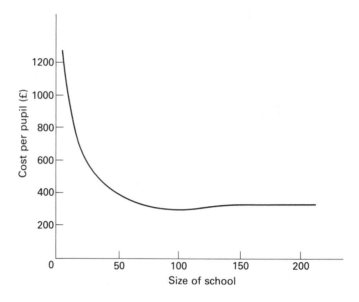

FIGURE 8.1   Primary school costs per pupil by size of school in Cumbria
Source: after Association of County Councils (1979)

rolls below 100. Almost all of these small primary schools were associated with the rural districts of the county, particularly the Cotswolds – there was only one primary school of fewer than 100 pupils in Gloucester and Cheltenham. It is these rural schools that will be the most vulnerable to closure if rolls fall, even if the Department of Education and Science has tended not to approve closures of schools until their rolls are in the low twenties (Gloucester County Council 1978).

Nevertheless, many small schools have closed as a result of investigations into cost effectiveness while some have literally died out as rolls have fallen. A basic statistic cited by Moseley (1979a) is that in 1963, 34 per cent of British primary schools had fewer than 100 pupils, while in 1973 this had fallen to 22 per cent, indicating that the small village school is gradually being phased out. In Norfolk 80 small primary schools closed between 1951 and 1971, so that by the early 1970s about 40 per cent of the county's parishes did not have a school (Moseley 1979a). The picture elsewhere is similar: in Suffolk, 46 out of 330 primary schools were closed in the decade after 1967 (Gilder 1979), and in many counties the introduction of middle schools between upper and primary schools has further reduced the numbers in primary schools. This has affected the viability of rural primary schools in particular since, although only 9 per

Closure of a village school in Scotland. This can happen wherever school rolls or finances fall too low (source: D. G. Lockhart)

cent of primary schools nationally have fewer than 50 pupils on their roll, 97 per cent of these were located in non-metropolitan counties. Some rural counties have a particularly high proportion of small schools; in 1979, in Powys, 42 per cent of primary schools had 50 pupils or fewer, Dyfed 38 per cent, North Yorkshire 30 per cent, Northumberland 28 per cent and Lincolnshire 27 per cent. This makes it very difficult for such counties to benefit from the economies of scale that may be derived from larger schools. In addition, savings from school closures may be offset by having to build new, larger schools and by the costs of transporting children further to schools (Association of County Councils 1979; Tricker 1982).

The main rural education debate concerns the primary school, since it is felt that younger children should be educated as near to home as possible. There is not much doubt that larger secondary schools are necessary to cover the required range of subjects and ability demanded in today's curriculum. However, there is by no means an agreement about what constitutes the ideal size even for a secondary school. Many survive with only 100 or 200 pupils, yet one of the largest comprehensive schools in Britain, with some 2,500 pupils, is to be found in Exmouth, in rural Devon. The major disadvantages of small schools for older age ranges seem to be a more limited curriculum, lack of interaction with a variety of teachers and pupils, a greater risk of problems from personality clashes between pupil and teacher, and general underpreparedness for transition to any larger institution.

It is also often claimed that moderately large schools are better educationally than small schools. But educational attainment is notoriously difficult to measure since it is influenced by so many factors external to school size, such as individual motivation, teacher quality and social background. In addition, there is no clear agreement as to what constitutes 'good education'; there are probably as many opinions on this as there are educationalists. As a result, the educational implications of small school closure are very unclear. Professional isolation, poor infrastructure, lack of books and teaching aids, the potential harmful effects of a single bad teacher and the narrow curricula that can be offered are all cited by various authors as indications of potentially poor education in small schools (Nash 1975; Martin 1976; Watkins 1978, 1979; Watkins and Derrick 1979). On the other hand, closer involvement of staff with pupils, a secure and familiar environment, greater individual attention and shorter travel time can all be very positive aspects (Mack 1978; Lewis 1980).

In spite of the numerous social and educational arguments, economic criteria are becoming increasingly paramount. As far back as 1967, the Plowden Committee stated unequivocally that it was the smallest schools that were the least defensible both financially and, except in special circumstances, on educational grounds (Gilder 1979). Today, because of falling rolls and financial retrenchment, the pressure for rationalization is even greater. In the current stringent financial and political climate, new constraints have to be faced by education, and these may well exacerbate existing differences among and within education authorities in various types of school provision (Williamson and Byrne 1979).

A social cost of school reorganization is the longer journeys to school that children often have to make, which may be considered undesirable especially for the very young. The suggestion that some young children may be psychologically or educationally disadvantaged by being educated at a distance from home is disturbing, although evidence is not conclusive (Lee 1957). Secondary schoolchildren can generally cope with a longer school day more successfully but, in spite of transport subsidies, Tricker (1982) found that some parents undoubtedly bore increased costs for school transport. In addition, the pattern of transport provision seems frequently to constrain the choice of alternative schools for families without daytime access to private transport, an aspect of the more general rural accessibility problem discussed in chapter 6.

Transport to schools can be a substantial item in educational expenditure and travelling can be a personal burden on the children. The

Education Act 1944 not only imposed upon local authorities the responsibility of preparing development plans for education (indicating where schools were to be opened, closed or expanded), but also required that school transport costs should, in certain circumstances, be borne by the state. The local authority must ensure and pay for adequate transport of children who live more than three miles from school, and two miles in the case of children between the ages of five and eight. This is undoubtedly an expensive but essential requirement in rural areas; for example, pupils in east Devon can travel up to 20 miles to attend their secondary school at Ottery St Mary, in a district where public transport is very infrequent. Long-distance journeys of over ten miles for secondary education are not uncommon in many rural locations. Figure 8.2 indicates this problem for Gloucestershire. Over one-half of the 55 secondary schools in the county were in Cheltenham, Gloucester and Stroud, and the restricted number of rural secondary schools tended to be of a larger size, a

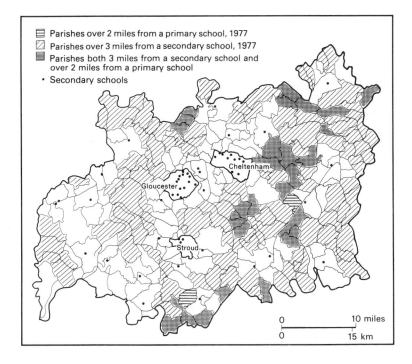

FIGURE 8.2   Access to schools in Gloucestershire, 1977. Distance is measured in straight line distance from the main settlement in the parish to the nearest primary or secondary school.
Source: based on Gloucestershire County Structure Plan 1978, Report of Survey, Technical Volume No. 7

contrast with the picture for primary provision, which exacerbates the accessibility problem.

Primary schools in villages have been cited as possible foci for out-of-hours activities, although many are too small to provide community education and recreation facilities (Moseley 1979a; Sigsworth 1980; Phillips and Williams 1982a). The existence of a school can give a real sense of 'community' to a village, but whether this should, or could, be subsidized by other parts of the constrained educational service is debatable.

More important, perhaps, is the fact that rural areas tend to be deficient in non-statutory education; for example, they often have very little pre-school nursery provision (Watkins and Derrick 1979). This can be a direct result of rural isolation, and, although it can be overcome by informal arrangements by parents, it must mean that many rural mothers cannot obtain nursery schooling for their children. Some counties are experimenting with mobile pre-school provision, using, for example, motorized caravans adapted as small classrooms and stores. In other counties some schemes have been started in village halls to provide nursery education for wide areas, although not all children may be able to attend (Association of County Councils 1979).

Rural areas also tend to be deprived of further or higher educational opportunities, particularly in special or technical education. Again in Devon, the Association of County Councils (1979) estimate that a 65-mile round trip would be needed for a resident of Beer or Seaton in east Devon to attend further education at the East Devon College at Tiverton. For adult education, journeys may be just as long. In the South West, Scottish and Welsh regions of the Open University, for example, round-trips of well over 100 miles are commonplace for students attending tutorials for some of the specialist, high-level courses. That students do attend is a measure both of their keenness to learn and of the fact that many residents in peripheral areas accept travel for services as a fact of life.

Because of the distances involved, it is frequently only block-release schemes that can enable young adults in rural areas to continue their training after the age of 16, whereas in urban locations day-release and evening study would be feasible. The provision of residential facilities for block-release courses is yet another burden that many rural authorities are currently unable to shoulder. At the same time, rural small firms often find it unacceptable to lose employees for block periods of time. These factors all reduce training opportunities. When this happens as a matter of course, the rural area as a whole will eventually suffer, since the local labour force will be less well trained, less employable and less mobile.

The picture drawn so far of rural education is somewhat depressing, with villages lacking pre-school provision, losing their primary schools (which may just be boarded-up, unsold) and requiring lengthy journeys of secondary schoolchildren who have little prospect of continuing education after school. Perhaps this is an unfair impression to leave. Many authorities are acutely aware of the problems, and within their spending limits try to maintain rural schools and accept the extra costs involved. Sometimes they can better utilize the time of staff by allowing peripatetic teachers to visit a number of schools. This increases the number of teachers and the range of subjects available at small schools and is a valuable way of enriching the curriculum. Parents can be involved in the work of small primary schools. In extreme cases, qualified teachers have set up their own village schools to replace those closed. Teacher supply is no longer a problem, as there are many well qualified recruits, eager to work in small rural schools.

Perhaps the most dismal aspect of education is the lack of access to specialist training for the rural school-leaver who wishes to continue living locally. The costs of providing such education and the distances involved may often mean that the choice is between leaving the locality, or abandoning the hope of further training. In either event, valuable human resources may be lost to the community.

HEALTH SERVICES AND ACCESS TO HEALTH CARE

Health services in Britain are financed mainly from central government expenditure. Gilder (1979) found that 94 per cent of the costs of community health services in West Suffolk were met from national taxation and less than 1 per cent by user charges. It might be expected, therefore, that these services would be influenced more directly by the policies of central government than local authority-funded social and education services, and that a greater uniformity of service provision would exist across the country. However, this is not necessarily so, and rural areas in particular have problems of distribution and accessibility of health services. A number of aggregate studies into resource allocation have identified some of the more rural regions of England and Wales as having low investment in health services, although certain urban areas also suffer in this respect (Phillips 1981; Whitelegg 1982). An assessment of resource allocation is very complex, since to be realistic it should involve an evaluation of the quality of care, about which it is almost impossible to be accurate. The Royal Commission on the National Health Service (1979) indicated that, even though an area appears to be adequately funded or staffed (and new facilities may therefore not be directed to it), the quality of the existing facilities may vary substantially. Rural locations often appear to be quite adequately staffed purely in terms of ratios of patients to health care professionals. For example, in 1976 East Anglia and the

South West were the regions of England which contained the smallest proportions of general practitioners (GPs) having list sizes of over 2,500 persons (Department of Health and Social Security, annual statistics). Similarly, apart from the South East, dentists in these two regions had the fewest patients on average. Therefore if such ratios have any meaning at all, which has been questioned, some rural areas seem on aggregate to be quite well-off in terms of absolute levels of provision of primary care.

To this may be added the feeling that rural (or non-urban) areas are somehow 'healthier' places. To some extent, this can be illustrated statistically in terms of lower morbidity (illness rates) and mortality (death rates) for some causes, although other ailments appear to be more rural in prevalence (Howe 1970, 1979). This is a notoriously difficult question, for accurate research and data concerning illness reporting and health service utilization rates may be misleading; they can be affected by matters such as distance to facility and social class of patients, as well as by less tangible factors such as attitudes to health and to health services (Phillips 1979, 1981). In addition, ill-health can be as much the result of lack of treatment facilities as of poor environment. Confoundingly, the establishment of new facilities almost inevitably causes an increase in demand as people become aware of their existence, so the problems of analysis can be almost insoluble. There is also the observation, however misplaced, that rural areas may have a greater community feeling, hardiness and resilience, which reduces the need for the entire range of health and general social service provision (Stockford 1978; Association of County Councils 1979). Hence almost any measures of need, resources and utilization can be proposed or rejected on differing criteria.

The scale of analysis is also very important because aggregate data (▪) service levels, which may show some standard region to be well provided with health services, will mean very little to individuals living in a village of that region without a doctor, dentist, chemist or cottage hospital. The problem again becomes one of availability and accessibility of services. These are usually arranged in an hierarchical manner, from primary and community services (general practitioners and dentists, community nurses and midwives), through to secondary facilities such as local and general hospitals. Finally, there are tertiary facilities: general hospitals and specialist institutions that concentrate on research and treatment at a high level or for unusual conditions. There will inevitably be some inequalities in accessibility and availability of secondary and tertiary facilities, major clinic and hospital facilities, especially those that have been designated as 'centres of excellence', because of the discrete location of individual facilities among spatially continuous, if unevenly distributed, populations (Dear 1974; Massam 1980).

A 20-bed cottage hospital. These often provide essential medical services for rural communities (source: authors and A. Teed)

The primary sector of care is growing in importance in the developed world since it is now recognized that many conditions are more efficiently and effectively treated in people's homes. Primary physicians can provide, in or near to the familiar home setting, accessible and continuing medical assistance for the individual and his family, which could be invaluable for rural residents. For many years Britain has been a world leader in primary care, which is provided increasingly by teams of doctors, nurses, midwives and social workers (Marsh and Kaim-Caudle 1976; Phillips 1981). However, this has had at least one locational aspect which some regard as detrimental: with the growth of group practices and larger health centres, even in rural areas, fewer doctors' and dentists' surgeries are available, with the inevitable consequence of longer journeys for some residents.

Such trends can exacerbate rural problems. A nationwide survey of health service provision in rural areas provided evidence, corroborated elsewhere, that the three main causes of problems of access to health care facilities for rural residents were transport difficulties, shortage of medical services, and the centralization of these services (Leschinsky 1977). Of the 226 settlements surveyed with populations of fewer than 500 people, 87 per cent had no doctor's surgery, 99 per cent no chemist and 100 per cent no dentist or optician. In addition, existing facilities in villages are often rudimentary and infrequent, such as a one-hour surgery held in a village hall or private house, or a branch surgery once or twice weekly. Such conditions are not conducive to exercising the best professional investigation or bestowing the best treatment. This contrasts with the dynamic growth of good primary care provision in other areas, and problems are almost certainly exacerbated by low investment per capita for rural areas.

Government policies have had the effect of reducing numbers of outlets for primary care by encouraging the formation of group practices comprising at least three doctors in urban or two in rural areas. The aim is to improve the quality of primary care, which is by far the most important level of care in terms of numbers of doctor–patient contacts. Rural practice allowances are payable to country doctors to offset the extra travelling costs in sparsely populated rural areas, but, as in education, there are problems of access, professional isolation and lack of further training for practitioners. An additional problem in recent years has been the decreasing numbers of retail pharmacists, particularly in small rural settlements (Pharmaceutical Society of Great Britain 1979). To overcome the difficulties of filling prescriptions, some rural GPs can dispense medicines for specified patients, but not all GPs wish to take on this responsibility because it can lead to problems in terms of supply and security of medicines. The problems and challenges offered to a general practitioner in a rural area are interestingly discussed by Berger and Mohr (1967).

Community health councils (CHCs), the patients' representatives in the National Health Service, have become more aware of rural health care problems. CHCs in Yorkshire and Devon have noted problems of prescription-filling and of access to services generally. A major survey of 180 rural parishes by the Exeter and District Community Health Council (1983) indicated typical difficulties: 52 per cent of respondent parishes reported problems or severe problems of access to GPs; 58 per cent experienced difficulties of access to chiropody services; and 35 per cent, problems in filling prescriptions. But the most pervasive problem, reported by over 75 per cent of parishes, was poor public transport to hospital, reflecting the difficulties of access to centralized facilities for many rural residents.

The disappearance of many essential local services from villages can particularly disadvantage the elderly (Standing Conference of Rural Community Councils 1978). Old people living alone make up quite large proportions in some villages, and their medical problems are often exacerbated by personal immobility (Greenberg 1982). Haynes and Bentham (1982) found that there were markedly lower consultation and attendance rates in more remote parishes without a GP surgery than in more accessible villages with a surgery. In addition, GPs in remote rural areas in their Norfolk study were much less likely to refer the elderly, males and those from manual worker households to an outpatient clinic than were GPs in more accessible rural areas. All these data appear to emphasize the importance of accessibility and service availability to utilization.

Distribution of GPs and other primary medical care services is therefore a major problem, closely linked with that of accessibility, which merely increasing numbers of doctors or dentists does not necessarily solve. In the rural areas of Cumbria, although there had been a three fold-increase in the number of GPs between 1949 and 1977, their spatial distribution was little changed and the trend was for concentration into existing sites (Whitelegg 1979). This is not surprising if settlement policy and the vast increase of health centres and group practices are considered (Phillips 1981). Although official policies may not have reduced the total numbers of rural practitioners, concentration of services can have socially detrimental effects, even if the 'quality' of care may increase. At the very least, there will be an increased demand for transport for essential trips to medical facilities, which not everyone will have access to.

Interestingly, Mackay and Laing (1982) did not find a great reduction recently in numbers of doctors in their 26 parishes in remote rural areas of Scotland. They noted the loss since 1960 of only two doctors' practices and one chemist. This was attributed to strenuous efforts by the Highland Health Board to maintain a service even in some very small settlements, especially in view of the increasingly elderly population of these areas. However, there were still respondents in their survey living in villages without a doctor or a dentist, and this comprised the most frequent complaint about health services. It is recognized that one of the deficiencies of dental treatment under the National Health Service is an inability to get treatment at all in some remote areas (Bramley 1980). The Scottish survey certainly indicated that rural areas are below the national average for dental as well as medical provision. This conclusion is supported by findings from a survey of access to health services in the Western Isles of Scotland (Williams *et al.* 1980) They found a shortage of dental, chiropodist and ophthalmic services, leaving little scope for 'preventive' care. Table 8.4 illustrates some of the more extreme problems of rural access to primary health facilities, compared with an urban area in London.

Hospital facilities are becoming increasingly inaccessible for the transport poor (Haynes *et al.* 1978). At one time, it appeared very likely that health service rationalization would concentrate virtually all hospital provision into larger units, which would effectively have eliminated any true rural hospitals. The extent to which this has occurred in Blackburn Health District, surprisingly rural in parts, is illustrated by figure 8.3, which shows most hospital facilities in the major centres, to the detriment of

Table 8.4   Access to health care: comparison of surveys in Hackney, West Cumbria and the Western Isles of Scotland (percentages)

	London (Hackney)		West Cumbria		Western Isles	
	Survey location					

	London (Hackney)	West Cumbria	Western Isles
Distance to GP's surgery			
1 mile	80	43	14*
1–5 miles	20	51	33*
> 5 miles	0	6	53*
Time to reach surgery			
10 minutes	62	41	37
11–30 minutes	26	36	38
31+ minutes	2	2	11
Cannot get to surgery	9	7	14

Other services	Children under 11 years	People over 70 years	Under 11	Over 70	Under 11	Over 70
Dentist visited in last 2 years	74	25	80	12	66	5
Eye test in last 2 years	56	53	70	39	58	57
Chiropody in last 2 years	4	39	4	26	5	23

* Includes 14 per cent who have to make a ferry journey
Source: after Williams *et al.* (1980)

rural residents in areas such as the Ribble Valley. Impressive technical, professional and economic arguments can be used to show that such a policy is correct in terms of efficiency, but during the 1970s the Department of Health and Social Security (DHSS) suggested retaining as community hospitals a number of small hospitals that might otherwise have faced closure. These are reminiscent of the general practitioner 'cottage hospitals', which have been provided in some rural areas since the mid-nineteenth century (While 1978), and many rural districts can now

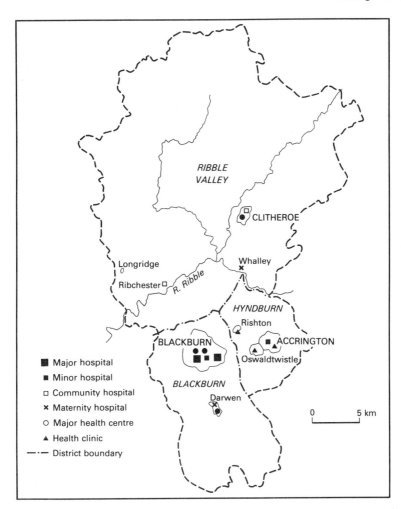

FIGURE 8.3   Major health facilities, Blackburn Health District
Source: Grime and Whitelegg (1982)

retain these as community hospitals for local needs. They will not, of course, provide a full range of diagnostic and treatment facilities, but they can provide very desirable local services for certain types of patients. The DHSS stressed that accessibility and convenience of patients were to be important factors determining where these hospitals should be retained and, funds permitting, any new facilities built. The recommended size for community hospitals was between 50 and 150 beds although many existing hospitals are below this size. It was hoped that the policy would provide flexibility for local needs, and utilize existing trained staff perhaps currently underemployed.

As Haynes and Bentham (1979) found, there can be considerable scope for community hospital development. In King's Lynn Health District, two groups of villages (accessible and more remote) were surveyed, highlighting the major problem in rural health care to be, predictably, access. Although special transport arrangements could be made for occasional visits to distant hospitals, for regular visits, whether for treatment or to see in-patients, community hospitals could be particularly beneficial. The authors considered that the establishment of community hospitals in rural Norfolk (and elsewhere) would decrease the average distances from patients' homes which should increase visiting to long stay patients such as those in pre-convalescence. (It was felt that little could be done to increase the number of visitors to the geriatric or mentally infirm patients who usually receive very few visits.) It was also evident that community hospitals would be welcomed by potential staff and patients and would be less forbidding and more socially and physically accessible.

What solutions are possible for rural communities that are deprived of medical facilities? Many authorities run mobile clinics of various kinds, and Mackay and Laing (1982) report requests for mobile dental clinics in remote parts of Scotland. Elsewhere, teams of professionals might be encouraged to visit certain localities on a regular basis. However, this does not get around the problem that primary care, in particular, needs to be accessible constantly. Since many dentists serve around 4,500–5,000 persons and it is estimated that a similar number is needed to suport a retail pharmacy, these will tend to be located only in larger settlements, so a journey seems to be inevitable for many rural residents. Many GPs run branch surgeries, although the unsatisfactory nature of many premises (such as village halls) discourages some, and their infrequent nature can also cause low usage. In the Western Isles of Scotland, opticians visit from the mainland occasionally and hold testing sessions in hotels and church halls (Williams *et al.* 1980) These and similar measures indicate that some strategies are being tried for improving health care in more remote locations.

Cottage community hospitals hold one avenue of hope for rural areas in providing medical facilities. In addition, various schemes have been tried to increase accessibility to clinics and hospitals for the less mobile. Community car and hospital car schemes have been supported by voluntary organizations and by local and central government funds, and a variety of ways of enabling rural residents to obtain prescribed medicines have developed, including deliveries by chemists and by other mobile services. However, many ventures are by nature *ad hoc* and are not always reliable or satisfactory.

Health services planners have an extremely important role to play in redressing local imbalances. At present, national planning is relatively well developed while local planning has been rather neglected because in many places, especially rural areas, problems often are quite specific to local areas so that blanket solutions are not always appropriate (Phillips 1981; Grime and Whitelegg 1982). In recognition of this, Exeter Health Care District is developing 'locality planning', in which local meetings are arranged to enable 'grass-roots' health and social services professionals to establish the nature of the problems in specific localities (Phillips and Court 1982). As mentioned earlier, community health councils can participate or assist by highlighting local shortcomings in medical care.

In addition, perhaps some fundamental changes are needed in financing. If it is recognized that a 'Rural Practices Fund' is essential to defray the higher travelling costs of rural doctors (Moseley 1979a), then perhaps some relaxation of the list size criterion for establishing new practices should be considered. Currently, areas with fewer than 1,800 patients per GP are 'closed' to new entrants. Many rural doctors have just such small numbers of patients but spread over vast distances, and it seems sensible for additional funding to be made available for the employment of more GPs in certain rural areas. It should be recognized, however, that some rural GPs attending very small numbers of patients could become under-utilized. This has been suggested in some remote Scottish areas where a number of practices of fewer than 1,000 (or even 500) patients were noted (Mackay and Laing 1982).

Perhaps in the long run, locality planning, imaginative solutions to transport problems and extra funding may solve the main rural health care problems. The picture is not very bright, however, in the light of financial stringencies in the early 1980s and in view of some proposals for 'privatization' of the British health service. Rural areas would be the least profitable for private medicine, and as a result they could be severely disadvantaged under a private health service, with serious social and medical implications.

SOCIAL AND WELFARE SERVICES

Social services departments and some voluntary agencies provide a variety of services ranging from children's homes, domiciliary and day care places for disabled and elderly persons to home helps, meals-on-wheels and several types of residential care for many client groups. While it is possible that some inhibitions do exist in rural areas about receiving statutory 'welfare' benefits, precise evidence is hard to find. Severe social problems certainly do exist rurally, yet the demand for social services seems to be substantially lower than in urban areas. This can lead to the erroneous conclusion that the need also is low (Association of Community Councils 1979).

Once again, physical accessibility to these services is identified as a major cause of low use. A particularly discouraging fact for preventive work is that over 15 per cent of the rural population live more than ten miles from an area social services office. However, low rates of spending on these services must also, at least in part, be blamed for low usage. Particularly notorious is the variation among local authorities in their provision of social services for the elderly. Bebbington and Davies (1982), for example, estimated that the rural localities of Devon and the Isle of Wight in 1977–78 spent less than £25 for each person aged over 65, compared with £137 in the London Boroughs of Camden and Islington.

Part of the reason for these differences in provision among authorities is that there is generally scope for interpretation of what is required, even under statutory duties. This contrasts with education, where duties are quite specific under the 1944 Act. That there are still differences among authorities in school provision implies that the picture will be even more diverse in social services provision. Many local authorities can decide 'in the light of local circumstances' what they wish to provide. Therefore comparisons are often made among services that, although nominally the same, are fulfilling different functions or intensities of work.

Many social services requiring large catchment populations will be sited only in larger centres and may therefore effectively not exist for many home-bound or village-bound rural residents. In addition, the running costs of services in rural areas may be higher than in urban areas, which means that any funds allocated will give less provision. For example, the Association of County Councils (1979) suggest that the limited opportunities for economies of scale in production and transport costs involved in delivery means that meals-on-wheels served in rural areas can cost 10 to 15 per cent more than those in towns, while the unit costs of social workers travelling to visit clients means that expenditure can be as much as 27 per cent higher in rural than in urban areas. Clearly, paying such costs out of limited budgets will mean that services will be very restricted in some rural areas. The fact that the budgets of many rural districts are smaller than those of many urban areas seems incontrovertible. The much-cited 'inverse care law', in which those in greatest need of care actually receive the least, may act physically in terms of resource provision and distance, and in terms of social access (Hart 1971; Phillips 1979). When expenditure itself is used as an indicator, however crude, then rural counties tended to be much less well provided than urban county boroughs.

Both Stockford (1978) and Bebbington and Davies (1982) indicate differences among authorities. Table 8.5 illustrates that 'rural' areas contrast with county boroughs, while table 8.6 highlights some variations among specific counties in expenditure for the elderly on residential care and meals-on-wheels. Rural counties such as Somerset, Cornwall and Devon come near the bottom of the list of these admittedly selective indicators for expenditure and provision. In the full tabulation prepared by Bebbington and Davies (1982), rural authorities are low providers of social services for the elderly with very few exceptions, which is indicative of their activities across the range of social services.

A consistent rural shortfall therefore appears on these per capita expenditure and provision figures. Admittedly, urban services are sometimes more costly to provide, even if the extra rural transport costs are taken into account, since premises, services, rates and wages will generally be more expensive in urban locations. However, the ostensiblty better resource allocation to social services in urban areas can be explained partly by the higher levels of expressed demand and political pressure evidenced in them. The myth of idyllic rural conditions and the rather mistaken belief that rural areas do not want government social aid all tend to reduce provision, with the result that people become resigned to lower standards.

Community and welfare rights information

People today need to have access to a range of information on economic,

Table 8.5   Expenditure on selected social services 1973–74

	Total expenditure	Residential child care	Residential elderly care	Home helps	Day nurseries
Rural (counties)	6,385	2,984	11,075	892	1,219
Urban (c. boroughs)	9,792	6,888	14,814	1,101	4,026
Percentage shortfall in rural areas	35	57	26	20	70

All expenditure is measured in £ per 1,000 population: residential child care is per 1,000 under 18; residential elderly care and home helps are per 1,000 over 65; day nurseries are per 1,000 under 5
Source: after Stockford (1978)

Table 8.6   Levels of provision and current expenditure on services for the elderly,
1977–78

Local authority	Residential care[a]	Meals-on-wheels[b]	Expenditure on elderly[c]
Camden	370	97	137
Islington	354	115	137
Southwark	291	107	97
Hounslow	176	73	53
Cumbria	182	30	40
Newcastle	227	54	77
Manchester	285	130	82
Salford	217	37	62
Liverpool	253	65	55
Coventry	160	57	55
Nottinghamshire	144	60	47
Berkshire	147	49	41
Dorset	145	23	30
Isle of Wight	142	13	20
West Sussex	164	38	28
Wiltshire	154	26	30
Cornwall	148	17	27
Devon	148	24	24
Gloucester	161	25	35
Somerset	149	26	29

[a]   Supported residents per 10,000 persons aged 65+
[b]   Meals delivered per 100 persons aged 65+
[c]   £ per person aged 65+
Source: after Bebbington and Davies (1982)

social and consumer matters. This has been increasingly recognized by the creation of bodies such as the Consumer Council and Scottish Consumer Council, citizens' advice bureaus and community councils. Even if rural residents on the whole may be grateful to be spared a barrage of spurious information, there are times when knowledge about entitlement to benefits or about new services may be very relevant to them. In an increasingly complex and competitive world, advice on welfare benefits, education, career opportunities and job vacancies are all increasingly important.

A considerable amount of information is available in printed form in libraries, schools, offices of various bodies and information centres, but physical and social distance can render much of this inaccessible to rural residents. A pilot survey of the information needs of some 500 individuals in six parishes in rural Lincolnshire revealed that almost 30 per cent of the information that was required concerned either rent and rates or transport matters. Planning, jobs, entertainment, social security and legal matters were the other leading categories for which information had been sought, each forming about 9 per cent of total requests (Clark and Unwin 1979). Unfortunately, specialist advice on most of these matters is rarely readily available in villages too small to support sub-offices of the relevant agencies.

A number of strategies have been examined to overcome this problem but none is entirely satisfactory. Non-personal contact via the telephone, the mass media and specialist media such as Freepost and PRESTEL can be available to those able to afford the facilities, some of which were referred to in chapter 4 as 'information technology'. Peripatetic mobile information services have an important role to play in disseminating information, particularly to rural gatherings at events such as fêtes and game fairs. Recreational information can be provided at tourist information centres and libraries; post offices, doctors' surgeries, chemists and other local services can provide display areas for poster and leaflet information. All these are essential for advertising available services, because only rarely will a fixed office be near enough for personal attendance in small- or even medium-sized villages. However, all such information channels are rather hit-or-miss, and there is an element of luck as to what is available at any particular place at any given time.

Rural inhabitants should be able readily to obtain reliable information from citizens' advice bureaus and organizations such as the National Council for Voluntary Organizations (formerly National Association of Social Service). Financial limitations will probably inhibit much expansion of these information services in the near future, but perhaps sub-post offices could become better used as official bases or distribution points. Post offices already provide a range of official information, but unfortunately even this is frequently inadequate or even out-of-date. Clark and Unwin (1979) report a survey of DHSS literature in village post offices in north-east Suffolk in which only 41 per cent of post offices were found to have the up-to-date leaflets requested, 33 per cent had out-of-date leaflets and 26 per cent had none available. At present, therefore, the post office does not seem to be a very efficient source of welfare information, and as this is now a detailed and complex subject, it cannot really be left to 'well-meaning amateurs' (Brogden 1978). Until adequate information on a wide range of topics is available to all rural residents, an improved knowledge of opportunities and prospects cannot be expected, and therefore the ability of people in rural areas to improve their lives will inevitably be impaired.

9 Recreation and Leisure

Rural areas are popular locations for a wide range of leisure and recreational activities, formal and informal, for people from all over the country. They are also, however, the homes of many people, and for them the opportunities for leisure activities may be surprisingly limited. This may be because of poor provision of facilities or because of social and economic disadvantage.

Demand for recreation can be appraised in a number of ways. In simple terms, it involves the number of people wanting to take part in a recreational activity. By this definition it is possible to envisage demand not as fixed or absolute but as variable, in that it may include people actually taking part in activities (effective demand), those who would and could participate but do not, either through lack of knowledge or lack of facilities (deferred demand), and those who cannot participate at present, for social or economic reasons, but might do so in the future (potential demand) (Lavery 1974). In many rural communities therefore much potential demand for recreation and leisure activities may exist that is currently frustrated by poor provision and accessibility problems.

Tourist trips have been defined as stays of one or more nights away from home for holidays, visits to friends or relations, business conferences and any purposes except such as boarding education or semi-permanent employment (English Tourist Board 1982). Recreation, unlike tourism, does not necessarily involve a stay away from home. It can involve any leisure activities (or 'inactivities', for relaxation) that may be carried out within or outside the home or while away on a 'tourist' holiday.

TRENDS

The popularity of countryside recreation is undoubted. It was found to be

Table 9.1　The relative popularity of countryside recreation

Activity	Percentages engaging in each activity during previous four weeks	
	OPCS[a]	CC[b]
Countryside trips, activities	46	54
Visits to seaside	18	17
Walking (two miles or more)	22	21
Visiting zoos/safari parks	4	5
Gardening	59	63
Do-it-yourself	40	34
Fishing	4	4
Horse riding/pony trekking	1	1
Sample size	4,531	5,150

[a] Office of Population Censuses and Surveys (1979)
[b] Countryside Commission (1979)
Sources: after Gilg (1980)

second only to gardening as the most popular form of outdoor recreation in two important surveys in the late 1970s (table 9.1), in both of which some 50 per cent of respondents had undertaken a countryside activity or trip during the previous month (Countryside Commission 1979; Office of Population Censuses and Surveys 1979). When the previous 12 months are considered, it becomes the most popular activity (figure 9.1), with over three-quarters of the population of Britain – some 37million people – having had a 'countryside day out' at least once in that period (Countryside Commission 1979). In addition, the 'leisure industry', associated in part with countryside recreation, has been one of the few growth sectors of the British economy in recent decades.

Demand for recreation of many kinds has been growing steadily in Britain (Bracey 1970; Patmore 1970; Coppock 1980; Blacksell 1983). This has continued into the 1980s, although a growing minority of families with unemployed breadwinners are losing their ability to enjoy increased leisure from lack of money. Nevertheless, in these times of international economic recession, demand for leisure activities is probably stronger than ever. Tourism (involving stays away from home for holidays) also witnessed a constant upward trend during the early 1970s until the energy crisis and resultant increased travel costs initiated a slight decline in 1974. Since then, there has been steady recovery and growth of inland tourism, the

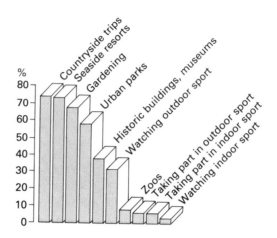

FIGURE 9.1   Relative popularity of countryside recreation over the year
Source: after the Countryside Commission (1979)

general trends being illustrated by figure 9.2 (Countryside Commission 1980). However, in 1981 there was a decrease of 2 per cent in inland tourism in Britain, probably because of the economic recession (English Tourist Board 1982). With the exception of the early 1980s, therefore, the scene is one of growth and expansion in leisure and holiday-making.

Although tourism and recreation are analytically distinct, the same underlying social trends account, in combination, for their growth. Throughout the 1970s over 80 per cent of Britain's employed population worked only a five-day week (Blacksell 1983). There is also a generally increasing holiday entitlement. In 1968, for example, no manual worker had an entitlement of four weeks' paid holiday; by 1978 over one-third had that much or even more. Paid holidays have now become more of a right rather than a privilege, and in the 1980s they will probably be more important than ever. Greater personal mobility and increased spending power (which may be reduced in the current recession) are two other important social trends influencing demand.

Surprisingly, increased demand for recreation and tourism has not been caused significantly by population growth, since this was low during the 1970s and the 34–44 age group (very active in countryside recreation) even decreased slightly in this decade. However, early retirement with good pensions and an increasing number of mobile and active elderly persons have been very important factors increasing demand both for

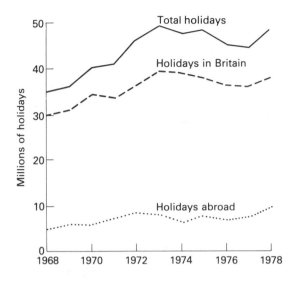

FIGURE 9.2   Trends in the number of holidays taken in Britain and abroad, 1968–78
Source: Countryside Commission (1980), after British National Travel Survey, 1979

From paper-mill to luxury holiday homes. Is the loss of jobs offset by the tourist receipts? Luxury development can be disruptive in an isolated community (source: authors)

Tourist honey-pot on Dartmoor. Social selection can occur at such places because only people with cars can reach them (source: authors and A. Teed)

tourism and for locally based recreation.

Who is most likely to participate in outdoor recreation? No socio-economic or age group has a monopoly on it, but its frequency certainly increases with income and car ownership (themselves highly intercorrel-ated) and is affected by age and family responsibilities. Almost two-thirds of people owning or having the use of a car visit the countryside, while fewer than one-third of those without cars do so. Figure 9.3 illustrates that families with children under 16 years of age use the countryside more than those with older children and older people with no children, even though these still make considerable use of it (Countryside Commission 1979). The picture generally accepted is of an active leisure-seeking population, a greater proportion of whom have increasing affluence and more time to devote to recreational activities. The following section considers where the participants in recreation and tourism originate from and where they visit.

Origins and destinations

The regional distribution of tourism is of some interest since it shows the

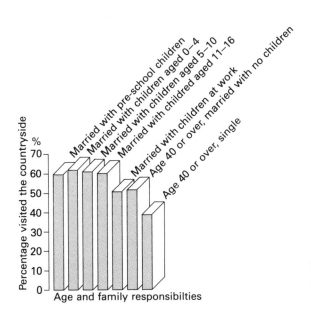

FIGURE 9.3   Age and family responsibilities of participants in countryside recreation
Source: after the Countryside Commission (1979)

marked attraction of many rural areas, particularly the West Country, south of England, East Anglia and Wales (figure 9.4). These tend to be the regions with greatest perceived attractiveness particularly in their coastal districts, although inland points of interest also seem to form foci for visitors. The data shown in the map are supported by more recent statistics, as the South West was the region in which 20 per cent of all holiday-makers spent at least one night of their holiday in 1981. Other popular regions in 1981 were the South (11 per cent), South East (9 per cent) and East Anglia and Yorkshire–Humberside, with 8 per cent each (British Tourist Authority 1982).

It is interesting to note the origins as well as the destinations of tourists and those pursuing local leisure activities. Many reports published in the 1970s, both general surveys and site-specific studies, included information on this theme. The degree of detail collected has varied considerably, as has the scale of analysis. Review publications, such as those by the English Tourist Board, have usually used broad regional scale analyses, while local studies have cited the towns of origin of visitors. Research in the Forest of Dean, for example, indicated that the majority of people visiting the area

FIGURE 9.4 Regions stayed in on British holidays, 1978. Numbers refer to percentages of holidays in which one or more nights were spent in that particular region.
Source: after the Countryside Commission (1980)

(77 per cent of a sample of about 1,000) were day-trippers. Although many of these came from within a 25-mile radius of a point designated within the Forest, about one-sixth had travelled over 40 miles and some had come from as far afield as Birmingham, some 70 miles away (Colenutt and Sidaway 1973). Whether the proportion of long-distance visitors has been reduced by increased petrols costs since 1973 is hard to say, although later surveys suggest there has been some reduction.

A survey in 1973 of less accessible sites in North Wales found that between 25 and 75 per cent of visitors to local attractions were tourists staying locally. However, in the better-known and more accessible sites, far fewer were locally based and more were on day-trips from the West Midlands (Jacobs 1976). Within the South West of England, over 40 per cent of tourists (as opposed to day-trippers) were from the South East of England and 15 per cent were from the West Midlands (table 9.2). Devon was the most popular 'target' county, with over 3¼ million tourists (40 per cent of the South West's total) in 1973. Cornwall received a further 30 per cent of the total (South West Economic Planning Council 1976). Recent figures confirm the popularity of the South West as a destination for visitors. The area accounts for 12 per cent of all nights spent away from home in 1981, or over 16 per cent if trips abroad are excluded. The South East of England was the origin of almost one-third of all holiday trips in Britain in 1981, and the East and West Midlands taken together were the next most important source regions with 21 per cent of the total (English Tourist Board 1982).

OPPORTUNITIES FOR RURAL RESIDENTS

Nationally Britain has a hierarchy of facilities for sport and recreation and for the arts, ranging from small multi-purpose halls with simple equipment to specialist centres with excellent facilities and spectator areas. However, the rural resident is likely to find that only the larger market towns or country seats can satisfy the sports requirements of the specialist or expert (Ventris 1979). Although the sports centre is now a commonplace feature in many small and medium-sized towns, villages rarely possess the resources to provide such facilities either publicly or privately. This effectively limits the type of leisure activities and standard of achievement open to many village residents.

Although rural areas are often the foci for visits, their permanent residents can fare relatively poorly in terms of recreation. When Family Expenditure Survey data are analysed, some predominantly rural areas such as East Anglia and Northern Ireland seem to have the lowest levels of expenditure per household on leisure, perhaps as a result of remoteness

Table 9.2 Tourists to the South West of England, by region of origin, 1973

| Region of origin | SWEPC surveys | | ETB survey[a] |
	Thousands	%	%
Scotland	140	2	1
Northern	220	3	2
Yorks/Humberside	440	5	5
North West	720	9	9
East Midlands	430	5	4
West Midlands	1,220	15	15
East Anglia	210	3	1
South East	3,260	40	44
Wales	280	3	4
South West	1,030	13	15
Overseas	170	2	–
Total	8,120	100	100

[a] Based on English Tourist Board surveys of West Country Tourist Board area
Source: after South West Economic Planning Council (1976)

and low overall levels of provision (Blacksell 1983). One particular problem is that different levels of local government can be responsible for the welfare and development of various recreation facilities. Public parks providing sports such as tennis or bowls can be the district's concern, while purpose-built centres will usually be the responsibility of the county. Therefore the vigour and involvement of the local authority with recreation can be all-important, and, unfortunately, the administrative structure for supporting recreation seems to be weakest in the more remote rural areas of East Anglia, Dyfed, Powys, Clwyd and the High-lands of Scotland. There are exceptions, such as Cornwall, Cumbria and West Sussex, although in these counties it could be tourism rather than locally based recreation that receives the most administrative attention. It seems that the initiative for integrated leisure provision throughout the 1970s remained with the cities, with the almost inevitable consequence that rural residents have a smaller range and poorer quality of formal recreation facilities than urban residents.

As in many other spheres of rural life, the problem is often one of access to facilities, particularly for those without personal transport. A study of sports provision in Norfolk suggested that, although per capita provision for villagers was actually at a reasonable level, access to major sports and spectator facilities was poor, particularly for the casual, short-term user.

The size of settlement was found to have a strong influence on the number and type of facilities, and there was a hierarchy of provision that seemed to follow, roughly, the costs of provision (table 9.3). In numerical terms, since the majority of inhabitants tend to be located in the larger settlements, the actual proportion of the population that is very distant from facilities can be relatively low, but for them it is a great disadvantage. In Norfolk, one-third or fewer of households were more than 10 km from an indoor public swimming pool, a cinema and a squash court, but this is still clearly a long distance to travel for 'casual' leisure activities (Ventris 1979).

Perhaps it is a combination of poor access to impulse leisure activities and a preference for informal recreation that explains the relatively low rates of external activities and a predominance of home-based leisure activities found in a study of six mid-Norfolk villages. Ninety per cent of respondents spent three or more evenings at home per week and 51 per cent were home for six or seven evenings. Television watching occupied some two-thirds of respondents as an evening pastime, even at the weekend. Afternoon activities were dominated by gardening. Although there were pursuits enjoyed away from home, participation tended to decline with family commitments. In the age-group 17–24, 37 per cent participated in non-home-based activities and in the age-group 25–29 34 per cent participated, while between the ages of 30 and 34 this fell to 31 per cent. There was a slight 'revival' among retired couples, presumably having fewer home ties (32 per cent). For almost all external pursuits, visits to friends dominated, while visiting pubs was the next most frequent activity, especially among younger age-groups (Hill 1978).

More importantly, perhaps, 44 per cent of the total sample of 300 persons indicated that they had experienced some degree of frustration in

Table 9.3   Hierarchy of rural recreation facilities in Norfolk

Facility	Population of smallest settlement possessing facility
Playing field	140
Community or village hall	130
Badminton court	1,140
Indoor pool	10,800
Squash court	14,800
Cinema	18,900
Theatre	120,000

Source: after Ventris (1979)

following leisure pursuits. Complaints were highest in the 25–29 age group and lowest among the retired. Outdoor sporting activities were placed first among 'frustrated' pursuits by all except the oldest age-groups, who tended to desire more social outings or formal entertainment. Elsewhere, in their consumer survey of 26 remote Scottish parishes, Mackay and Laing (1982) found similar results. Overall, 40 per cent of their respondents expressed some measure of dissatisfaction with sports facilities, and, although there was not great variation across age groups, the dissatisfied proportion was highest among the under-25s, at 51 per cent. The 26 parishes were on average some 35 per cent below the norm for a composite leisure and recreation index calculated for the Scottish districts although the range from well provided to poorly provided parishes was greater than for other services. Top of the list of consumers' complaints in this survey were, predictably, lack of facilities or unsuitable facilities. Interestingly, some parishes that had poor facilities but seemed to possess a strong 'community spirit' were active in using the facilities they did have, while others, with better facilities, were not so active. This was especially noticeable in raising teams for playing local inter-parish games such as football. The influence of the church was felt by some to be restrictive towards sport, leisure and recreation, especially in some of the Western Isles parishes. Among the survey's main recommendations were that schools and community centres should be designed to allow access for recreation and that commercial sponsorship for providing leisure facilities should be more actively sought.

Further recent evidence has been given, again in six mid-Norfolk villages, on social aspects of leisure for country residents (Hill 1982). In particular, the leisure activities of newcomers to the villages sometimes seemed to differ from those of older longer term residents. Newcomers appeared to have to make some adaptations to their previous activities, although these might have been related as much to life-cycle changes as to residential relocation in a rural environment. Most newcomers had taken up pursuits different from those they previously enjoyed, such as walking and gardening, while others had engaged in the sometimes limited local social activities. However, many still seemed to want access to indoor sports activities, and often were willing to travel to reach them. This is in contrast to the wishes of longer term residents, who would have preferred to pursue somewhat 'lower-status' outdoor sport or social outings (table 9.4). Over one-fifth of newcomers indicated that they now undertook fewer part-time pursuits, particularly of the evening class, theatre or cinema variety, presumably mainly as a result of limited local facilities.

Hill (1982) therefore found varying degrees of frustration of leisure requirements. Newcomers more frequently looked beyond their immedi-

Table 9.4   Types of 'frustrated' leisure activities among newcomers and long-term residents in six mid-Norfolk villages

Types of activities	Percentage wanting to take part	
	Newcomers	Long-term residents
Outdoor sport	33.7	51.6
Social outings (incl. popular entertainment)	18.6	22.6
Indoor sport	18.6	6.4
Cultural/educational	15.1	8.1
Indoor general	5.8	8.1
Outdoor general	8.2	3.2
Total	100.0	100.0
No. of activities	86	62

Source: after Hill (1982)

ate village for activities than did long-term residents. The latter were more likely to meet with friends in pubs or social clubs than were newcomers, to whom family life seemed more important, perhaps because of their younger average age. Newcomers also often seemed to attempt to maintain links with friends or activities outside the villages, sometimes in their previous areas of residence. Nearly 60 per cent of recent arrivals mentioned some degree of frustration in attempting to follow certain away-from-home activities of a more specialist type, notably sports and cultural–educational activities. This was much higher than for long-term residents (33 per cent) and perhaps suggests an initial disappointment with local facilities which longer-term residents had come to accept – or perhaps those most dissatisfied had moved away.

These aspects of leisure and recreation for rural residents form an important area of further research. More needs to be known about the expectations of community life that people of different social groups may possess before moving into villages. Will the relatively fewer opportunities for formal or specialist pursuits lead to frustration or resentment, and will this lead to deterioration of relations between new arrivals and established residents? This is very much related to more general social and economic change in the village. In Norfolk, the newcomers were generally younger, better educated and presumably more well-to-do than the longer-term residents. Would their leisure and recreational activities, which tend to be focused at least partly outside the local community or otherwise on their families, lead to a gradual erosion of more traditional village activities or at least to a decreasing rate of participation in such activities? This seems to be an area of potential conflict between newcomers and longer-term residents that might be overcome only by careful recreational planning and an expansion of appropriate village leisure provision, although what is 'appropriate' is very debatable.

In spite of a variety of research and published material on these aspects of recreation and its management, there is a surprising paucity of detailed information concerning the leisure pursuits of rural residents. This is worrying, since the poor levels of formal facilities available to them may be a further manifestation of rural deprivation (Walker 1978b).

THE IMPORTANCE OF TOURISM AND RECREATION IN RURAL AREAS

Some authors, such as Clawson and Knetsch (1966), stress the importance that tourism can have in maintaining the economy of more remote rural areas; other writers are more cautious in assessing financial benefits. In any case, it seems that many of the poorer rural areas of Britain are not fully exploiting their tourist potential (Burton 1967).

Tourist expenditure is notoriously difficult to estimate, but in 1980 the value of tourist spending to the national economy (mainly by overseas visitors) put it well within Britain's top ten leading exports (British Tourist Authority 1982). Bodies and agencies such as the tourist boards can help to attract visitors to the more remote areas, but, as observed in the following chapter, their advertising campaigns can sometimes have adverse social effects by perpetuating or even creating feelings of remoteness, isolation and backwardness for residents of these regions. Financially, there is little doubt that visitors are extremely valuable to many rural areas (and especially to 'rural' coastal settlements), even if the exact contribution is hard to establish. This is illustrated by the dismay shown in 'bad' tourist years. In addition, it is difficult to judge whether the seasonal influx of tourists to smaller settlements, causing congestion, placing strain on services and increasing accommodation prices, has socially damaging effects. It may be felt that the 'demonstration effect' to local youngsters may increase out-migration but, in an age of mass media coverage, a vivid picture of the outside world can be conveyed in any event. The seasonal employment that tourism brings can be valuable; equally, it can lead to unemployment in winter months and lower average annual wages.

The considerable growth in self-catering and caravan holidays since the early 1970s can be regarded as part of the desire for flexible leisure, in which Dower *et al.* (1981) see people as 'their own providers'. Such holidays are especially attractive for families with children. They are undoubtedly cheaper than the conventional hotel or guest house holiday, and as a result, it may be argued that they contribute less to the local economy. However, they can support the economy of the areas in which they are located if the holiday-makers purchase food and other items locally rather than bringing all their requirements from home.

Similarly, second home owners can bring in considerable amounts of money to localities if they purchase their goods and services locally. In a study in rural Wales, 64 per cent were found to buy their main supplies in local shops (Thomas 1977). They will undoubtedly contribute to the local rate base and this may help to maintain the viability of services in areas of rural depopulation. The arguments in favour of and against second homes were mentioned in chapter 5 and need not be repeated here. Suffice it to say that Thomas (1977) suggests that the benefits of second homes to rural areas tend to be measurable mainly in economic terms while the disadvantages, being largely social, are not easily quantified. The complaints that second home owners do not integrate into local societies or institutions, that they may not fit linguistically into the local culture (in Wales for example) and that they create winter 'ghost' villages are very difficult to validate or disprove. However, it is now quite clear that the second home is a well established recreational feature of many rural areas.

Tourism can bring outsiders into rural localities but, as we have stressed, there are also permanent residents living in what some may regard as holiday areas. Many more rural parts are not holiday venues at all but are the everyday working environments for their local residents. In small or isolated settlements the opportunities for cultural activities or entertainment may be very restricted. Positive social planning for recreation and tourism should ensure that, while conserving the countryside for mass enjoyment, the legitimate requirements of these permanent residents are not prejudiced or forgotten. Unfortunately, the worthy intentions of much conservation and planning activity seem to have resulted only in a constraint or sterilization of the opportunities available in some areas, either by restrictive zoning or by increased overall costs. And in spite of these restrictions, Green (1981) suggests that the battle to protect the countryside of Britain is being lost. It is only to be hoped that, as the 'battle' progresses, the needs and requirements of rural residents will be appreciated and that a form of rural deprivation – the lack of recreation and leisure facility provision – will be rectified. If this is achieved, it might even assist the conservation movement in focusing the disparate energies of leisure seekers into more formalized pursuits, and countryside management may be enhanced.

10 Deprivation

NEED AND DEPRIVATION

This chapter considers the proposition that deprivation in rural areas results from an inequality in access to, and availability of, jobs, services and opportunities. The issue is complex, not least because there is no single accepted and unequivocal definition of the term 'deprivation', so that any measures will be relative and based on value judgements. This is almost unavoidable since measures and definitions of deprivation are certain to be couched in terms of personal experience and aspirations although these are notoriously unreliable and non-objective in this matter.

Let us assume that deprivation, as a concept, relates not to the presence or absence of any single characteristic (although this in itself can be distressing) but to a generally poor 'range of life opportunities'. Just what these are, or should be, involves making a number of explicit and implicit value judgements, for not everyone's idea of what should be on a list of 'life needs and opportunities' would be the same, although there is usually a common core of items.

Related to the idea of a range of life opportunities is that of 'social well-being', which Coates *et al.* (1977) use as a generic term for a family of overlapping concepts including level of living, quality of life, social satisfaction, social welfare and standard of living. Various components contribute to these concepts and the potential list is almost infinite, although it is possible to identify the most obvious:

I (UN Research Institute for Social Development 1966)
1 Nutrition
2 Shelter
3 Health
4 Education
5 Leisure

6 Security
7 Social stability
8 Physical environment
9 Surplus income

II (Smith 1973)
1 Income, wealth and employment
2 The living environment
3 Health
4 Education
5 Social order
6 Social belonging
7 Recreation and leisure

III (OECD 1976)
1 Health
2 Individual development through learning
3 Employment and the quality of life
4 Time and leisure
5 Personal economic situation
6 Physical environment
7 The social environment
8 Personal safety and the administration of justice
9 Social opportunity and participation
10 Accessibility

Research into the 'distribution' of well-being, which underlies social justice and territorial justice, has broadly been termed the 'welfare approach' in human geography. Put simply, this approach is about 'who gets what, where and how' (Smith 1974, 1977, 1979b). It is useful here to distinguish between economic welfare and social welfare; the former usually refers to what people get for the money they spend on goods and services, while the latter embraces all things contributing to the quality of life in general (Smith 1973; Coates *et al.*1977). Therefore, deprivation could relate to an absence, or in a rural context unavailability because of distance, of goods and services, but it can also relate to a 'lack' of well-being. This could be caused by an uneven distribution or unavailability of 'impure' public goods such as health care, education and welfare services, but also by the lack of choice, say, for rural dwellers to obtain good housing at a fair price, to enjoy cultural and recreational activities and to have access to the range of jobs, services and information available to urban residents.

Deprivation can be said to exist when needs that society or individuals feel should be satisfied are not met. Various types of need can be identified (Bradshaw 1972); *normative needs* are defined by professional administrators or social scientists; *felt needs* are more akin to personal 'wants'; *expressed needs* are more akin to demands (felt needs expressed as actions); while *comparative needs* involve a more academic approach to measuring the characteristics of those requiring or receiving a specific service or group of services. As Shaw (1979b) writes, it is clear that deprivation is closely connected with ideas of equality and inequality in relation to need. However, a list of those in need or deprived will be very much influenced by the way in which need has been defined. This can be further complicated since, in some instances, notions of equity rather than equality may be invoked, demanding recourse to 'natural justice': i.e. that some people or places be allocated more than their proportional share of resources because their need is greater. Indeed, many attempts in the Western world to alleviate need have been based on these concepts of unequal but 'fair' resource allocation.

Deprivation can be measured purely in terms of the lack of specific services or facilities, such as proportions of households living in over-crowded conditions, lacking household amenities, or lacking education. More popular in the 1970s was the specification of areas of multiple deprivation, those suffering deprivation on a number of indices (Brooks 1975). Rural geography has been particularly interested in researching quantitative model-building and behaviouralism, that is the in-depth study of individuals' attitudes and behaviour. Such studies have as their focus the manifestations and victims of deprivation, rather than a study of managerialism or political economy (Moseley 1980a; Knox and Cottam 1981a, 1981b). Whatever the focus, however, we still have to specify the nature and locales of deprivation, particularly since research into this topic is relatively new in rural areas, and to explain social aspects of deprivation and suggest causes (and remedies) for it.

There are a number of general theories of poverty and deprivation that place greater or lesser responsibility on the individual, social group, residential area, allocative system or social formation (Herbert and Thomas 1982). Deprivation can be viewed as part of a vicious cycle or circle and its components (poverty of education, housing, opportunity, health, physical possessions, income and the like) can be identified even if not precisely quantified. They form the individual pieces of what Cloke (1980c) calls the 'rural deprivation jigsaw'. The 'culture of poverty' theory (Lewis 1966) suggests that the lack of aspiration among the poor results from their marginal position in society, which in turn contributes to deprivation on specific items or components of the jigsaw. However, inefficient bureaucracies and an uneven distribution of resources can be perpetuated by managerial elitism and low welfare inputs. At the higher level of analysis, deprivation can stem from structural class conflict, resulting from an unequal distribution of power and a maintenance of disparities and class distinctions (Herbert and Thomas 1982), which in turns leads to an inequality of ability, means and opportunity.

It has been somewhat difficult to initiate research into rural deprivation, since its existence was for long not generally recognized or admitted. Until the 1970s in Britain, there was a tendency to imagine that rural areas were pleasant, attractive and untroubled; 'a rigorous assessment of the social well-being of rural Britain has been bedevilled by the romanticism which tends to be associated with descriptions of the English countryside. . .' (Shaw 1979a, p. 1). This 'traditional' view of rural society prevailed well into the post-war period so that the majority of references to the needs and requirements of rural communities and to the nature and causes of rural social problems are from the late 1970s.

COMPONENTS OF RURAL DEPRIVATION

For purely practical purposes, rural deprivation can be envisaged as comprising three components: household deprivation, opportunity deprivation and mobility deprivation (Association of County Councils 1979). As will be discussed later, these components sometimes afflict individuals and localities in combination, so that it is hard to isolate their specific effects.

Household deprivation

The personal characteristics and attributes of country dwellers that affect the extent to which they may be able to take advantage of any available facilities or services may be called 'household factors'. One of the major constraints on a person's ability to enjoy a reasonable standard of living is income and, as seen in chapters 2 and 3, there often tends to be a large proportion of low-income groups in many rural areas such as agricultural workers, pensioners, the unemployed and the economically inactive, including those families in which, because of location, only one member is able to obtain work. Low income is often associated with other types of household deprivation, such as inadequate housing (owing to substandard infrastructure, lack of basic amenities or inappropriate space provision), poor standard of household goods and inadequate food supply. The plight of rural low-income families is exacerbated by the fact that prices in village shops are often higher than elsewhere, making a small income worth even less to the household.

Opportunity deprivation

Perhaps the most obvious form of rural deprivation is simply a lack of the basic opportunities available to residents in the rest of Britain – education, health and social services, employment, shops and information. Not only do many of these provide essential services, but the quality and choice add immeasurably to the overall quality of life in any given areas.

It has already been shown that, in spite of policies to introduce small manufacturing and service firms to rural areas in recent years in an attempt to replace jobs lost in the primary sector, employment opportunities remain severely restricted, especially for the younger and older members of the workforce. The choices may be to remain unemployed (or in low-wage jobs), to travel long distances to alternative work, or to leave the area altogether.

There are often ostensibly very practical reasons for the declining service availability in rural areas. Modern techniques and ideas often favour concentration, or 'rationalization', rather than dispersal of services, and threshold catchment populations are therefore raised. Because of the dispersed nature of population in many rural areas and large catchment areas for certain fixed services such as schools, banks, hospitals and clinics, it is inevitable that many persons will live at a distance from them. Some facilities, specialized professional services in particular, are rarely found in rural areas and those that do exist may provide only a limited and occasional service. In addition, purchases such as food and consumer goods will tend to be more expensive, although to an extent this can be offset by lower rates on rural than urban homes, even if the differential is not as great now as it used to be. However, unless definite attempts are made by service providers (public and private) to overcome the problems of distance and dispersed populations, a continuing decline of opportunities is almost inevitable in rural areas.

Opportunity deprivation can be obvious in the lack of a village school, shop, doctor's surgery or bank, but it can also be more subtle. The cumulative effect of planning policies that aim to concentrate services in key locations can be to make other villages seem less attractive except to a few well-to-do, mobile families. This can result in a changing social composition of some villages that lose their services; they may become depopulated, second home sites or commuter homes. The resulting lack of services and of information can make rural residents feel very isolated.

Mobility deprivation

This is perhaps the most distinctive component of rural deprivation. It can afflict a community as a whole, as for example when public transport is withdrawn or curtailed, but some individuals in the community will always be affected more than others. The changing levels of public and private transport availability were discussed in chapter 6, and it was suggested that the lack of a car is probably the main single factor identifying those rural dwellers who are disadvantaged in terms of mobility and accessibility (Moseley 1979a). In addition, many living in car-owning households do not have the use of a car and these can be added to the other 'transport poor' who include the elderly, young children, teenagers, the poor and the infirm. Therefore, mobility deprivation requires research at a number of scales ranging from the community to the individual.

MULTIPLE DEPRIVATION

In the late 1960s and early 1970s it became fashionable for academic researchers and planners to talk of 'multiple deprivation': this usually meant the identification of areas (streets, enumeration districts or neighbourhoods) where a number of different types of deprivation were to be found, and which compounded each other. The focus moved quickly from the delimitation of measures of well-being to the identification of problem areas and areas of social stress, almost exclusively within cities, where deprivation was considered to be at its worst. As Knox (1982), Herbert (1975) and others have pointed out, a major reason for identifying areas of deprivation is that they represent an important facet of the social geography of the city. In addition, there was the impetus of urban redevelopment resulting in demands from professional planners who needed quantifiable indices for resource allocation purposes. Recently, Cullingford and Openshaw (1982) have suggested that social area analysis, a type of multivariate statistical technique originally developed to classify urban sub-areas, could be adapted as a practical means of defining areas of rural deprivation.

Such ideas have often been termed 'area-based' explanations and policies. Where patterns of deprivation are 'accumulative', that is where there is a high degree of spatial overlap in the distribution of deprivations, there are to be seen areas of multiple deprivation. However, the ecological fallacy has to be guarded against constantly. Area-based definitions are necessarily based on averages of information gathered about a group of people and houses in a given area. An area is said to be suffering from multiple deprivation if it exceeds some arbitrarily chosen cut-off point on a scale of deprivation that itself is not absolute. However, the size of area chosen (street, enumeration district, ward) will very much affect the nature of policies that can be carried out; and the further removed is the analysis from the individual household (for which information is rarely available), the less can be inferred from the index. Not all households even in the most deprived areas will be deprived, and not every deprived household will be multiply deprived or live in a designated area. Therefore, blanket policies that give aid to all residents or households within a defined area may not be efficient; worse still, they will miss households that may be multiply deprived but are outside the designated areas.

There is no satisfactory and universally accepted definition of multiple deprivation in either urban or rural areas. Usually, readily available surrogate indices are chosen, since it is almost impossible to measure deprivation directly. Many only marginally relevant indices or variables have been 'thrown into the statistical melting pot' (Edwards 1975) to define deprived areas; and because of the uncertainty of the nature of deprivation itself, there is a crucial lack of a generally accepted model or theory of deprivation on which to base empirical measurement (Knox 1982). Perhaps even more important than this is the finding by Smith (1979a) that there is not a convincing overlap between different types of deprivation even in the 'more deprived' areas of inner London.

One of the few aspects of agreement is that area-based, blanket policies such as GIAs, HAAs and the Community Development Projects (CDPs) are not ideal, although they frequently have to be used for want of anything better (Eyles 1979). However, there has been a growing recognition, particularly by the CDPs, that inner-city areas were not isolated urban pockets suffering an unfortunate combination of circumstances (problems of housing, income, education and employment) but areas that had lost out in the competition in the urban system for jobs, housing and education: they were almost redundant in terms of the space economy. Area-based policies of positive discrimination are favoured largely by those who see deprivation as a result of the maldistribution of resources (Knox 1982). If, on the other hand, it is the result of structural class conflict or redundancy of persons and places in terms of the space economy, such marginal tinkerings as positive discrimination to throw funds at supposed 'problem areas' will have little relevance and little long-term influence.

If it is difficult to define multiple deprivation in urban areas, where defects may be readily visible in the physical fabric and employment structure of densely populated areas, is it possible to identify it at all in rural localities? An enumeration district (ED) with a population of perhaps 1,500 persons can be an area of some few hundred square metres in a town: in a rural area it can be as large as a parish (although some are subdivided into EDs), and can cover many square kilometres. Can it therefore be possible to draw such a tight boundary around the unit and apply blanket area-based policies? The village population will often mirror the nation's population: there will be some well-to-do persons, some poor, some moderately well-off. Therefore, there will be insufficiently fine data and spatial nets to define those localities within the village or countryside that are suitable for area-based policies. With regard to mobility deprivation, for example, rural areas present problems to the administrator seeking to implement blanket policies; 'certainly an area focus is insufficient: very marked disparities exist cheek by jowl in the same village. Nor even is a family focus adequate: the family as a unit has few travel needs and the circumstances of its members can also differ considerably. . .' (Moseley 1979a, p. 51). This is one of the major reasons (apart from lack of funds and political will) why the mainly area-based GIA and HAA housing improvement programmes discussed in chapter 5 were not much implemented in rural areas. Certainly, the problem of defining people and places in rural localities that are deprived has not yet been resolved.

LOCATION AND ISOLATION

Deprivation, it has been suggested, can be both personal and areal. A basic rural problem is that many communities and individuals are isolated: even if they have financial resources, they lack adequate access to opportunities. Therefore, accessibility is a key to understanding the nature of rural deprivation. Parts of Britain demonstrate peripherality to a marked degree, and consequent underdevelopment because of their disadvantage in the core–periphery relationship. The whole 'celtic fringe' has 'long experienced poverty and deprivation as a result of its subordinate role in the regional division of labour. . .' (Knox and Cottam 1981b, p. 435). Hechter (1975), Geddes (1979) and others view this situation as the product of 'internal colonialism'. Places such as the Highlands of Scotland or parts of Wales are relatively desolate not simply because of their terrain, climate and remoteness, but also because of their position in a system of economic and social relations. In this, they may be viewed almost as internal colonies, producing wool, mutton, beef, wood and labour to sustain urban industrial growth in the English south while acting as recreational areas for the limited few who can reach them. Structural shifts in the economy, notably the decline of primary employment, have reduced parts of Scotland, Wales, the North and the South West to the official status of problem regions of high unemployment, low incomes and old age structures. Falling population thresholds make the withdrawal of services increasingly likely, and as a result exacerbate the feelings of remoteness and isolation of rural inhabitants.

'Remote Scotland', according to Mackay and Laing (1982), could be defined as districts being at least ten miles from urban areas of 2,000 or more people. Such areas comprised more than 350 parishes and 6 per cent of Scotland's population. The less extreme definition of 'rural Scotland' by the Scottish Office covered 644 parishes in which over 1 million persons, or 21 per cent of Scotland's population, lived: these parishes are distant from urban centres of 100,000 or more and have at least 10 per cent of their economically active population employed in agriculture. Therefore, substantial numbers of people in Scotland were living in 'rural' districts and over 300,000 were in 'remote' areas.

Similar calculations have been carried out in England and Wales, although not, perhaps, with such spectacular results. It is estimated that there are over 9,000 settlements in England and Wales with populations below 1,000, of which 80 per cent have fewer than 500 persons. Table 10.1 illustrates the total numbers of people living some distance from their nearest large town of 20,000 or more persons. Some 3.3 million people (10 per cent of the population of the non-metropolitan counties) live in settlements of fewer than 1,000 persons and 1.4 million of these are more than ten miles from their nearest main town. If the definition of village is raised from 1,000 to 2,000 persons, then 2 million people in England and Wales live in what may be termed 'deep rural' locations, more than ten miles from a town (Association of County Councils 1979).

The dispersed geographical nature of such rural communities naturally underlies the rural accessibility problem and makes public services costly to provide and private services sparsely located because of threshold requirements. For example, some of the Scottish glens and parts of Wales form the approximately 1 per cent of Britain that does not receive television broadcasts or colour transmissions. It is physical distances and accessibility problems that make rural deprivation somewhat different from urban deprivation even if, as will be argued later, their underlying causes can be very similar.

Table 10.1 Total populations of small and remote settlements in non-metropolitan counties of England and Wales

Population size of settlements	Distance from an urban centre with a population over 20,000		
	0–4.9 miles	*5–9.9 miles*	*10+ miles*
1,000–4,999	2,300,000	1,500,000	1,300,000
500–999	400,000	500,000	600,000
0–499	400,000	600,000	800,000

Source: after Association of County Councils (1979)

Isolation

A 'level of living' index for England and Wales, has been compiled which, while not directly measuring 'deprivation', does illustrate some aspects of the aggregate quality of life in counties of England and Wales (figure 10.1). This was based on four variables: average numbers of persons per room; possession of a fixed bath; economic activity rates; and percentage of elderly persons. Knox (1974, 1975) presents a picture that shows the more peripheral areas to have the 'worst' levels of living, notably Cornwall, West and mid-Wales, the Isle of Wight, parts of East Anglia and parts of the North of England. London also tends to have poor levels on this index although the Home Counties fare the best. At a gross scale, therefore, the accepted ideas about the social geography of England and Wales illustrated by writers such as Coates and Rawstron (1971) are not seriously challenged, and peripherality, isolation and low levels of living seem to go hand in hand.

Extreme isolation on Jura, Scotland. The main road is a single track and the journey to the mainland involves a circuitous ferry trip (source: D. G. Lockhart)

A more up-to-date example has been produced for Scotland, at the finer spatial scale of the 644 parishes in the Scottish Office's 1978 *Rural Indicators Study* referred to earlier (Knox and Cottam 1981a). A ranking of the worst 10 per cent of the parishes was produced, based on standardized scores for a number of variables:

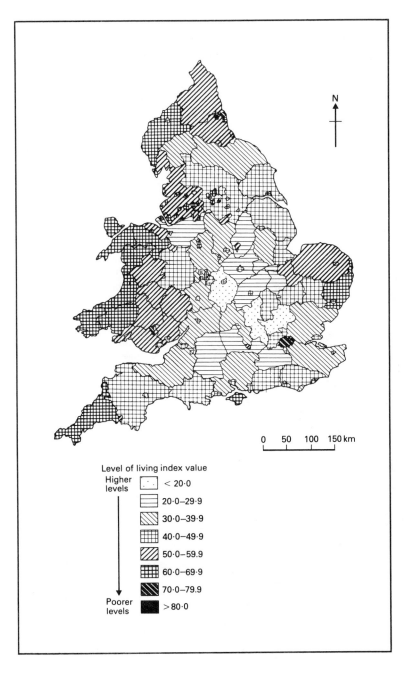

Level of living index value

Higher levels

[.·]	< 20·0
	20·0–29·9
	30·0–39·9
	40·0–49·9
	50·0–59.9
	60·0–69·9
	70·0–79.9
	> 80·0

Poorer levels

0   50   100   150 km

FIGURE 10.1   An index of level-of-living for England and Wales
Source: Knox (1975)

1 percentage of households lacking exclusive use of all basic amenities;
2 percentage of households with no car;
3 percentage of economically active males seeking work;
4 percentage of population in retired age groups;
5 percentage of households living at more than 1.5 persons per room.

Figure 10.2 shows a very distinctive spatial distribution, with the most

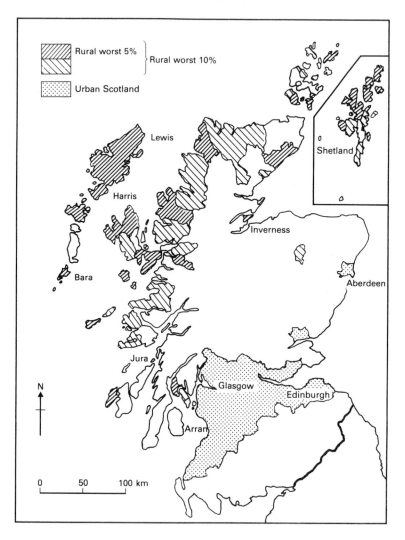

FIGURE 10.2   Spatial patterns of rural deprivation in Scotland
Source: after Knox and Cottam (1981a)

deprived parishes (the worst 5 per cent) coinciding with the more remote and inaccessible parts of the North and West Highlands and parts of the outer Islands. Some 9 or 10 of the 26 survey parishes in Mackay and Laing's (1982) study of rural consumers were in the 10 per cent identified above. Over half of these come low down in the ranking of the 26 parishes on a composite index of service provision levels. All but one were below the norm for the 26, and it should be noted that the norms set very low standards of service provision in the first place. All in all, the idea of remoteness and deprivation is confirmed by both studies, and the parishes identified by Knox and Cottam mainly represent the area that is occupied by the remnants of Scotland's peasant population (Carter 1974); here, apart from the limited opportunities offered by tourism, the local economy is still based on crofting, a marginal form of subsistence farming (Knox and Cottam 1981a).

The Scottish Highlands

In spite of the acknowledged problems of using aggregate measures to define social well-being, Knox and Cottam (1981b) have identified certain Highland 'settlement zones' which do appear to be deprived on a few key indices of social well-being. Selecting as indices the proportion of dwellings lacking either a hot water supply, a fixed bath or shower or an inside toilet, alarmingly high percentages of dwellings in the remote region of the central Highlands appear to be multiply deprived. In the west, in particular, there is a high proportion of older housing stock, and although subject to considerable improvement, there are areas in which over one-third of houses lack one or more of the three amenities, compared with the Scottish average of 13.5 per cent. Therefore, there is a marked contrast between the western more remote areas and the growth areas of the eastern seaboard (figure 10.3).

In addition, evidence of financial hardship was gained from the percentage of children receiving free school meals, or of households without a car. By these measures, there was a relatively high level of financial hardship throughout the Highlands in 1979: 15 out of 62 settlement zones had a higher proportion of children receiving free school meals than the Scottish average. Again, the western areas fared badly, but so did many settlements of the more industrial eastern coast. Public transport in the Highlands is expensive and infrequent, so lack of a car represents a key dimension of social well-being. Outside Inverness the worst-off areas coincided with the remote and isolated parts of the region. The less prosperous areas of the west, which rely on upland farming, tourism and fishing, were localities 'where problems of poor housing conditions and low personal mobility compound the disadvantages of economic stag-

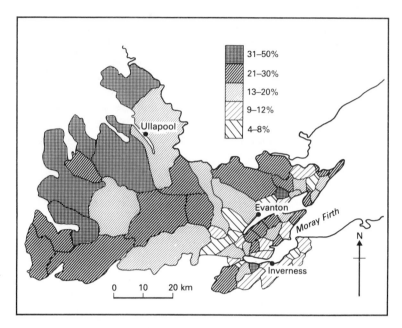

FIGURE 10.3   Scottish Highland dwellings lacking three or more basic
amenities, 1971
Source: after Knox and Cottam (1981b)

nation and physical isolation. . .' (Knox and Cottam 1981b, p. 441).
However, lest a biased picture be presented, it should also be noted that
even the more urbanized areas enjoying the best accessibility to services
and the best housing conditions also exhibited an above-average incidence
of overcrowding, social problems and car-less households. Therefore
perhaps the region as a whole could be regarded as rural and deprived.

These aggregate data give a rather bleak outlook, which was not much
improved by a detailed survey of 429 households in two settlements,
Ullapool on the west coast and Evanton, towards the east of the region. In
an essentially materialistic society, Knox and Cottam (1981b) see the
ownership or consumption of goods and services and the amount of money
available to a household as fundamental criteria of people's welfare. Both
the areas surveyed showed very limited affluence although Evanton is the
better-off. Very few households reported possession of all nine items
shown in table 10.2, and those possessing four or fewer can be regarded in
Britain today as being materially deprived. By what is recognized to be an
arbitrary criterion, Knox and Cottam found 25 per cent of Ullapool's
households and 16 per cent of Evanton's to be materially deprived. 'The
only item reported by a majority of deprived households is a hot water

Table 10.2   Material deprivation in the central Highlands, 1981

Amenities	Percentage of households deprived	
	Ullapool area	*Evanton area*
Hot water supply	20.8	3.7
Car	74.6	74.0
Telephone	59.7	70.3
Washing machine	58.2	59.2
Central heating	86.5	70.3
Freezer	80.5	85.2
Colour television	86.5	77.7
Holiday (> 4 days away)	73.1	77.7
Income > £50 per week (gross)	80.5	70.3

	Percentage of households with 0–9 items	
	Ullapool area *(n = 267)*	*Evanton area* *(n = 162)*
All 9 items	7.5	11.6
8	24.7	21.3
7	16.5	22.6
6	14.6	15.2
5	11.6	12.8
4	10.9	6.1
3	4.5	7.3
2	4.5	1.8
1	3.7	1.2
None	1.5	0.0

Source: after Knox and Cottam (1981b)

supply. Even so, over 20 per cent of those households in the Ullapool area did not have even this rudimentary household amenity . . .' (Knox and Cottam 1981b, p. 444). The commonest material deprivation involved low incomes and the absence of central heating and freezers. Perhaps surprisingly, the deprived households were to be found among owner-occupiers (the property-owning poor), as well as council tenants and private renters, but there was a higher incidence among semi-skilled and unskilled workers and a particularly high incidence among the elderly; 49 per cent of deprived households in Ullapool and 37 per cent in Evanton were aged 66 or over. This has very important implications for public policy and public service provision. However, also surprisingly, people's general levels of satisfaction, their 'perceived' quality of life, was quite high. Only public transport scored a consistently very low rating compared with attitudes to other services. This again supports the contention that accessibility is a major and problematic dimension of the quality of rural life (Moseley 1979a; Shaw 1979b; Knox and Cottam 1981b).

It is clear that the issues of household, opportunity and mobility deprivation require further research, if only to dispel some of the myths and romantic imagery that confound analysis of rural social welfare.

> The popular image of rural Scotland – a spectacular heather-clad landscape dotted with picturesque cottages and inhabited by hardworking but unimaginative ginger-haired people who love accordion music, dressing up in kilts and sporrans, and live on whisky and porridge – has been particularly effective in obscuring some of the harsher aspects of rural living conditions. [Knox and Cottam 1981b, p. 163].

Ironically, this image has been fostered in many rural localities by some of the very institutions and agencies responsible for their development (such as the regional councils and the Highlands and Islands Development Board in Scotland), with the intention of stimulating tourism, which is often the only growth sector of the local economy. Such propaganda portraying idyllic rural living conditions has become so successful in diverting attention away from problems of rural deprivation that it can now be difficult to convince policy-makers that it exists.

REALITIES IN RURAL DEPRIVATION

Results from studies such as Knox and Cottam's and from research reported by Walker (1978a), Shaw (1979a) and others indicate a rich potential for investigating specific facets of rural deprivation, the components of the 'deprivation jigsaw' (Cloke 1980c). The total number of residents in non-metropolitan counties of England and Wales that may be considered deprived in terms of certain specific services has been estimated (see table 10.3), and can be a cause for serious concern. There do appear to be substantial areas, households and individuals afflicted by real deprivation.

In many of the more accessible lowland areas, however, a type of rural gentrification is occurring as many villages are becoming middle-class enclaves of commuters or the retired. At the other end of the accessibility spectrum, some of the more remote villages are dying (White 1972; Norman 1978). It can be argued convincingly that farmers and landowners dominate rural local government as effectively as they did in the past (Rose *et al.* 1979). This particularly accords with the managerialist mode of

Table 10.3   Estimated total population of parishes lacking selected facilities in non-metropolitan counties in England and Wales, 1979

Facility	Population lacking facility in responding counties	No. of responding counties (out of a total of 47)	Estimated total population lacking facility in England and Wales
Health			
Doctor's surgery	3,300,000	41	3,800,000
Dispensing chemist	5,300,000	40	6,300,000
Infant welfare clinic	4,100,000	38	5,200,000
Utilities			
Mains sewerage	600,000	34	900,000
Mains gas	3,100,000	32	4,900,000
Mains water	7,000	32	12,000
Electricity	0	34	0
Local facilities			
Sub-post office	700,000	42	800,000
Food shop	600,000	39	700,000
Village hall	1,100,000	37	1,400,000
Public transport			
Any bus or rail service	200,000	42	250,000

	Population more than 10 miles from facility in responding counties	No. of responding counties	Estimated total population more than 10 miles from facility
Information and advice			
Area social service office	1,800,000	41	1,000,000
DHSS office	1,900,000	40	2,200,000
Citizens' Advice Bureau	1,400,000	39	1,700,000

Source: after Association of County Councils (1979)

analysis of the role of 'gatekeepers' to scarce resources, discussed in chapter 1. Local councillors may see issues only in an individual and personalized way: they can understand the inability of an individual family to obtain a house (a reality to them); but they sometimes cannot or will not see that it is the overall housing shortage (which they believe to be a myth) that underlies the problem and that this is caused by a combination of planning and financial policies and low wages (Rose *et al.* 1978; Phillips and Williams 1982a). Since there is conspicuous lack of opposition, local

An isolated settlement in lowland England, with no shops, buses or local jobs (source: authors)

'gatekeepers' and politicians may continue to believe that they are acting non-politically and in the public interest in resource allocation.

Results from studies of deprivation will in future give a much sharper edge to critical social policy in rural areas. In time, rural social geography will catch up with its urban counterpart behind which it has lagged for so long in matters of welfare and deprivation research (Cloke 1980c; Moseley 1980a). In particular, rural deprivation must be viewed as being inextricably linked with the whole issue of urban deprivation, even if somewhat different analytical techniques may be required to establish this. Both are the products of the same forces that emerged from the dynamics of late industrial capitalism – structural shifts in the economy and a changing demand for, and role of, labour (Moseley 1980a; Knox and Cottam 1981a). It can be pointed out that both are manifestations of the same forces although characterized by distinctive syndromes of social problems.

11 Policy Issues and the Future

A METHODOLOGICAL REFLECTION

We have proposed that a political economy orientation is essential to furthering the understanding of rural social geography. Such an approach could be based on research explaining the roles of various social groups and various types of rural areas in terms of changes in the national and international economies. At the present, however, the theoretical under-standing of political economy as it affects rural areas is inadequate to develop far such a research methodology, and data are lacking with which to test empirically many propositions. Instead, most of the book has concentrated on the effects of resource allocation at a national level and in part at the local level. Therefore, many of the substantive chapters are based upon managerialist and behavioural studies of social processes, with the implicit (rather than explicit) notion that these are located within the larger social formation.

Nevertheless, we have attempted to highlight the influence of national policies on local rural areas. Housing, transport and services are particu-larly amenable to such analysis, and it is in these specific fields that the major methodological advances might be expected in the near future. National legislation, resource allocation decisions and managerial de-cisions all have effects on rural localities, but in themselves they are part of a structure of economic and social relationships. As yet, a full understand-ing of how changes in production, consumption and ideology affect rural areas has not been achieved. Perhaps the very attempt to discern the operation of such processes in specific geographical areas is not possible and will fail in the analysis of an essentially aspatial and holistic social science.

This can be even more important at a time when there is a changing relationship between central and local government within Britain. With the reduction of much financial and administrative autonomy, the local

State's influence and ability to modify resource allocation and service provision may be substantially reduced. The national State, being in ascendancy, will become increasingly the focus of explanation, and perhaps this will, in practice, lessen the relevance of a specific spatial focus.

However, at a different level it can be argued that spatial structure is part of, and does affect, the workings of a capitalist society (Harvey 1982). Rural areas have distinctive spatial structures which influence their contribution to processes such as capital accumulation and the reproduction of labour power. At the same time, it is essential to discern the effects of such processes on the ground. In times of international recession and national retrenchment, it is particularly important to appreciate the implications for local areas of policy changes. Therefore, in spite of some theoretical reservations, this is a recognition of the value of structuralist research but applied to specific areas.

THE FUTURE

Employment

One of the key issues in the future of rural Britain is the employment prospects of various areas. This is not a problem that can be easily isolated in analytical terms since it is intricately bound with the question of the competitive position of the various types of rural areas and industries in national and international economies. Britain, for example, is part of the European Economic Community, and as such potential rural employers could be mobile in a larger space economy than the purely domestic one. This has implications for the ability of British rural areas to attract and retain employers if it is accepted that the 'traditional' rural employment base, agriculture and forestry, will nationally remain at its current low level (both relatively and absolutely).

There is uncertainty in all British employment at present, but one feature that seems to be assured is the growth of new technology, especially in the secondary and service industries. It has generally been argued that technological changes, particularly the application of microelectronics, will lead to further major reductions in the demand for labour. Rural areas are likely to share equally with urban areas in this decline. However, the new industrial revolution may create new links between home and the workplace as developments in information technology enable more activities, especially of a service type, to be carried on in almost any physical location including people's homes. The attraction of rural living may then produce a breed of 'footloose' employees who do not have to be tied to central office locations for much of their work. In the shorter term, however, the maintenance of current employment levels in particular areas is still very much dependent on physical accessibility. Therefore, to maintain economic and community viability in the remoter rural areas, a good transport network must be retained or, more likely, re-established.

Good communications still exist in much of the accessible countryside, and of course this is itself partly responsible for the pressure on these 'reachable' rural areas. The prospects for the more remote areas in the 1980s are not bright, however. For example, if some of the more extreme strategies proposed in the 1983 Serpell Report on British railways are adopted, many non-central areas will be totally deprived in a rail network that would be essentially inter-major-city. To this is added the move towards privatization of bus transport, which will leave many rural routes unattractive for commercial operators. Each route is now treated on its own merits rather than receiving automatic cross-subsidization from profitable routes, so the explicit social function envisaged for public transport in the Transport Act 1978 has been replaced by economic criteria in the 1980 Act. The general feeling is that rural bus services in particular may become more limited in the future (Banister 1983) and rail services may become even fewer than they are in the early 1980s. If this does occur, the future of the more remote rural areas in terms of 'conventional' employment is bleak indeed.

Welfare regions

It is possible to foresee a time when certain rural areas will become almost entirely dependent on the state for support because they are economically defunct. If any population at all remains in these places, the areas must continue to be a part of the consumption process even though they may effectively disappear from the production process. Their consumption levels will then be maintained only by subsidies from urban-generated income or from urban residents who bring monetary resources to their second or retirement homes. As such, they may be considered to be 'welfare regions'. This may relegate the existing population of some rural areas (or perhaps those in pockets of particular isolation) to a high degree of dependency on 'national benevolence'; and in terms of personal pride and expectations, let alone national equity, this can hardly be felt to be a 'just' development.

Another side to this argument is that some rural areas may be viewed as 'internal colonies' (Hechter 1975; Knox and Cottam 1981a, 1981b). These may provide, as did the overseas colonies, raw materials and some labour supply, and thereby retain a role in the reproduction of labour power.

However, they may be used as fossilized economic areas which fulfil the functions of being recreational areas for individual consumption by the well-to-do from urban or accessible rural locations. The argument is persuasive, and this does seem to be occurring in some areas already. The planning process can be used to sterilize such areas when, for example, conservationists argue against establishing a skiing centre in an area of the Scottish Highlands in order to preserve its 'wild and natural' appearance. The centre would, of course, provide jobs for local inhabitants as well as bringing spin-offs in demand for local services and, perhaps as crucial, 'importing' some element of dynamism to a depressed region.

Planning

In view of these arguments, it seems relevant to question the role of planning in rural areas. Does it reallocate resources to the rural poor, or does it raise the needs of individual consumption over those of collective consumption? The answer must be couched in terms of the different types of rural region already identified. Planning itself, being based largely on restrictive and negative powers, will probably do little either to ease substantially the lot of groups such as the transport poor, or to prevent the development of welfare-dependent regions. In pressurized rural areas, it may have a marginal influence on preserving landscape and amenity, but the social implications for both individual and collective consumption are less predictable. It is interesting to see Blacksell and Gilg (1981) still echoing Clout's (1972) call for 'integrated management of the country-side'; if this involves linking more effectively the planning of spatial and social structures, it would be welcome. However, planning legislation will inevitably take on a political colour, which, given the alternating nature of British politics, is hardly conducive to the development of long-term strategies.

From the standpoint of this book, however, one of the greatest failures of planning in terms of its impact on the countryside must be the relatively poor co-ordination of physical and social policies. Physical planning, in spite of years of lip-service to social planning, still dominates the legislative and public arena. Admittedly, many of the county structure plans approved up to the early 1980s have contained explicit elements of social planning, but the extent to which these will remain pious statements of intent is as yet unclear. It is apparent, however, that some structure plans contain little evidence of awareness and little of substance which might be used in the social planning for rural areas. Even where structure plans have provided positive frameworks for an integration of physical, economic and social planning, economic recession and financial stringency are ever likely to hamper implementation. Many British planning institutions and organizations were developed in an era of growth and their relevance for an era of decline is questionable.

Self-help

In the absence of official responses or strategies to cope with many rural needs, can self-help measures be expected to fill the gap? Some have argued that many traditional rural inhabitants are averse to the welfare orientation of the national or even the local state, and perhaps local community involvement can reduce the need for it. This seems, however, to be an over-optimistic expectation at present. The voluntary housing movement, for example, has been slow to take off in most rural areas, and many successful schemes have depended on the input of energy and expertise from outsiders and newcomers. It has already been suggested that the local state can be dominated by interests that do not correspond with those of traditional rural social groups. Will the managers of factory farms and agribusinesses or the wealthy semi-retired urbanites adopt local social and political responsibilities in the same patriarchal manner as did the old farming squirearchy? Suggestions to date are that they do not and will not. In any event, the resources available to the self-help movement are, arguably, totally inadequate in relationship to the extent of need.

So, in the absence of positive planning and state intervention and the denial that self-help is a way ahead for anything but very small-scale, local developments, the prospects for the rural poor seem discouraging. Perhaps a rural counterpart may develop of the type of 'more-caring' official identified in some urban areas, the 'bureaucratic guerrilla' (Knox 1982), working covertly in the interests of deprived communities while in the employment of the bureaucracy. Such a type certainly does exist in some rural local authorities and can be particularly effective because at that scale relationships between officials and community can be reduced to a remarkably 'personal' level, unlike that attained in many larger urban authorities. This is not to say that a widespread outbreak of rebellion or even positive advocacy on behalf of the underprivileged is likely among rural council officers; but in particular areas and for specific issues, it could become significant.

In conclusion, it may be apposite to question matters of resource allocation. It may certainly be questioned whether 'society' should be expected to subsidize and maintain a settlement pattern and way of life that arguably is anachronistic and perhaps is redundant in terms of the modern economy; or whether villages can be 'afforded' by the nation (Shaw 1976; Phillips and Williams 1982a). It is also open to debate whether sufficient resources exist to enable a positive and effective response to rural problems (Cloke 1983), and especially whether new resources could be attracted to areas in times of recession. It is unfortunate that there has not been a sustained national debate on these issues, and that there has not been a coherent national strategy in Britain that views the space economy in an integrated form or in its totality. Until a system of just priorities is achieved, both between rural and urban areas and within rural areas, the problems and prospects of different localities are likely to remain as manifold and as confused, and as much subject to *ad hoc* policies, as they are today.

Bibliography

Adams, L., Daly, A. J. and Pilgrim, B. (1977) *Problems and solutions in rural transport*. Report D28, Local Government Operational Research Unit, Royal Institute of Public Administration, Reading and Manchester.

Age Concern (1973) *Age Concern on transport*. London: Age Concern.

Aldcroft, D. H. (1968) *British railways in transition*. London: Macmillan; New York: St Martin's Press.

Allison, L. (1975) *Environmental planning: a political and philosophical analysis*. London: George Allen and Unwin.

Allon-Smith, R. D. (1982) The evolving geography of the elderly in England and Wales. In A. M. Warnes (ed.), *Geography perspectives on the elderly*. Chichester: John Wiley.

Ambrose, P. (1974) *The quiet revolution*. London: Chatto and Windus.

(1977) Accessibility and spatial inequality. D204 *Fundamentals of Human Geography*, Unit 24. Milton Keynes: Open University Press.

Anderson, J. (1976) *The political economy of urbanism: a bibliography*. London: Architectural Association.

Arensberg, C. M. and Kimball, S. T. (1940) *Family and community in Ireland*. London: Peter Smith.

Ashton J. and Cracknell, B. E. (1961) Agricultural holdings and farm business structure in England and Wales. *Journal of Agricultural Economics* 14, 472–506.

and Long, W. H. (1972) *The remoter rural areas of Britain*. Edinburgh: Oliver and Boyd.

Ashworth, W. A. (1954) *The genesis of modern British town planning*. London: Routledge and Kegan Paul.

Association of County Councils (1979) *Rural deprivation*. London: Association of County Councils.

Ayton, J. B. (1976) Rural settlement policy: problems and conflicts. In P. J. Drudy (ed.), *Regional and rural development: essays in theory and practice*. Chalfont St Giles: Alpha Academic.

Bailey, J. (1975) *Social theory for planning*. London: Routledge and Kegan Paul.

Baker, A. R. H. (1969) The geography of rural settlements. In R. U. Cooke and

J. H. Johnson (eds.), *Trends in geography: an introductory survey*. Oxford: Pergamon.

Baker, C. V. (1976) *Housing associations*. London: Estates Gazette.

Banister, D. J. (1983) 'Transport and accessibility'. In M. Pacione (ed.), *Progress in rural geography*. London: Croom Helm.

and Hall, P. G. (eds.), (1981) *Transport and public policy planning*. London: Mansell.

Barr, J. (1969) Durham's murdered villages. *New Society* 340, 523–5.

Barrass, R. (1979) The first ten years of English Structure Planning: current progress and future directions. *Planning Outlook* 22, 19–23.

Bassett, K. and Short, J. R. (1980) *Housing and residential structure: alternative approaches*. London: Routledge and Kegan Paul.

Bean, R. and Peel, D. A. (1976) A cross-sectional analysis of regional strike activity in Britain. *Regional Studies* 10, 299–306.

Bebbington, A. C. and Davies, B. (1982) Patterns of social service provision for the elderly. In A. M. Warnes (ed.), *Geographical perspectives on the elderly*. Chichester: John Wiley.

Bell, C. and Newby, H. (1971) *Community studies: an introduction to the sociology of the local community*. London: George Allen and Unwin.

(1974a) Capitalist farmers in the British class structure. *Sociologia Ruralis* 14, 86–107.

(eds.) (1974b) *The sociology of community: a selection of readings*. London: Frank Cass.

Bell, M. (ed.) (1975) *Britain's national parks*. Newton Abbot: David and Charles.

Bellerby, J. R. (1956) *Agriculture and industry: relative income*. London: Macmillan.

(1958) The distribution of manpower in agriculture and industry, 1851–1951. *Farm Economist* 9, 1–11.

Bennett, S. (1976) *Rural housing in the Lake District*. Lancaster: University Press.

Berger, J. and Mohr, J. (1967) *A fortunate man*. London: Allen Lane.

Berry, B. J. L. (1976) Urbanization and counterurbanization. *Urban Affairs Annual Review*.

Berry, F. (1974) *Housing: the great British failure*. London: Charles Knight.

Best, R. H. (1968) Competition for land between rural and urban uses. In *Land use and resources: studies in applied geography*. London: Institute of British Geographers, Special Publication 1.

(1976) The extent and growth of urban land. *The Planner* 62, 8–11.

(1977) Agricultural land loss: myth or reality? *The Planner* 63, 15–16.

(1981) *Land use and living space*. London: Methuen.

and Champion, A. G. (1970) Regional conversions of land to urban use in England and Wales, 1945–1967. *Transactions of the Institute of British Geographers* 49, 15–31.

and Rogers, A. W. (1973) *The urban countryside: the land use structure of small towns and villages in England and Wales*. London: Faber and Faber.

Bielckus, C. L., Rogers, A. W. and Wibberley, G. P. (1972) *Second homes in England and Wales*. Studies in Rural Land Use no. 11, Wye College, University of London.

Birch, A. H. (1959) *Small town politics*. Oxford: University Press.

Blacksell, M. (1983) Leisure, recreation and environment. In R. J. Johnston and J. Doornkamp (eds.), *The changing geography of the United Kingdom*. London: Methuen.

— and Gilg. A. (1981) *The countryside: planning and change*. London: Allen and Unwin.

Blowers, A. (1972) The declining villages of County Durham. In A. Blowers (ed.), *Social geography*. Milton Keynes: Open University Press.

— Brook C., Dunleavy, P. and McDowell, L. (eds.) (1982) *Urban change and conflict: an interdisciplinary reader*. London: Harper and Row.

Boddy, M. J. (1976) The structure of mortgage finance: building societies and the British social formation. *Transactions of the Institute of British Geographers* New Series 1, 58–71.

— (1980) *The building societies*. London: Macmillan.

Bollom, C. (1978) *Attitudes and second homes in rural Wales*. Cardiff: University of Wales Press.

Bowler, I. R. (1979) *Government and agriculture: a spatial perspective*. London: Longman.

Bracey, H. E. (1958) Some aspects of rural depopulation in the United Kingdom. *Rural Sociology* 23, 385–91.

— (1959) *English rural life, village activities, organizations and institutions*. London: Routledge and Kegan Paul.

— (1963) *Industry and the countryside: the impact of industry on amenities in the countryside*. London: Faber and Faber.

— (1970) *People and the countryside*. London: Routledge and Kegan Paul.

Bradshaw, J. (1972) The concept of social need. *New Society* 19, 640–3.

Bramley, P. (1980) *Dental health*. London: King's Fund Centre.

Brett, M. (1972) A new route to agricultural investment. *Investors Chronicle and Stock Exchange Gazette* 19, 481–2.

British Railways Board (1963) *The reshaping of British railways*. London: HMSO.

British Tourist Authority (1982) *Digest of tourist statistics no. 10*. London: British Tourist Authority.

Britton, D. K. (1974) The structure of agriculture. In A. Edwards and A. Rogers (eds.), *Agricultural resources: an introduction to the farming industry of the United Kingdom*. London: Faber and Faber.

Broady, M. (1980) Mid-Wales: a classic case of rural self-help. *The Planner* 66, 94–5.

Brockway, F. (1932) *Hungry England*. London: Gollancz.

Brogden, G. (1978) Welfare rights and access to information. In A. Walker (ed.), *Rural poverty*. Poverty Pamphlet 37. London: Child Poverty Action Group.

Brooks, E. (1975) Development problems of the inner-city. *Geographical Journal* 141, 355–62.

Brown, M. and Winyard, S. (1975) *Low pay on the farm*. London: Low Pay Unit.

Brownrigg, M. and Greig M. A. (1974) *The economic impact of tourist spending in Skye*. Special Report 13, Highlands and Islands Development Board.

Bryant, C. R., Russwurm, L. H. and McLellan, A. G. (1982) *The city's countryside*. London: Longman.

Bryden, J. and Houston, G. (1976) *Agrarian change in the Scottish Highlands: the role of the Highlands and Islands Developement Board in the agricultural economy of the crofting counties.* London: Martin Robertson.

Buchanan, S. (1982) Power and planning in rural areas: preparation of the Suffolk county structure plan. In M. J. Moseley (ed.), *Power, planning and people in rural East Anglia.* Norwich: Centre of East Anglian Studies, University of East Anglia.

Building Societies Association (1982) *Housing facts.* London: Building Societies Association.

Buller, H. and Lowe, P. (1982) Politics and class in rural preservation: a study of the Suffolk Preservation Society. In M. J. Moseley (ed.), *Power, planning and people in rural East Anglia.* Norwich: Centre of East Anglian Studies, University of East Anglia.

Burgess. J. A. (1982) Selling places: environmental images for the executive. *Regional Studies* 16, 1–17.

Burke, G. (1981) *Housing and social justice.* London: Longman.

Burton, T. L. (1967) *Outdoor recreation enterprises in problem rural areas.* Ashford: Wye College.

Butler, D. and Stokes, D. (1971) *Political change in Britain: forces shaping electoral choice.* Harmondsworth: Penguin.

Buttimer, A. (1968) Social geography. In *International encyclopedia of the social sciences, vol 6.* New York: Macmillan and Free Press.

(1969) Social space in interdisciplinary perspective. *Geographical Review* 59, 417–26.

Byrne, D. S. (1976) Allocation, the council ghetto, and the political economy of housing. *Antipode* 8, 24–9.

Cairncross, A. K. (1949) Internal migration in Victorian England. *The Manchester School* 17, 67–87.

Campbell, M. (1981) *Capitalism in the UK: a perspective from Marxist political economy.* London: Croom Helm.

Carlstein, T., Parkes, D. and Thrift, N. (eds.), (1978) *Human activity and time geography.* London: Edward Arnold.

Carney, J. G. and Hudson, R. (1978) The Scottish Development Agency. *Town and Country Planning* 46, 507–10.

(1979) The Welsh Development Agency. *Town and Country Planning* 48, 15–16.

Carter, C. (1973) Agricultural land drainage. *Power Farming* 51.

Carter, I. (1974) The Highlands of Scotland as an underdeveloped region. In E. de Kadt and G. Williams (eds.), *Sociology of development.* London: Tavistock Press.

Castells, M. (1976) Is there an urban sociology? In C. G. Pickvance (ed.), *Urban sociology: critical essays.* London: Tavistock.

(1977a) *The urban question: a Marxist approach.* London: Edward Arnold.

(1977b) Towards a political urban sociology. In M. Harloe (ed.), *Captive cities.* London: John Wiley.

Catchpole, L. (1982) The local government, planning and land act, 1980. In A. W. Gilg (ed.), *Countryside planning yearbook 1982.* Norwich: Geo Books.

Central Statistical Office (1982) *Social trends*. London: HMSO.

Champion, A. G. (1976) Evolving patterns of population distribution in England and Wales, 1951–71. *Transactions of the Institute of British Geographers* New Series 1, 401–20.

—— (1983) Land use and competition. In M. Pacione (ed.), *Progress in rural geography*. London: Croom Helm.

Cherry, G. E. (1974a) The development of planning thought. In M. J. Burton (ed.), *The spirit and purpose of planning*. London: Hutchinson.

—— (1974b) *The evolution of British town planning*. London: Leonard Hill.

—— (ed.) (1976) *Rural planning problems*. London: Leonard Hill.

Clark, D. and Unwin, K. (1979) Community information in rural areas. In J. M. Shaw (ed.), *Rural deprivation and planning*. Norwich: Geo Books.

—— (1981) Telecommunications and travel: potential impact in rural areas. *Regional Studies* 15, 47–56.

Clark, D. (1981) *Rural housing initiatives*. London: National Council for Voluntary Organisations.

Clark, G (1982a) *Housing and planning in the countryside*. Chichester: John Wiley/ Research Studies Press.

—— (1982b) Housing policy in the Lake District. *Transactions of the Institute of British Geographers* New Series 7, 59–70.

Clawson, M. and Knetsch, J. L. (1966) *Economics of outdoor recreation*. Baltimore: Johns Hopkins University.

Clements, L. M. (1978) The 'demise' of tied cottages – Rent (Agriculture) Act 1976. *The Conveyancer and Property Lawyer* 42, 259–76.

Clifton, R. F. and Creigh, S. W. (1977) Regional strike-proneness: a research note. *Regional Studies* 11, 79–86.

Cloke, P. J. (1977a) An index of rurality for England and Wales. *Regional Studies* 11, 31–46.

—— (1977b) In defence of key settlement policies. *The Village* 17, 19–31.

—— (1979) *Key settlements in rural areas*. London: Methuen.

—— (1980a) The key settlement approach: the theoretical argument. *The Planner* 66, 98–9.

—— (1980b) Key settlements. *Town and Country Planning* 49, 187–9.

—— (1980c) New emphases for applied rural geography. *Progress in Human Geography* 4, 181–217.

—— (1983) Resource evaluation and management. In M. Pacione (ed.), *Progress in rural geography*. London: Croom Helm.

Clout, H. D. (1972) *Rural geography: an introductory survey*. Oxford: Pergamon.

Coates, B. E., Johnston, R. J. and Knox, P. L. (1977) *Geography and inequality*. Oxford: University Press.

Coates, B. E. and Rawstron, E. M. (1971) *Regional variations in Britain*. London: Batsford.

Colenutt, R. J. and Sidaway, R. M. (1973) *Forest of Dean day visitor survey*. Forestry Commission Bulletin no. 46. London: HMSO.

Coles, O. (1978) Transport and rural deprivation. In A. Walker (ed.), *Rural poverty*. Poverty Pamphlet 37. London: Child Poverty Action Group.

Colletti, L. (1975) Introduction. In K. Marx, *Early writings*. Harmondsworth: Penguin.

Community Development Project (1977) *The costs of industrial change*. London: CDP Inter-Project Team.

Conference of Socialist Economists (1979) *Struggle over the state: cuts and restructuring in contemporary Britain*. CSE State Apparatus and Expenditure Group. London: CSE Books.

Connell, J. (1974) The metropolitan village: spatial processes in discontinuous suburbs. In J. H. Johnson (ed.), *Suburban growth*. London: John Wiley.

Coppock, J. T. (1976) *An agricultural atlas of England and Wales*. London: Faber and Faber.

(ed.) (1977) *Second homes: curse or blessing?* Oxford: Pergamon Press.

(1980) The geography of recreation and leisure. In E. H. Brown (ed.), *Geography, yesterday and tomorrow*. Oxford: University Press.

Cornwall County Council (1966) *Survey of the holiday industry*. Truro: Cornwall County Council.

(1979) *County structure plan: report of survey*. Truro: Cornwall County Council.

Countryside Commission (1974) *New agricultural landscapes*. Cheltenham: Countryside Commission.

(1977) *New agricultural landscapes: issues, objectives and action*. Cheltenham: Countryside Commission.

(1979) *Leisure and the countryside*. Cheltenham: Countryside Commission.

(1980) *Trends in tourism and recreation, 1968–1978*. Cheltenham: Countryside Commission.

(1982) *Fourteenth report of the Countryside Commission*. London: HMSO.

Countryside Review Committee (1977a) *Rural communities*. London: HMSO.

(1977b) *Leisure and the countryside*. London: HMSO.

Cowan, R. (1982) In the face of prosperity. *Town and Country Planning* 51, 218–21.

Cowie, W. J. G. and Giles, A. K. (1957) An inquiry into the reasons for 'the drift from the land'. *Selected papers in agricultural economics* 5, 70–113.

Cripps, J. (1980) The Countryside Commission: its first decade. In A. W. Gilg (ed.), *Countryside Planning Yearbook* 1, 38–48.

Cross, M. (1981) *New firm formation and regional development*. Farnborough: Gower.

Cullingford, D. and Openshaw, S. (1982) Identifying areas of rural deprivation using social area analysis. *Regional Studies* 16, 409–17.

Daly, A. (1975) Measuring accessibility in a rural context. In P. R. White (ed.), *Rural transport seminar 1975*. London: Transport Studies Group, Polytechnic of Central London.

Damette, F. (1980) The regional framework of monopoly exploitation: new problems and trends. In J. Carney, R. Hudson and J. Lewis (eds.), *Regions in crisis*. London: Croom Helm.

Daniels, P. (1978) Service sector office employment and regional imbalance in Britain, 1966–71. *Tijdschrift voor Economische en Sociale Geografie* 69, 286–95.

Dartmoor National Park Authority (1977) *Dartmoor National Park Plan*. Exeter: Devon County Council.

Davey, B, Josling, T. E. and McFarquhar, A. (1976) *Agriculture and the state: British policy in a world context*. London: Macmillan.

Davidson, J. and Lloyd, R. (eds.) (1978) *Conservation and agriculture*. Chichester: John Wiley.

and Wibberley, G. (1977) *Planning and the rural environment*. Oxford: Pergamon Press.

Davies, R. B. and O'Farrell, P. N. (1981) A spatial and temporal analysis of second home ownership in Wales. *Geoforum* 12, 161–78.

Dawson, J. A. (1980) Retail activity and public policy. In J. A. Dawson (ed.), *Retail Geography*. London: Croom Helm.

and Kirby, D. A. (1979) *Small scale retailing in the U.K.* Farnborough: Saxon House.

Dear, M. (1974) A paradigm for public facility location. *Antipode* 6, 46–50.

Denman, R. (1978) *Recreation and tourism on farms, crofts and estates*. Edinburgh: Scottish Tourist Board.

Dennis, N. (1972) *Public participation and planning blight*. London: Faber and Faber.

Henriques, F. and Slaughter, C. (1956) *Coal is our life*. London: Eyre and Spottiswoode.

Dennis, R. and Clout, H. (1980) *A social geography of England and Wales*. Oxford: Pergamon Press.

Department of Health and Social Security (annual) *Health and personal social service statistics for England*. London: HMSO.

Department of the Environment (1971a) *Study of rural transport in West Suffolk*. London: HMSO.

(1971b) *Study of rural transport in Devon*. London: HMSO.

(1976) *British cities: urban population and employment trends 1951–71*. Research Report 10. London: Department of Environment.

(1977a) *Inner area studies*. London: HMSO.

(1977b) *Housing policy: a consultative document*. London: HMSO.

(1977c) *Mobile homes in England and Wales, 1975*. London: HMSO.

(1978) *English house condition survey, 1976: Part 1; report of the physical condition survey*. London: HMSO.

(1981) *Housing and construction statistics 1970–1980*. London: HMSO.

(1982) *English house condition survey, 1981: Part 1; report of the physical condition survey*. London: HMSO.

Derounian, J. (1980) The impact of structure plans on rural communities. *The Planner* 66, 87–8.

Desai, M. (1974) *Marxian economics*. Oxford: Basil Blackwell.

Devon County Council (1977) *Country structure plan: report of the survey* Exeter: Devon County Council.

Dicken, P. and Lloyd, P. E. (1981) *Modern Western society: a geographical perspective on work, home and well-being*. London: Harper and Row.

Dobbs, B. (1979) Rural public transport: the economic stranglehold. In D. A. Halsall and B. J. Turton (eds.), *Rural transport problems in Britain*. Transport Geography Study Group, Institute of British Geographers. Department of

Geography, University of Keele.

Dower, M. (1972) Amenity and tourism in the countryside. In J. Ashton and W. H. Long (eds.), *The remoter rural areas of Britain*. Edinburgh: Oliver and Boyd.

— (1977) Planning aspects of second homes. In J. T. Coppock (ed.), *Second homes: curse or blessing?* Oxford: Pergamon Press.

Rapoport, R., Strelitz, Z. and Kew, S. (1981) *Leisure provision and people's needs*. London: HMSO.

Downing, P. and Dower, M. (1973) *Second homes in England and Wales*. London: HMSO for the Countryside Commission.

Drudy, P. J. (1978) Depopulation in a prosperous agricultural sub-region. *Regional Studies* 12, 49–60.

— and Drudy, S. M. (1979) Population mobility and labour supply in rural regions: North Norfolk and Galway. *Regional Studies* 13, 91–9.

— and Wallace, D. B. (1971) Towards a development programme for remote rural areas: a case study in North Norfolk. *Regional Studies* 5, 281–8.

Duclaud-Williams, R. H. (1978) *The politics of housing in Britain and France*. London: Heinemann.

Duncan, S. S. (1976) Research directions in social geography: housing opportunities and constraints. *Transactions of the Institute of British Geographers* New Series 1, 10–9.

— (1977) *Urban studies in Britain – developments on the housing question*. Paper no 34. Institutionen Kulturgeografi ach Ekonomisk Geografi. Lunds Universitet.

Dunleavy, P. (1982) Perspectives on urban studies. In A. Blowers, C. Brook, P. Dunleavy and L. McDowell (eds.), *Urban change and conflict: an interdisciplinary reader*. London: Harper and Row.

Dunn, M. C. (1976) Population change and the settlement pattern. In G. E. Cherry (ed.), *Rural planning problems*. London: Leonard Hill.

— (1979) Patterns of population change and movement in Herefordshire 1951–71 and their implications for rural planning. Unpublished PhD thesis, University of Birmingham.

Rawson, M. and Rogers, A. (1981) *Rural housing: competition and choice*. London: Allen and Unwin.

Durant, R. (1959) *Watling: a survey of social life on a new housing estate*. London: King.

Economides, K. (1982) Legal services and rural deprivation. *Bracton Law Journal* 15, 41–78.

Edwards, A. (1974) Resources in agriculture: land. In A. Edwards and A. Rogers (eds.), *Agricultural resources: an introduction to the farming industry of the United Kingdom*. London: Faber and Faber.

— and Rogers, A. (eds.) (1974) *Agricultural resources: an introduction to the farming industry of the United Kingdom*. London: Faber and Faber.

Edwards, J. A. (1964) The settlement factor in the rural problems of North-east England. Unpublished PhD thesis, University of Newcastle.

— (1971) The viability of lower size-order settlements in rural areas: the case of north-east England. *Sociologia Ruralis* 11, 247–75.

Edwards, J. (1975) Social indicators, urban deprivation and positive discrimination. *Journal of Social Policy* 4, 275–87.

Elson, M. (1981) Structure plan policies for pressurised rural areas. In A. W. Gilg (ed.), *Countryside Planning Yearbook 1981*. Norwich: Geo Books.

English Tourist Board (1982) *British home tourism survey 1981*. London: English Tourist Board.

Evans, M. (1975) *Karl Marx*. London: Allen and Unwin.

Eversley, D. (1973) *The planner in society*. London: Faber and Faber.

Exeter and District Community Health Council (1983) *Medical services in rural areas*. Report of a survey of rural parishes' health services. Exeter: Exeter and District CHC.

Eyles, J. (1974) Social theory and social geography. *Progress in Geography* 6, 27–87.

—— (1978) Social geography and the study of the capitalist city: a review. *Tijdschrift voor Economische en Sociale Geografie* 69, 296–305.

—— (1979) Area-based policies for the inner city: context, problems and prospects. In D. T. Herbert and D. M. Smith (eds.), *Social problems and the city*. Oxford: University Press.

Fletcher, P. (1969) 'The control of housing standards in a rural district: a case study'. *Social and Economic Administration* 3, 106–20.

Ford, J. (1975) The role of the building society manager in the urban stratification system. *Urban Studies* 12, 295–302.

Forsythe, D. E. (1980) Urban incomers and rural change. *Sociologia Ruralis* 20, 287–305.

Fothergill, S. and Gudgin, G. (1979) Regional employment change: a subregional explanation. *Progress in Planning* 12, 155–219.

Frankenberg, R. (1957) *Village on the Border*. London: Cohen and West.

—— (1966) *Communities in Britain: social life in town and country*. Harmondsworth: Penguin.

Garbett-Edwards, D. P. (1972) The establishment of new industries. In J. Ashton and W. H. Long (eds.), *The remoter rural areas of Britain*. Edinburgh: Oliver and Boyd.

Gasson, R. (1966) *The influence of urbanization on farm ownership and practice; some aspects of the effects of London on farms and farm people in Kent and Sussex*. Report no. 7, Studies in Rural Land Use, Wye College.

—— (1969) Occupational immobility of small farmers. *Journal of Agricultural Economics* 20, 279–88.

—— (1971) Relative deprivation and attachment to farming. *Sociological Review* 19, 557–83.

—— (1974a) Resources in agriculture: labour. In A. Edwards and A. Rogers (eds.), *Agricultural resources: an introduction to the farming industry of the United Kingdom*. London: Faber and Faber.

—— (1974b) *Mobility of farm workers: a study of the effects of towns and industrial employment on the supply of farm labour*. Occasional Paper no. 2, Department of Land Economy, Univerity of Cambridge.

—— (1975) *Provision of tied cottages*. Occasional Paper no. 4, Department of Land Economy, University of Cambridge.

Gavin, W. (1967) *Ninety years of family farming*. London: Hutchinson.

Geddes, M. (1979) *Uneven development and the Scottish Highlands*. Working Paper no. 17, School of Urban and Regional Studies, University of Sussex.

Geddes, P. (1915) *Cities in evolution*. London: Tyrwhitt, Williams and Norgate.

Gilder, I. M. (1979) Rural planning policies: an economic appraisal. *Progress in Planning* 11, 213–71.

Gilg, A. (1974) Regional planning in the South West. *Social and Economic Administration* 8, 220–4.

(1976) Rural employment. In G. E. Cherry (ed.), *Rural planning problems*. London: Leonard Hill.

(1978) *Countryside planning: the first three decades 1945–1976*. Newton Abbot: David and Charles.

(1980) Planning for rural employment in a changed economy. *The Planner* 66, 91–3.

(ed.) (1981) *Countryside Planning Yearbook 1981*. Norwich: Geo Books.

(1982) Politics and the countryside: the British example. Paper presented to Anglo-Dutch Symposium, University of East Anglia, Norwich, September 1982.

(1983a) Population and employment. In M. Pacione (ed.), *Progress in rural geography*. London: Croom Helm.

(ed.) (1983b) *Countryside Planning Yearbook 1983*. Norwich: Geo Books.

Glass, R. (1955) Urban sociology in Great Britain: a trend report. *Current Sociology* 4, 5–19 .

(1962) Urban sociology. In A. T. Welford (ed.), *Society: problems and methods of study*. London: Routledge and Kegan Paul.

(1968) Urban sociology in Great Britain. In R. E. Pahl (ed.), *Readings in urban sociology*. Oxford: Pergamon Press.

Gloucester County Council (1978) *Community facilities*. County structure plan, Draft Report of Survey, Technical Volume no. 7. Gloucester: Gloucester County Council.

Glyn-Jones, A. (1979) *Rural recovery: has it begun? A study of a parish in north-west Devon 1964–1978*. Exeter: Devon County Council and the University of Exeter.

Goddard, J. B. (1975) *Office location in urban and regional development*. London: Oxford University Press.

(1978) Office location and urban and regional development. In P. Daniels (ed.), *Spatial patterns of office growth and location*. Chichester: John Wiley.

Goodman, R. (1972) *After the planners*. Harmondsworth: Penguin.

Gough, I. (1979) *The political economy of the welfare state*. London: Macmillan.

Gould, P. (1969) *Spatial diffusion*. Washington DC: Commission on College Geography, Association of American Geographers.

Gray, F. (1976a) Selection and allocation in council housing. *Transactions of the Institute of British Geographers* New Series 1, 34–46.

(1976b) The management of local authority housing. In Political Economy of Housing Workshop, *Housing and class in Britain*. Brighton: School of Cultural and Community Studies, University of Sussex.

Greaves, A. M. (1979) Population change and settlement policy. In P. Hall (ed.),

Population and employment in rural areas. Forum Report 15. Glasgow: The Planning Exchange.

Green, B. (1981) *Countryside conservation.* London: Allen and Unwin.

Green, R. (1971) *Country planning: the future of rural regions.* Manchester: University Press.

Greenberg, L. (1982) The implications of an ageing population for land-use planning. In A. M. Warnes (ed.), *Geographical perspectives on the elderly.* Chichester: John Wiley.

Gregory, D. G. (1970) *Green belts and development control.* Birmingham: Centre for Urban and Regional Studies.

Grieve, R. (1973) Scotland: Highland experience of regional government. *Town and Country Planning* 41, 172–6.

Grime, L. P. and Whitelegg, J. (1982) The geography of health care planning: some problems of correspondence between local and national policies. *Community Medicine* 4, 201–8.

Gyford, J. (1976) *Local politics in Britain.* London: Croom Helm.

Hadden, T. (1979) *Housing: repairs and improvements.* London: Sweet and Maxwell.

Haddon, R. (1970) A minority in a welfare state: the location of Indians in the London housing market. *New Atlantis* 1, 80–133.

Hägerstrand, T. (1970) What about people in regional science? *Papers and Proceedings of the Regional Science Association* 24, 7–21.

Hall, C. (1975) Rural transport: a poor relation? *Built Environment* 1, 119–20.

Hall, J. M. (1974) Forests as recreation resources. In P. Lavery (ed.), *Recreational geography.* Newton Abbot: David and Charles.

—— (1982) *The geography of planning decisions.* Oxford: University Press.

Hall, P. R., Thomas, R., Gracey, H. and Drewett, R. (1973) *The containment of urban England.* London: George Allen and Unwin.

Halsall, D. A. (1979) Railway network contraction in rural North Wales, 1948–1972. In D. A. Halsall and B. J. Turton (eds.), *Rural transport problems in Britain.* Transport Geography Study Group, Institute of British Geographers. Department of Geography, University of Keele.

—— and Turton, B. J. (eds.) (1979) *Rural transport problems in Britain.* Transport Geography Study Group, Institute of British Geographers. Department of Geography, University of Keele.

Hancock, T. (1976) Planning in rural settlements. *Town and Country Planning* 44, 520–3.

Hannan, D. F. (1970) *Rural exodus.* London: Geoffrey Chapman.

Harloe, M. (1977) Introduction. In M. Harloe (ed.), *Captive cities.* London: John Wiley.

Harman, R. G. (1978) Retailing in rural areas: a case study in Norfolk. *Geoforum* 9, 107–26.

Harris, M. (1973) Some aspects of social polarization. In D. V. Donnison and D. E. C. Eversley (eds.), *London: urban patterns, problems and policies.* London: Heinemann.

Harrison, M. L. (1972) Development control: the influence of political, legal and ideological factors. *Town Planning Review* 43, 254–74.

Hart, J. T. (1971) The inverse care law. *Lancet i*, 405–12.

Harvey, D. (1970) Social processes and spatial form: an analysis of the conceptual problems of urban planning. *Papers and Proceedings of the Regional Science Association* 25, 47–69.

(1973) *Social justice and the city*. London: Edward Arnold.

(1978a) The urban process under capitalism. *International Journal of Urban and Regional Research* 2, 101–31.

(1978b) Labour, capital and class struggle around the built environment in advanced capitalist societies. In K. R. Cox (ed.), *Urbanization and conflict in market societies*. London: Methuen.

(1982) *The limits to capital*. Oxford: Basil Blackwell.

Haynes, R. M. and Bentham, C. G. (1979) *Community hospitals and rural accessibility*. Farnborough: Saxon House.

(1982) The effects of accessibility on general practitioner consultations, out-patient attendances and in-patient admissions in Norfolk, England. *Social Science and Medicine* 16, 561–9.

Spencer, M. B. and Spratley, J. M. (1978) Community attitudes towards the accessibility of hospitals in West Suffolk. In M. J. Moseley (ed.), *Social issues in rural Norfolk*. Norwich: Centre of East Anglian Studies, University of East Anglia.

Hebbert, M. and Gault, I. (1978) *Green belt issues in local plan preparation*. Oxford: Oxford Polytechnic.

Hechter, M. (1975) *Internal colonialism: the celtic fringe in British national development 1536–1966*. London: Routledge and Kegan Paul.

Heller, T. (1978) Health and health services. In A. Walker. (ed.), *Rural poverty* Poverty Pamphlet 37. London: Child Poverty Action Group.

(1979) Rural health and health services. In J. M. Shaw (ed.), *Rural deprivation and planning*. Norwich: Geo Books.

Herbert, D. T. (1972) *Urban geography: a social perspective*. Newton Abbot: David and Charles.

(1975) Urban deprivation: definition, measurement and spatial qualities. *Geographical Journal* 141, 362–72.

and Johnston, R. J. (eds.) (1976) *Social areas in cities: spatial perspectives on problems and policies*. London: John Wiley.

and Thomas, C. J. (1982) *Urban geography: a first approach*. Chichester: John Wiley.

Hill, A. B. (1925) *Internal migration and its effects upon the death rates with special reference to the County of Essex*. London: Medical Research Council.

Hill, B. (1974) Resources in agriculture: capital. In A. Edwards and A. Rogers (eds.), *Agricultural resources: an introduction to the farming industry of the United Kingdom*. London: Faber and Faber.

Hill, C. M. (1978) Leisure behaviour in six mid-Norfolk villages. In M. J. Moseley (ed.), *Social issues in rural Norfolk*. Norwich: Centre of East Anglian Studies, University of East Anglia.

(1982) Newcomers and leisure in Norfolk villages. In M. J. Moseley (ed.),

Power, planning and people in rural East Anglia. Norwich: Centre of East Anglian Studies, University of East Anglia.

Hillman, M., Henderson, I. and Whalley, A. (1973) *Personal mobility and transport policy.* Broadsheet 542, Vol. XLII. London: Political and Economic Planning.

Hillman, M. and Whalley, A. (1977) *Fair play for all.* Broadsheet 571, Vol. XLIII. London: Political and Economic Planning.

(1980) *The social consequences of rail closures*, Report no. 587. London: Policy Studies Institute.

Hislop, M. (1975) Improving rural bus services. *Local Council Review* 26, 149–52.

Hodge, I. D. and Whitby, M. C. (1979) *New jobs in the Eastern Borders: an economic evaluation of the Development Commission factory programme.* Monograph 8, Agricultural Adjustment Unit, University of Newcastle, Newcastle.

(1981) *Rural employment: trends, options, choices.* London: Methuen.

Hodges, M. W. and Smith, C. S. (1954) The Sheffield estate. In C. D. Mitchell, T. Lupton, M. W. Hodges and C. Smith (eds.), *Neighbourhood and community.* Liverpool: University Press.

Holding, D. M. (1979) Levels of rural bus provision and fares policy. In D. A. Halsall and B. J. Turton (eds.), *Rural transport problems in Britain.* Transport Geography Study Group, Institute of British Geographers. Department of Geography, University of Keele.

Hookway, R. J. S. (1978) National park plans. *The Planner* 64, 20–2.

House, J. W. (1965) *Rural North-East England 1951–61.* Papers on migration and mobility in N.E. England no. 1, Geography Department, University of Newcastle.

and Knight, E. M. (1965) *Migrants of North-East England, 1951–1961.* Geography Department, University of Newcastle.

Houston, J. M. (1963) *A social geography of Europe.* London: Gerald Duckworth.

Howarth, R. W. (1969) The political strength of British agriculture. *Political Studies* 17, 458–69.

Howe, G. M. (1970) *National atlas of disease mortality in the United Kingdom.* London: Nelson.

(1979) Mortality from selected malignant neoplasms in the British Isles: the spatial perspective. *The Geographical Journal* 145, 401–15.

Howes, R. and Law, D. (1973) Manufacturing industry and rural areas. *Journal of the Royal Town Planning Institute* 59, 406–10.

Hughes, D. J. (1981) *Public sector housing law.* London: Butterworths.

Irving, B. L. and Hilgendorf, E. L. (1975) *Tied cottages in British agriculture.* Working Paper no. 1. London: Tavistock Institute of Human Relations.

Jackson, V. J. (1968) *Population in the countryside: growth and stagnation in the Cotswolds.* London: Cass.

Jacobs, C. A. J. (1976) *Countryside recreation site survey*, vol. 1. Mold: Clwyd County Council.

John, B. (1981) A plea from the Welsh wilderness. *Town and Country Planning* 50, 256–60.

Johnston, R. J. (1967) A reconnaissance study of population change in Nidderdale 1951–61. *Transactions of the Institute of British Geographers* 41, 113–23.

Jones, A. (1975) *Rural housing: the agricultural tied cottage*. Occasional Papers on Social Administration no. 56. London: Bell.

Jones, E. (ed.) (1975) *Readings in social geography*. London: Oxford University Press.

and Eyles, J. (1977) *An introduction to social geography*. Oxford: University Press.

Jones, G. (1973) *Rural life*. London: Longman.

Jones, H. R. (1965) A study of rural migration in Central Wales. *Transactions of the Institute of British Geographers* 37, 31–45.

(1981) *Population geography*. London: Harper and Row.

Keeble, D. (1976) *Industrial location and planning in the United Kingdom*. London: Methuen.

Kennett, S. and Spence, N. (1979) British population trends in the 1970s. *Town and Country Planning* 48, 221–3.

Kirby, A. (1977) *Housing action areas in Great Britain, 1975–1977*. Geographical Papers, no. 60, Department of Geography, University of Reading.

Kirby, D. A. (1974) The decline and fall of the small retail outlet: a geographical study. *Retail and Distribution Management* 2, 14–18.

Kirk, J. H. (1974) The agricultural industry: an introduction. In A. Edwards and A. Rogers (eds.), *Agricultural resources: an introduction to the farming industry of the United Kingdom*. London: Faber and Faber.

Knox, P. L. (1974) Spatial variations in levels of living in England and Wales. *Transactions of the Institute of British Geographers* 62, 1–24.

(1975) *Social well-being: a spatial perspective*. Oxford: University Press.

(1982) *Urban social geography: an introduction*. London: Longman.

and Cottam, M. B. (1981a) Rural deprivation in Scotland: a preliminary assessment. *Tijdschrift voor Economische en Sociale Geografie* 72, 162–75.

(1981b) A welfare approach to rural geography: contrasting perspectives on the quality of Highland life. *Transactions of the Institute of British Geographers* New Series 6, 433–50.

Knox, P. and Cullen, J. (1981) Planners as urban managers: an exploration of the attitudes and self-image of senior British planners. *Environment and Planning* 13, 885–98.

Lambert, J., Paris, C. and Blackaby, B. (1978) *Housing policy and the state: allocation, access and control*. London: Macmillan.

Lansley, S. (1979) *Housing and public policy*. London: Croom Helm.

Larkin, A. (1978a) Inner-city infatuation – rural areas must fight it. *Municipal and Public Services Journal* 86, 1277–8.

(1978b) Housing and the poor. In A. Walker (ed.), *Rural poverty*. Poverty Pamphlet no. 37. London: Child Poverty Action Group.

(1979) Rural housing and housing needs. In J. M. Shaw (ed.), *Rural deprivation and planning*. Norwich: Geo Books.

Lavery, P. (1974) The demand for recreation. In P. Lavery (ed.), *Recreational geography*. Newton Abbot: David and Charles.

Law, C. M. (1980) *British regional development since World War One*. Newton Abbot: David and Charles.

and Warnes, A. M. (1973) The movement of retired people to seaside resorts. *Town Planning Review* 4, 373–90.

(1975) Life begins at sixty: the increase in regional retirement migration. *Town and Country Planning* 43, 531–4.

(1976) The changing geography of the elderly in England and Wales. *Transactions of the Institute of British Geographers* New Series 1, 453–71.

(1982) The destination decision in retirement migration. In A. M. Warnes (ed.), *Geographical perspectives on the elderly*. Chichester: John Wiley.

Lawton, R. (1973) Rural depopulation in nineteenth century England. In D. R. Mills (ed.), *English rural communities: the impact of a specialised economy*. London: Macmillan.

(1977) Regional population trends in England and Wales, 1750–1971. In J. Hobcraft and P. Rees (eds.), *Regional demographic development*. London: Croom Helm.

Lee, T. (1957) On the relation between the school journey and emotional adjustment in rural infant children. *British Journal of Educational Psychology* 27, 101–14.

(1960) A test of the hypothesis that school reorganisation is a cause of rural depopulation. *Durham Research Review* 3, 64–73.

Leschinsky, D. (1977) *Health services in rural areas*. London: National Federation of Women's Institutes.

Lever, W. (1974) Regional multipliers and demand leakages at establishment level. *Scottish Journal of Political Economy* 21, 111–22.

(1978) Company dominated labour markets: the British case. *Tijdschrift voor Economische en Sociale Geografie* 69, 306–12.

Lewis, G. (1969) A study of socio-geographical change in the Welsh borderland. Unpublished PhD thesis, University of Leicester.

Lewis, G. (1980) The disadvantages and advantages of small rural schools. In *Educational disadvantage in rural areas*. Manchester: Centre for Information and Advice on Educational Disadvantage.

Lewis, O. (1966) The culture of poverty. *Scientific American* 215, 19–25.

Liell, P. (1981) *Council houses and the Housing Act 1980*. London: Butterworths.

Lipietz, A. (1980) The structuration of space, the problem of land and spatial policy. In J. G. Carney, R. Hudson and J. R. Lewis (eds.), *Regions in crisis*. London: Croom Helm.

Littlejohn, J. (1964) *Westrigg: the sociology of a Cheviot parish*. London: Routledge and Kegan Paul.

Lockhart, D. G. (1982) Contemporary rural settlement planning in Scotland: a study of key village and related policies. Paper presented to Anglo-Dutch Symposium, University of East Anglia, Norwich, September 1982.

Low, N. (1973) Farming and the inner green belt. *Town Planning Review* 44, 103–16.

(1975) Centrism and the provision of services in residential areas. *Urban Studies* 12, 177–91.

Lowenthal, D. and Comitas, L. (1962) Emigration and depopulation: some neglected aspects of population geography. *Geographical Review* 52, 195–210.

Lupton, T. and Mitchell, D. (1954) The Liverpool estate. In C. D. Mitchell, T. Lupton, M. W. Hodges and C. Smith (eds.), *Neighbourhood and community*. Liverpool: University Press.

McAuslan, P. (1980) *The ideologies of planning law*. Oxford: Pergamon Press.

McCrone, G. (1976) *Regional policy in Britain*. London: George Allen and Unwin.

MacIver, R. M. and Page, C. H. (1952) *Society: an introductory analysis*. London: Macmillan.

Mack, J. (1978) The village school. *New Society* 44, 660–2.

Mackay, G. A. and Laing, G. (1982) *Consumer problems in rural areas*. Glasgow: Scottish Consumer Council.

McLaughlin, B. P. (1976) Rural settlement planning: a new approach. *Town and Country Planning* 44, 156–60.

Manners, G., Keeble, D., Rodgers, B. and Warren, K. (1972) *Regional development in Britain*. London: John Wiley.

Marquand, J. (1979) *The service sector and regional policy in the United Kingdom*, Research Series 29. London: Centre for Environmental Studies.

Marsh, G. and Kaim-Caudle, P. (1976) *Team care in general practice*. London: Croom Helm.

Marshall, J. N. (1979) Ownership, organization and industrial linkage: a case study in the Northern Region of England. *Regional Studies* 13, 531–57.

Martin, I. (1976) Rural communities. In G. Cherry (ed.), *Rural planning problems*. London: Leonard Hill.

Massam, B. (1980) *Spatial search*. Oxford: Pergamon Press.

Masser, F. I. and Stroud, O. C. (1965) The metropolitan village. *Town Planning Review* 36, 111–24.

Massey, D. B. (1979) In what sense a regional problem? *Regional Studies* 13, 233–44.

Matthews, J. D., Philip, M. S. and Cumming, D. G. (1972) Forestry and forest industries. In J. Ashton and W. H. Long (eds), *The remoter rural areas of Britain*. Edinburgh: Oliver and Boyd.

Mellor, J. R. (1977) *Urban sociology in an urbanized society*. London: Routledge and Kegan Paul.

Metcalf, D. (1969) *The economics of agriculture*. Harmondsworth: Penguin.

Miliband, R. (1969) *The state in capitalist society*. London: Weidenfeld and Nicolson.

Ministry of Agriculture, Fisheries and Food (1982) *Annual review of agriculture 1982*. London: HMSO.

Ministry of Housing and Local Government (1964) *Depopulation in Mid-Wales: report of the committee*. London: HMSO.

Mitchell, C. G. B. and Town, S. W. (1976) *Accessibility of various social groups to different activities*. Crowthorne, Berkshire: Transport and Road Research Laboratory.

Mitchell, G. D. (1950) Depopulation and rural social structure. *Sociological Review* 42, 69–85.

 (1951) The relevance of group dynamics to rural planning problems. *Sociological Review* 43, 1–16.

Mogey, J. (1956) *Family and neighbourhood*. London: Oxford University Press.

Morgan, B. S. (1976) The bases of family status segregation: a case study. *Transactions of the Institute of British Geographers* New Series 1, 83–108.

Moseley, M. J. (1973) The impact of growth centres in rural regions: II – an analysis of spatial flows in East Anglia. *Regional Studies* 7, 77–94.

(1974) *Growth centres in spatial planning*. Oxford: Pergamon Press.

(ed.) (1978) *Social issues in rural Norfolk*. Norwich: Centre of East Anglian Studies, University of East Anglia.

(1979a) *Accessibility: the rural challenge*. London: Methuen.

(1979b) Rural mobility and accessibility. In J. M. Shaw (ed.), *Rural deprivation and planning*. Norwich: Geo Books.

(1980a) Is rural deprivation really rural? *The Planner* 66, 97.

(1980b) *Rural development and its relevance to the inner-city debate*. Inner City in Conflict, Paper 9. London: Social Science Research Council.

(ed.) (1982) *Power, planning and people in rural East Anglia*. Norwich: Centre of East Anglian Studies, University of East Anglia.

Harman, R. G., Coles, O. B. and Spencer, M. B. (1977) *Rural transport and accessibility*, 2 vols. Norwich: Centre of East Anglian Studies, University of East Anglia.

and Spencer, M. B. (1978) Access to shops: the situation in rural Norfolk. In M. J. Moseley (ed.), *Social issues in rural Norfolk*. Norwich: Centre of East Anglian Studies, University of East Anglia.

and Townroe, P. M. (1973) Linkage adjustment following industrial movement. *Tijdschrift voor Economische en Sociale Geografie* 64, 137–44.

Mulligan, C. A. (1979) The Snowdon sherpa: public transport and National Park management experiment. In D. A. Hallsall and B. J. Turton (eds.), *Rural transport problems in Britain*. Institute of British Geographers. Transport Geography Study Group. Department of Geography, University of Keele.

Munton, R. J. C. (1976) Agricultural land prices in 1974: some observations. *Chartered Surveyor, Rural Quarterly* 4, 14–16.

(1977) Financial institutions: their ownership of agricultural land. *Area* 9, 29–37.

and Clout, H. D. (1975) The geographical implications of changing patterns of personal mobility for the spatial organization of central places in rural Norfolk. In B. Sarfalvi (ed.), *Urbanization in Europe*. Budapest: Akademiai Kiado.

Nalson, J. S. (1968) *Mobility of farm families: a study of occupational and residential mobility in an upland area of England*. Manchester: University Press.

Nash, R. (1975) The one-teacher school. *British Journal of Education Studies* 24, 12–32.

National Council of Social Service (1979) *Structure plans and rural communities*. London: National Council of Social Service.

Neate, S. (1981) *Rural deprivation: an annotated bibliography of economic and social problems in rural Britain*. Norwich: Geo Abstracts.

Newby, H. (1972a) The low earnings of agricultural workers: a sociological approach. *Journal of Agricultural Economics* 23, 15–24.

(1972b) Agricultural workers in the class structure. *Sociological Review* 20, 413–39.

(1977) *The deferential worker: a study of farm workers in East Anglia*. London: Allen Lane.

(1979) *Green and pleasant land?* London: Hutchinson.

Bell, C., Rose, D. and Saunders, P. (1978) *Property, paternalism and power.* London: Hutchinson.

Niner, P. (1975) *Local authority housing policy and practice – a case-study approach,* Occasional Paper no. 31, Centre for Urban and Regional Studies, University of Birmingham.

Norman, P. (1975) *Managerialism: review of recent work,* Conference Paper 14. London: Centre for Environmental Studies.

Norman, P. (1978) Is there life after death? *The Sunday Times,* 29 January, 33–4.

Nutley, S. D. (1979) Patterns of regional accessibility in the NW Highlands and Islands. *Scottish Geographical Magazine* 95, 142–54.

(1980) Accessibility, mobility and transport-related welfare: the case of rural Wales. *Geoforum* 11, 335–52.

(1982) The extent of public transport decline in rural Wales. *Cambria* 9, 27–48.

Oakenshott, R. (1979) The call of the Shires. *The Economist* 272, 31–7.

O'Connor, J. (1973) *The fiscal crisis of the state.* New York: St Martins Press.

Office of Population Censuses and Surveys (1979) *General household survey, 1977.* London: HMSO.

Organisation for Economic Cooperation and Development (1976) *Measuring social well-being.* Paris: OECD.

Pacione, M. (ed.) (1983) *Progress in rural geography.* London: Croom Helm.

Packman, J. (1979) Rural employment: problems and planning. In J. M. Shaw (ed.), *Rural deprivation and planning.* Norwich: Geo Books.

Pahl, R. E. (1965a) Trends in social geography. In R. J. Chorley and P. Haggett (eds.), *Frontiers in geographical teaching.* London: Methuen.

(1965b) *Urbs in rure,* Geographical Paper 2. London: London School of Economics.

(1966) The social objectives of village planning. *Official Architecture and Planning* 29, 1146–50.

(1967) Sociological models in geography. In R. J. Chorley and P. Haggett (eds.), *Models in geography.* London: Methuen.

(1968) The rural-urban continuum. In R. E. Pahl (ed.), *Readings in urban sociology.* Oxford: Pergamon Press.

(1970) *Whose city?* London: Longman.

(1975) *Whose city?* Harmondsworth: Penguin.

(1977) Managers, technical experts and the state: forms of mediation, manipulation and dominance in urban and regional development. In M. Harloe (ed.), *Captive cities.* London: John Wiley.

(1979) Socio-political factors in resource allocation. In D. T. Herbert and D. M. Smith (eds.), *Social problems and the city: geographical perspectives.* Oxford: University Press.

Palmer, C. J., Robinson, M. E. and Thomas, R. W. (1977) The countryside image – an investigation of structure and meaning. *Environment and Planning A* 9, 739–750.

Paris, C. and Lambert, J. (1979) Housing problems and the state: the case of Birmingham, England. In D. T. Herbert and R. J. Johnston (eds.),

Geography and the urban environment, vol. II. Chichester: John Wiley.

Patmore, J. A. (1970) *Land and leisure in England and Wales*. Newton Abbot: David and Charles.

Peak Park Joint Planning Board (1978) *Peak District National Park Plan*. Bakewell, Derbyshire: Peak Park National Park Office.

Penfold, S. F. (1974) *Housing problems of local people in rural pressure areas: the Peak District experience and discussion of policy options*. Sheffield: Department of Town and Regional Planning, University of Sheffield.

Perry, M. and Chalkley, B. (1982) The geography of recent small-factory provision in Cornwall. In G. Shaw and A. M. Williams (eds.), *Economic development and policy in Cornwall*. South West Papers in Geography, no. 2. Plymouth-Exeter: Plymouth Polytechnic, College of St. Mark and St. John and University of Exeter.

Perry, P. J. (ed.) (1973) *British agriculture 1875–1914*. London: Methuen.

Perry, R. (1979) Why do manufacturing firms come to Cornwall? In Cornwall Industrial Development Association, *Summary of studies of the Cornish economy*. Camborne: CIDA.

(1982) The role of the small manufacturing business in Cornwall's economic development. In G. Shaw and A. M. Williams (eds.), *Economic development and policy in Cornwall*. South West Papers in Geography no. 2. Plymouth-Exeter: Plymouth Polytechnic, College of St. Mark and St. John and University of Exeter.

Pharmaceutical Society of Great Britain (1979) Survey of pharmacy closures, 1978. *Pharmaceutical Journal* 8 December, 598–9.

Phillips, D. R. (1979) Public attitudes to general practitioner services: a reflection of an inverse care law in intraurban primary medical care? *Environment and Planning A* 11, 815–24.

(1981) *Contemporary issues in the geography of health care*. Norwich: Geo Books.

and Court, M. (1982) 'Grassrooting': an experiment in planning health care. *The Health Services* no. 35, 14–15.

and Williams, A. M. (1981) Council house sales and village life. *New Society* 58, 367–8.

(1982a) *Rural housing and the public sector*. Aldershot: Gower.

(1982b) The need for rural council houses. *Housing* 18, 16–9.

(1982c) Local authority housing and accessibility: evidence from the South Hams, Devon. *Transactions of the Institute of British Geographers* New Series 7, 304–20.

(1982d) A positive approach to transfer management? *Housing Review* 31, 13–16.

(1983) The social implications of rural housing policy: a review of developments in the past decade. In A. Gilg (ed.), *Countryside Planning Yearbook 1983*. Norwich: Geo Books.

Pickvance, C. G. (1976) *Urban sociology: critical essays*. London: Methuen.

Pinch, S. P. (1978) Patterns of local authority housing allocation in Greater London between 1966 and 1973: an inter-borough analysis. *Transactions of the Institute of British Geographers* New Series 3, 35–54.

Planning Advisory Group (1965) *The future of development plans*. London: HMSO.

Pred, A. and Palm, R. (1978) The status of American women: a time-geographic view. In D. A. Lanegran and R. Palm (eds.), *An invitation to geography*. New York: McGraw Hill.

Price Commission (1975) *Food prices in outlying areas*. London: HMSO.

Pulling, L. and Speakman, C. (1974) *Changing directions: the report of the Independent Commission on Transport*. London: Coronet Books.

Quaini, M. (1982) *Geography and Marxism*. Oxford: Basil Blackwell.

Randolph, W. and Robert, S. (1981) Population redistribution in Great Britain, 1971–1981. *Town and Country Planning* 50, 227–30.

Rapoport, R. and Rapoport, R. N. (1975) *Leisure and the family life cycle*. London: Routledge and Kegan Paul.

Rees, A. D. (1950) *Life in a Welsh countryside*. Cardiff: University of Wales Press.

Reissman, L. (1964) *The urban process*. New York: Free Press.

Rettig, S. (1976) An investigation into the problems of urban fringe agriculture in a green belt situation. *Planning Outlook* 19, 50–74.

Rex, J. and Moore, R. (1967) *Race, community and conflict*. London: Oxford University Press.

Rhind, D. and Hudson, R. (1980) *Land use*. London: Methuen.

Rich, R. C. (1979) Neglected issues in the study of urban service distributions: a research agenda. *Urban Studies* 16, 143–56.

Richmond, P. (1983) *Housing associations in rural areas*. South West Papers in Geography no. 7. Plymouth-Exeter: Plymouth Polytechnic, College of St. Mark and St. John and University of Exeter.

Robert, S. and Randolph, W. (1983). Beyond decentralization: the evolution of population distribution in England and Wales, 1961–1981. *Geoforum* 14, 75–102.

Robins, D. L. J. (1983) Rural planning. In M. Pacione (ed.), *Progress in rural geography*. London: Croom Helm.

Robinson, D. G. (1976) Rural landscape. In G. E. Cherry (ed.), *Rural planning problems*. London: Leonard Hill.

Robson, B. T. (1979) Housing, empiricism and the state. In D. T. Herbert and D. M. Smith (eds.), *Social problems and the city*. Oxford: University Press.

Rogers, A. (1974) The pattern of farming. In A. Edwards and A. Rogers (eds.), *Agricultural resources: an introduction to the farming industry of the United Kingdom*. London: Faber and Faber.

—— (1983) Housing. In M. Pacione (ed.), *Progress in rural geography*. London: Croom Helm.

Rose, D., Saunders, P., Newby, H. and Bell, C. (1978) Landownership and the politics of rural areas. In A. Walker (ed.), *Rural poverty*. Poverty Pamphlet 37. London: Child Poverty Action Group.

—— (1979) The economic and political basis of rural deprivation: a case study. In J. M. Shaw (ed.), *Rural deprivation and planning*. Norwich: Geo Books.

Rossi, P. H. (1955) *Why families move*. New York: Free Press of Glencoe.

Roth, A. (1973) The business backgrounds of MPs. In J. Urry and J. Wakeford (eds.), *Power in Britain*. London: Heinemann.

Royal Commission on Legal Services (1979) *Report of the Royal Commission on Legal Services (the Benson report)*. London: HMSO.

Royal Commission on the National Health Service (1979) *Access to primary health care*. Research Paper no. 6, Royal Commission on the National Health Service. London: HMSO.

Rural Planning Services (1979) *The Oxford green belt*. Oxford: Rural Planning Services.

Russell, A. J. (1975) *The village in myth and reality*. London: Chester House Publications.

Samuel, R. (ed.) (1975) *Village life and labour*. London: Routledge and Kegan Paul.

Samuels, A. (1978) Give me planning permission to replace my country cottage. *Journal of Planning and Environmental Law*, 94–7.

Sarre, P. (1981) *Second homes: a case study in Brecknock*. Milton Keynes: Faculty of Social Science Publications, Open University.

Saunders, P. (1978) Domestic property and social class. *International Journal of Urban and Regional Research* 2, 233–51.

—— (1979) *Urban politics: a sociological interpretation*. London: Hutchinson.

Newby, H., Bell, C. and Rose, D. (1978) Rural community and rural community power. In H. Newby (ed.), *International perspectives in rural sociology*. Chichester: John Wiley.

Saville, J. (1957) *Rural depopulation in England and Wales 1851–1951*. London: Routledge and Kegan Paul.

Schifferes, S. (1980) Tied accommodation: letting without strings. *Housing and Planning Review* 36, 12–14, 25.

Scottish Development Department (1980) *Allocation and transfer of council houses*. Edinburgh: HMSO.

Self, P. and Storing, H. (1962) *The state and the farmer*. London: Allen and Unwin.

Shaw, G. (1982) Structure plan policies for retail provision in rural areas: a case-study of South West England. *Service Industries Review* 2, 38–50.

—— and Toyne, P. (1978) Manpower demands, labour supplies and employment aspirations: a problem with implications for the formulation of regional policy. *Geoforum* 9, 149–59.

—— and Williams, A. M. (1980) Structure plans and retail planning. *Retail Distribution and Management* 8, 43–7.

—— (1981) The regional structure of structure plans. *Planning Outlook* 23, 2–7.

—— (1982a) Approaches to structure planning in South West England. *Planning and Administration* 9, 74–84.

—— (1982b) Industrial estates and the recession: the Cornish experience 1973–1982. In G. Shaw and A. M. Williams (eds.), *Economic development and policy in Cornwall*. South West Papers in Geography no. 2. Plymouth-Exeter: Plymouth Polytechnic, College of St. Mark and St. John and University of Exeter.

Shaw, J. M. (1976) Can we afford villages? *Built Environment* 2, 135–7.

—— (1978) The social implications of village development. In M. J. Moseley (ed.), *Social issues in rural Norfolk*. Norwich: Centre of East Anglian Studies, University of East Anglia.

—— (ed.) (1979a) *Rural deprivation and planning*. Norwich: Geo Books.

—— (1979b) Rural deprivation and social planning: an overview. In J. M. Shaw (ed.), *Rural deprivation and planning*. Norwich: Geo Books.

(1982) The development of statutory rural planning in the 1970s. In A. Gilg (ed.), *Countryside Planning Yearbook 1982*. Norwich: Geo Books.

and Stockford, D. (1979) The role of statutory agencies in rural areas: planning and social services. In J. M. Shaw (ed.), *Rural deprivation and planning*. Norwich: Geo Books.

Shaw, M. (1972) The coming crisis of radical sociology. In R. Blackburn (ed.), *Ideology in social science*. London: Fontana.

Sheail, J. (1975) The concept of national parks in Britain 1900–1950. *Transactions of the Institute of British Geographers* 66, 41–56.

(1981) *Rural conservation in inter-war Britain*. Oxford: Clarendon Press.

Shelter (1974) *Tied accommodation*. London: Shelter.

Shoard, M. (1980) *The theft of the countryside*. London: Maurice Temple Smith.

Short, J. R. (1978) Residential mobility in the private housing market of Bristol. *Transactions of the Institute of British Geographers* New Series 3, 533–47.

Shucksmith, M. (1981) *No homes for locals?* Aldershot: Gower.

and Lloyd, G. (1982) The Highlands and Islands Development Board, regional policy and the Invergordon closure. *National Westminster Bank Quarterly Review* May, 14–24.

Sigsworth, A. (1980) The rural school – in, of, or for the community. In *Educational disadvantage in rural areas*. Manchester: Centre for Information and Advice on Educational Disadvantage.

Smith, D. M. (1973) *The geography of social well-being in the United States*. New York: McGraw-Hill.

(1974) Who gets what where and how: a welfare focus for human geography. *Geography* 59, 289–97.

(1977) *Human geography: a welfare approach*. London: Edward Arnold.

(1979a) The identification of problems in cities: applications of social indicators. In D. T. Herbert and D. M. Smith (eds), *Social problems and the city*. Oxford: University Press.

(1979b) *Where the grass is greener*. Harmondsworth: Penguin.

Smith, J. and Gant, R. (1981) Transport provision and rural change: a case study from the Cotswolds. In J. Whitelegg (ed.), *The spirit and purpose of transport geography*. Lancaster: Institute of British Geographers, Transport Geography Study Group, Department of Geography, University of Lancaster.

(1982) The elderly's travel in the Cotswolds. In A. M. Warnes (ed.), *Geographical perspectives on the elderly*. Chichester: John Wiley.

Smith, P. F. (1981) *The Housing Act 1980*. London: Butterworths.

South West Economic Planning Council (1974) *A strategic settlement pattern for the South West*. London: HMSO.

(1975) *Survey of second homes in the South West*. London: HMSO.

(1976) *Economic survey of the tourist industry in the South West*. London: HMSO.

Spence, N., Gillespie, A., Goddard, J., Kennett, S., Pinch, S. and Williams, A. (1982) *British cities: an analysis of urban change*. Oxford: Pergamon Press.

Spooner, D. J. (1972) Industrial movement and the rural periphery: the case of Devon and Cornwall. *Regional Studies* 6, 197–215.

Stacey, M. (1960) *Tradition and change: a study of Banbury*. Oxford: University

Press.

(1974) The myth of community studies. In C. Bell and H. Newby (eds.), *The sociology of community: a selection of readings*. London: Frank Cass.

Stamp L. D. (1949) The planning of land use. *The Advancement of Science* 6, 224–33.

Standing Conference of Rural Community Councils (1978) *The decline of rural services*. London: National Council of Social Service.

(1979) *Whose countryside?* London: National Council of Social Service.

Stein, M. (1964) *The eclipse of community*. New York: Harper Torch Books.

Stockford, D. (1978) Social service provision. In A. Walker (ed.), *Rural poverty*. Poverty Pamphlet 37. London: Child Poverty Action Group.

Thomas, C. J. (1976) Sociospatial differentiation and the use of services. In D. T. Herbert and R. J. Johnston (eds.), *Social areas in cities: spatial perspectives on problems and policies*. London: John Wiley.

Thomas, C. and Winyard, S. (1979) Rural incomes. In J. M. Shaw (ed.), *Rural deprivation and planning*. Norwich: Geo Books.

Thomas, D. St J. (1963) *The rural transport problem*. London: Routledge and Kegan Paul.

Thomas, D. (1964) Components of London's green belt. *Journal of the Town Planning Institute* 50, 434–9.

(1970) *London's green belt*. London: Faber and Faber.

(1974) The urban fringe: approaches and attitudes. In J. H. Johnson (ed.), *Suburban growth*. Chichester: John Wiley.

(1977) Tourist Wales. In D. Thomas (ed.), *Wales: a new study*. Newton Abbot: David and Charles.

Thomas, J. G. (1972) Population changes and the provision of services. In J. Ashton and W. H. Long (eds.), *The remoter rural areas of Britain*. Edinburgh: Oliver and Boyd.

Thorburn, A. (1971) *Planning villages*. London: Estates Gazette.

Thorns, D. C. (1968) The changing system of rural stratification. *Sociologia Ruralis* 8, 161–77.

Tönnies, F. (1963) *Community and society*. New York: Harper and Row.

Townsend, A. R. (1980) Unemployment geography and the new government's 'regional' aid. *Area* 12, 9–18.

Townsend, P. (1976) Area deprivation policies. *New Statesman* 92, 168–71.

Toyne, P. (1977) Recruiting for industry in a non-industrial area: the businessman's view. *Area* 9, 133–7.

Tracy, M. E. (1976) Fifty years of agricultural policy. *Journal of Agricultural Economics* 27, 331–49.

Tricker, M. (1982) Rural education services: the social effects of reorganization. Paper presented to Anglo-Dutch Symposium, University of East Anglia, Norwich, September 1982.

Turnock, D. (1969) Regional development in the crofting counties. *Transactions of the Institute of British Geographers* 48, 189–204.

(1974) *Scotland's Highlands and Islands*. Oxford: University Press.

Tyler, G. J. (1974) The mobility, replacement and wage rates of farm workers – a note. *Oxford Agrarian Studies* 3, 151–3.

Tyler, M. (1979) Implications for transport. In *Impacts of telecommunications on planning and transport*, Research Report no. 24. London: Department of the Environment and Transport.

United Nations Research Institute for Social Development (1966) *The level of living index*, Report no. 4. Geneva: UNRISD.

de Vane, R. (1975) *Second home ownership: a case study*. Bangor: Occasional Papers in Economics no. 6, University of Wales.

Varwell, A. (1973) Scotland: highland and island communities. In M. Broady (ed.), *Marginal regions, essays on social planning*. London: Bedford Square Press.

Ventris, N. (1978) Access to recreational opportunities. In A. Walker (ed.), *Rural poverty*. Poverty Pamphlet 37, London: Child Poverty Action Group.

 (1979) Recreational and cultural provision in rural areas. In J. M. Shaw (ed.), *Rural deprivation and planning*. Norwich: Geo Books.

Vince, S. W. (1952) Reflections on the structure and distribution of rural population in England and Wales, 1921–31. *Transactions of the Institute of British Geographers* 18, 224–33.

Wagstaff, H. R. (1971) Recruitment and losses of farm workers. *Scottish Agricultural Economics* 21, 7–16.

Walker, A. (ed.) (1978a) *Rural poverty*. Poverty Pamphlet 37. London: Child Poverty Action Group.

 (1978b) Introduction and background. In A. Walker (ed.), *Rural poverty*. Poverty Pamphlet no. 37. London: Child Poverty Action Group.

Wallace, D. B. (1981) Rural policy: a review article. *Town Planning Review* 52, 215–22.

Warnes, A. M. (1982) Geographical perspectives on ageing. In A. M. Warnes (ed.), *Geographical perspectives on the elderly*. Chichester: John Wiley.

Watkins, R. (1978) Deprivation and education in rural schools. In A. Walker (ed.), *Rural poverty*. Poverty Pamphlet 37. London: Child Poverty Action Group.

 (1979) Educational disadvantage in rural areas. In J. M. Shaw (ed.), *Rural deprivation and planning*. Norwich: Geo Books.

 and Derrick, D. (1979) Educational disadvantage in rural areas. *Disadvantages in Education* 2, 4–6.

Watson, J. W. (1957) The sociological aspects of geography. In G. Taylor (ed.), *Geography in the twentieth century*. New York: Philosophical Library.

Watts, H. D. (1981) *The branch plant economy: a study of external control*. London: Longman.

Webber, R. and Craig, J. (1976) Which local authorities are alike? *Population Trends* 5, Autumn, 13–19.

 (1978) *Socio-economic classification of local authority areas*. Office of Population Censuses and Surveys, Studies on Medical and Population Subjects no. 35. London: HMSO.

While, A. E. (1978) The vital role of the cottage community hospital. *Journal of the Royal College of General Practitioners* 28, 485–91.

Whitby, M. A. and Willis, K. G. (1978) *Rural resource development*. London: Methuen.

White, D. (1972) Dying village. New Society 19, 108–9.

Whitelegg, J. (1979) Access to health care facilities in Cumbria. In D. A. Halsall and B. J. Turton (eds.), *Rural transport problems in Britain*. Keele: Transport Geography Study Group. Institute of British Geographers. Department of Geography, University of Keele.

(1982) *Health care: inequalities of access and provision*. Retford, Notts.: Straw Barnes Press.

Wibberly, G. (1978) Mobility and the countryside. In R. Cresswell (ed.), *Rural transport and country planning*. London: Leonard Hill.

Williams, P. R. (1976) The role of institutions in the inner London housing market. *Transactions of the Institute of British Geographers* New Series 1, 20–33.

(1978) Building societies and the inner city. *Transactions of the Institute of British Geographers* New Series 3, 23–34.

Williams, R. (1973) *The country and the city*. London: Chatto and Windus.

Williams, R. (1976) The idea of social planning. *Planning Outlook* 19, 11–18.

Williams, R., Bloor, M., Horobin, G. and Taylor, R. (1980) Remoteness and disadvantage: findings from a survey of access to health services in the Western Isles. *Scottish Journal of Sociology* 4, 105–24.

Williams, W. M. (1956) *The sociology of an English village: Gosforth*. London: Routledge and Kegan Paul.

(1973) The social study of family farming. In D. R. Mills (ed.), *English rural communities: the impact of a specialised economy*. London: Macmillan.

Williamson, W. and Byrne, D. S. (1979) Educational disadvantage in an urban setting. In D. T. Herbert and D. M. Smith (eds.), *Social problems and the city*. Oxford: University Press.

Willmott, P. and Young, M. (1960) *Family and class in a London suburb*. London: Routledge and Kegan Paul.

Wilson, G. K. (1977) *Special interests and policy making*. Chichester: John Wiley.

Winter, G. (1971) Plenty of space – too few people: the anomaly of rural depopulation. *Country Life* 4, 236–8.

Winyard, S. (1978) Low pay and farmworkers. In A. Walker (ed.), *Rural poverty*. Poverty Pamphlet 37. London: Child Poverty Action Group.

Wirth, L. (1938) Urbanism as a way of life. *American Journal of Sociology* 44, 1–24.

Wood, S. (ed.) (1982) *Degradation of work?* London: Hutchinson.

Woodruffe, B. J. (1976) *Rural settlement policies and plans*. London: Oxford University Press.

Worsley, P. (1970) *Introducing sociology*. Harmondsworth: Penguin.

Young, M. and Willmott, P. (1957) *Family and kinship in East London*. London: Routledge and Kegan Paul.

Index